Free to Be God's Woman

Free to Be God's Woman

Building a Solid Foundation
for a Healthy Self-Image

JANET CONGO

Regal Books

A Division of GL Publications
Ventura, California, U.S.A.

Published by Regal Books
A Division of Gospel Light
Ventura, California 93006
Printed in U.S.A.

Second Edition
Formerly published under the title *Finding Inner Security*

Library of Congress Cataloging in Publication Data

Congo, Janet, 1949-
    Free to be God's Woman.
    1. Women, Christian—religious life. 2. Self-perception. I. Title.
BV4527.C643   1988   248.8'43   88-6679
ISBN: 0-8307-1270-4

4 5 6 7 8 9 10 11 12 13 14 15 16 17 18 / 99 98 97 96 95 94 93

Rights for publishing this book in other languages are contracted by Gospel Literature International (GLINT). GLINT also provides technical help for the adaptation, translation, and publishing of Bible study resources and books in scores of languages worldwide. For further information, contact GLINT, Post Office Box 488, Rosemead, California, 91770, U.S.A., or the publisher.

To my husband Dave
with whom
I'm continually discovering and celebrating
the joys of interdependence.

To my son Christopher and daughter Amy
who are choosing their own styles
of relating.

I offer my love,
my thoughts and
my thanks.

Contents

Preface

Have you ever experienced the shock of seeing all your well-thought-out plans disintegrate before your eyes? Precisely seven years ago this happened to me. Because of this disguised blessing you are now reading my first book.

I had recently left my homeland of Canada, with my family, to pursue a dream of my husband's in Southern California. Dave was beginning his work toward a doctoral degree in clinical psychology at the Rosemead Graduate School of Psychology on the Biola University campus. I had received the welcome news that Biola was interested in having me join their faculty. I was thrilled because I had been a university instructor for the past seven years. After arriving we enthusiastically set out to find a home. We soon settled into a new life-style and culture and a home, confident of God's direction in our future.

Three months after I began teaching, I received word from the United States Immigration Department that I would have to stop. Because I was a Canadian, I was taking a job away from American teachers who needed work. Frantically, we appealed the decision three times, only to receive the same answer.

We found ourselves facing quite a crisis. Dave was deeply involved in his doctoral program, we had two children to support and had purchased a small house with much larger house payments than we had ever assumed while in Canada. Dave possessed a student visa which entitled him to work 20 hours a week on campus, but any of you who have worked on a college campus know that means minimum wage! Because of our Canadian citizenship we could not qualify for American student loans. Neither could we qualify for Canadian loans because we were studying outside the country. What were we to do?

Being pretty normal, I hit the pits. Not only was there phenomenal financial pressure but I was forced to admit that my self-esteem had been tied into that prestigious university job—along with the nice little pay check I received at the end of the month.

From my beautiful office on the college campus I had always said that being a homemaker was the highest of all professions. When I found myself forced to be a full-time homemaker my self-esteem plummeted. Not only did I feel sorry for myself and afraid of what the future would hold, but I felt very insecure about not being able to fit into the mold of the "successful" woman.

I responded by making an intellectual decision to be a superwoman. The Proverbs 31 woman would have nothing on me! She may have acquired her qualities over a lifetime, but I was going to get them overnight. I struggled constantly to prove my value. It got so bad that if I didn't have something concrete to show my husband and children at the end of every day, I felt like a failure.

Externally, everything looked fine. The house was immaculate, the meals were nourishing and often gourmet, the children's needs were met and my husband was happy. But internally I was absolutely miserable. There was no time to cultivate my personal interests. I felt as though I lived constantly for everyone else's approval, under everyone else's control. I shudder even now as I recall this stage. I enjoyed very little. Nothing was ever quite perfect, on my part or anyone else's. And because I was so hard on myself it wasn't long until I was equally hard on others. Why couldn't they live up to my standards?

At this time I was offered the opportunity to lead a Bible study and I accepted the position—not because I wanted to know more of my wondrous Lord or because of any concern for hurting women. I took it because I believed this was the way I could prove I was worthwhile, even if I didn't have a career. I'm so glad I took on this assignment. If I hadn't I probably would never have found the time to be in the Word—there were just too many fires to put out. Very quickly I began to comprehend just how different God's standards are from those promoted in our Western culture.

When I first studied God's Word I really believed that the Christian woman had only two relational options: she could either be a dependent woman or an independent woman. Somehow dependency sounded more Christian and less selfish. Independency sounded a great deal more interesting.

What you are holding in your hands is the result of the journey on which the Lord led me. It is my prayer you will read this book slowly and take the time to work through the personalized exercises in a thoughtful and prayerful manner. Be aware, as you read and question, that the concepts presented and *you* are covered in prayer.

I hope you find the journey towards "interdependency" a challenging and exciting one. We, as Christian women, can offer our hurting world an exciting alternative.

Acknowledgments

It is with deep gratitude and appreciation that I acknowledge the contributions of the following people to this manuscript:

Dave Congo for his extensive theological and psychological counsel;

Joan Bay Klope, a gifted editor at Gospel Light Publications, for her sensitive and professional assistance;

Anne Ortlund for her willingness to review the manuscript.

The numerous women who willingly attended seminars based on this content—I'm grateful for your questions, comments and prayers;

My parents and Dave's parents for their loving support and affirmation;

Jean Coffin for being a thoughtful critic and a cherished friend;

Alberta Smith for her timely help in typing the final manuscript.

If I Love God, Why Don't I Feel Good About Myself?

Identifying Four Faulty Foundations

The young woman walked briskly into the counselor's office. At first glance it was obvious that she cared about her appearance. Her body was trim beneath the attractive outfit she wore. Rays of sunlight from a nearby window danced on her shining, carefully styled hair. Her makeup had been deftly applied. As she lowered herself into the overstuffed chair her body seemed to stiffen and a controlled reserve crept quietly over her face. Slowly she started to share her story.

She was a mother with three children under the age of six and at this point in her life she had chosen to stay at home with them. Her husband believed that family was her first responsibility, but her responsibilities and his seemed worlds apart. He was a pastor, an active man with little time for his family. Everyone else's needs seemed more urgent and important than those of his own family. She felt there was no social status in her job as a stay-at-home wife and mother. There seemed to be plenty of status connected with *his* job. At church she taught a children's Sunday School class and helped out in the nursery when needed. But she could not find joy in service like that performed by her husband because of an overwhelming fear of getting up in front of adults. Academically she had done well in college and had graduated with a degree in a well-respected field. But for years she had been laboring under a burden of inferiority because she felt she wasn't as intelligent as her husband.

What can she do? She is in crisis and needs to make some changes. There is no one to whom she can pour her heart out. After all, to whom does a pastor's wife go when her life is falling to pieces at her feet?

There are many competent, creative, educated, attractive women today who have similar feelings of emptiness, depression and failure. Each one condemns herself for her feelings. And as each one experiences the results of this steady diet of self-condemnation it eats away at her self-esteem until she is left a crumbled mass of humanity, denying her very worth as a person. Is this what the Lord envisioned when He created woman? Definitely not!

What has gone wrong? Have we truly appropriated the life of freedom and fulfillment for which God created us? Is it possible we have let society squeeze us ever so subtly into its mold?

Perhaps you are uncomfortable with the idea that secular society has molded us. Perhaps you don't believe this is the case at all. May I challenge both responses by asking you to pretend for a moment that we have just been introduced to one another. I turn to you and say, "Tell me about yourself." If you are like the majority of women, your description of yourself will probably sound a little bit like this: "I am so and so's wife, so and so's mother and I do such and such a job." If you are a proud grandmother you might let me know that, and if we have a mutual acquaintance you might let me know that you are so and so's friend.

Does this sound remotely familiar? Are you aware that you have used labels to define your identity? You have told me *what you do* rather than *who you are* as a woman. Labels should be used to describe the spheres in which you operate. They cannot describe who we are. Is there security in using a label? I think there is—the security of not really having to answer the question of who we are. I believe secular society, particularly in the West, has influenced us to such an extent that we not only describe ourselves but we give ourselves value based on a summary of what we do. This is a foundation, a faulty and destructive one which undermines what the Lord teaches us in Scripture. Most of us have frequently built our self-esteem on this and three other types of foundations. The disastrous results we'll learn about in chapter two. For now I'd like to tell you about this foundation and unearth three others of which you need to be aware.

Faulty Foundation 1:

The value of a woman's life is based on a summation of the things she does.
Essential to this belief is the unwritten law that says the things you do hold a certain status rating. If, for example, you are active in a career outside the home, your status rating is definitely higher than if you devote yourself to full-time home management. Have your values been affected by this philosophy? Please take the time to ask yourself these questions before you read any further.

How do you feel about yourself at the end of a day when you have scheduled 10 things to accomplish and you haven't completed one?

If, for any number of reasons, you have chosen not to pursue a career outside the home at the present time, how do you feel when someone asks you what you do?

Do you feel more valuable when you are bringing home a paycheck?

In her book *A Woman's Worth,* Eileen Stedman asks the question, "Have you ever given thought to why God rested on the seventh day?" I am fond of her answer: "God rested not because He was tired but rather to show us that in His essence He is apart from, more than His creation—more than His works."[1] As God's children we are much more than what we create, much more than what we do. Our relationship with our Creator God is the basis for our sense of dignity, not what we are able to accomplish. How easy it is to fall into the trap of focusing on what we do rather than on what God did for us on the cross. And when we're out of focus we drive ourselves to do more in order to gain God's approval and the approval of others. Before long we start believing that God's standards are the same as the world's.

The result of our misdirected energies is to create a monster—the superwoman. You've heard of her, haven't you? She can leap over tall buildings, solve any problem, overcome any enemy in her path. And she accomplishes all this within the confines of an immaculately kept house. How foolish she sounds to us, doesn't she? But many of us labor under the burden of being God's superwomen in our homes, our churches, and our communities. We try to be the best possible woman, wife, mother and career person—just to mention a few hats that we choose. We take self-improvement course after self-improvement course. Unfortunately, it ends up being self-enslavement rather than self-improvement. Why do we do this? It is because we have adopted the world's standard that our value comes as a direct result of what we do.

When we find ourselves focused on our accomplishments we slip into the trap of becoming results oriented. Scripturally, results in and of themselves are not necessarily an indicator of God's blessing. In the Old Testament (see Num. 20:2-13) we read about the angry, negative, complaining Israelites. They lashed out with fury at Moses when they accused him of bringing them into the desert to let them die. Moses and Aaron, no doubt totally overcome by the cruelty of the people's accusations, fell prostrate and God showed Himself in His great love to these two hurting leaders. Instructions were given for Moses to take his staff and gather the Israelites together. Then he was to speak to the rock out of which would flow life-giving water, enough for all the people and their livestock. Rising to his feet, an overwhelming flood of emotion must have burst into Moses' consciousness. He had had it with these ungrateful people! How had he gotten himself into this mess in the first place? Instead of talking to the rock as God had commanded, he hit the rock with his rod. The water flowed and the people were ecstatic with joy and relief. Was Moses a success? Well, there was water in the wilderness wasn't there? But only in man's eyes was Moses a success. This great leader had disobeyed God, and even though it brought apparent success it also brought God's punishment. Success is not necessarily a barometer of God's pleasure.

In his book *There's a Lot More to Health Than Not*

Being Sick, Bruce Larson writes:

> Most of us think that it proves that God is with
> us when we go from success to success. Actu-
> ally most of us will fail more than we succeed,
> and the real proof that God is with us is that we
> no longer have to defend our failures and pre-
> tend that we have succeeded. If I'm not defen-
> sive about my failures but own them, God can
> redeem them and make compost out of them to
> nourish the soul out of which wisdom and com-
> passion and insight can grow. [2]

As a Christian woman my sense of self-worth need not
increase if I succeed in my endeavors or decrease if I meet
failure head-on. Rather its roots are grounded in my relationship with my heavenly Father. Fundamentally important to me is whose I am, rather than what I do or do not
succeed in doing. A high sense of self-worth is available to
the Christian woman who grasps the incredible truth that
she is created in the image of the Almighty God of the universe.

Faulty Foundation 2:

The value of a woman's life is based on what she possesses.

Do you struggle with a tendency to compare your possessions and finances to those of others? Is your sense of
worth found in the type of possessions you have, the
clothes you wear or the amount of money you have? Such
comparisons always result in envy and discontent and will
cause some of us to buy and buy and buy—ever searching
but never satisfied.

It is so easy for this comparison game to lead us into
bondage to the social status of our friends. Most of us

have been there, haven't we! I came face-to-face with this
issue in my own life when I stopped teaching college to
have our first child. I hadn't realized up to that point how
much my self-worth was tied to receiving a paycheck
every month. As precious as newborn babies are I discovered that they do not score high in their ability to give
mothers needed quantities of affirmation or financial remuneration.

My feelings were a little shaky when a friend would
stop by at least three times a week wearing a cute little
something she had just picked up at the store. My inability
to handle being low woman on the social totem pole drove
a wedge into our relationship. I finally began to understand
that our society's lie opposes God's affirmation of our
value. This knowledge freed me to confess my jealousy
and begin to build bridges instead of walls.

As we all know money is both legitimate and necessary. Yet it is too easy for us to feel that unless we have
lots of money or possessions, we will be left out or not be
recognized as worthwhile by other people. We feel we are
not worthwhile individuals in and of ourselves.

As a Christian woman, is it my finances that commend
me to God? Matthew 6:19-21 in *The Living Bible* reads:

> Don't store your treasures here on earth where
> they can erode away or may be stolen. Store
> them in heaven where they will never lose their
> value, and are safe from thieves. If your profits
> are in heaven your heart will be there too.

First John 2:15-17 in *The Living Bible* also warns us
against the world:

> Stop loving this evil world and all that it offers
> you, for when you love these things you show

that you do not really love God; for all these
worldly things, these evil desires—the craze
for sex, the ambition to buy everything that
appeals to you, and the pride that comes from
wealth and importance—these are not from
God. They are from this evil world itself.

Are you tempted to cut this out of your Bible? My feelings of self-worth must not be based on the tottering comparison of my possessions or my finances. If it is I will find myself trapped in the blackness of my own jealousy and in bondage to other people's standards.

Faulty Foundation 3:

The value of a woman's life is based on who she knows.

If we hold to this philosophy we soon find ourselves using people to fulfill our own selfish ends. And it isn't long before we become a name dropper. Sometimes even in our Christian circles the insinuation is made that God is particularly impressed by celebrities or by people who are trying to become celebrities. As a result we walk around either threatened by the status of other people or become a threat to our fellow Christians. This must not be! God is impressed by only one man—Jesus Christ. Only those of us who accept Jesus Christ as our personal Saviour by faith receive God's approval.

The insidious part of this particular comparison is the implication that some people are worth knowing and some are not. Francis Schaeffer wrote a book entitled *No Little People.* I love that title. In God's eyes there are no little people—no one worth more than anyone else. God places such a high value on each of us that He has given us everything He has—His only son, Jesus Christ. Can we then as Christian women adopt the world's philosophy that only some people are worth knowing? Can we use people that way to make ourselves feel good?

It would do us well to remember our Saviour's words, as recorded in Matthew 25:40 *(NKJV)* "Inasmuch as you did it to one of the least of these My brethren, you did it to Me." Any time we base our identity on human relationships we end up using other people. Our relationships will become shallow and the security we seek will transform into insecurity. Scripture is excruciatingly clear; we are to have no part in this particular comparison game:

> My [sisters], as believers in our glorious Lord Jesus Christ, don't show favoritism. Suppose a man [or woman] comes into your meeting wearing a gold ring and fine clothes, and a poor man [or woman] in shabby clothes also comes in. If you show special attention to the man [or woman] wearing fine clothes and say, 'Here's a good seat for you,' but say to the poor man [or woman], 'You stand there' or 'Sit on the floor by my feet,' have you not discriminated among yourselves and become judges with evil thoughts? (Jas. 2:1-4, *NIV*).

Suppose two women fitting the above descriptions came into one of your church groups. Would you welcome the obviously well-to-do woman into your group, would you introduce her to your friends and extend a personal invitation to the next women's luncheon? How about the poorly dressed woman? Would you show as much warmth to her? Or would you only pause long enough to acknowledge her presence and then turn away and ignore her?

> Listen, my dear [sisters]: Has not God chosen those who are poor in the eyes of the world to

be rich in faith and to inherit the kingdom he promised those who loved him? But you have insulted the poor. Is it not the rich who are exploiting you? Are they not the ones who are dragging you into court? Are they not the ones who are slandering the noble name of him to whom you belong?

If you really keep the royal law found in Scripture, 'Love your neighbour as yourself,' you are doing right. But if you show favoritism, you sin and are convicted by the law as lawbreakers. For whoever keeps the whole law and yet stumbles at just one point is guilty of breaking all of it (Jas. 2:5-10, *NIV*).

As committed Christians we must reject the cruel comparison game based on who we know.

An interesting sideline to this pastime has to do with whether or not we are involved in a relationship. In order to be accepted in some circles, we feel the need to be married. In other circles we seem to gain more identity by remaining single.

Imagine a group informing us we are not complete without a man. Some women will begin to believe men are superior and they are only half people. When these women search out relationships they often find half men, for a woman who believes she is only half a person never finds a man capable of completing her. Once this dear woman finds the man of her dreams she lives her life through him and takes on not only his name but also his identity. If this philosophy permeates a church there is an unspoken agenda which says, "You haven't really discovered God's will for your life unless you are married." So the single woman flounders, feeling as if she has no value of her own.

In many secular circles your sanity is questioned if you have chosen to be married to only one man. "How old fashioned! How dull! You certainly aren't ever-changing and ever-growing or you would realize that one person can not possibly meet all your needs!"

Instead of our value being a gift from a loving God, we try to earn the affirmation of our peers by either choosing to be married or single. Comparisons with others is always a dead-end route. Our value has been declared! We should have no part in these degrading games that compare what we do, what we own and who we know. Each of us must follow Jesus individually. The path we choose will be considered successful by some and unsuccessful by others. Regardless, Christ's command to us is always the same: "You follow me" (see John 21:22).

Faulty Foundation 4:

The value of a woman's life is based on how she looks.

The beauty propaganda begins when we are very young. Think about those fabulous fairy tales we all enjoy. They reinforce the concept that says the good girl is beautiful and the wicked girl is ugly. The beautiful one always gets her dream, usually in the form of a man. But the story always ends before we discover whether he turns out to be a dream or a nightmare!

Young mothers are made particularly aware of the beauty cult. That precious baby of yours gets so much attention and so many smiles when he or she is all dressed up. Suddenly the child bangs his head on the corner of your coffee table. Now when that same dear child goes out with you with a bruised forehead or a black eye, he is either ignored or stared at. And you as a parent are viewed as either neglectful or a child beater. No one has to announce to you that approval has been removed. You can feel it.

Have you been influenced by this beauty propaganda?

What would you change about your physical appearance if you could?

How valuable do you feel when your hair needs to be done, when you have acne, when you are 10 pounds overweight?

Why are we so dissatisfied with our physical appearance? Isn't this yet another area where our focus is on what we don't have instead of being thankful for what we do have? What a folly it is to compare ourselves to the flawless beauty on the magazine cover who, by the way, had her hair styled by the same hairdresser who is still hovering in the wings making certain that the natural look is achieved.

Lest you think that I don't believe making the most of your appearance is important—I do. The way we appear is a sign to God, to ourselves and to others about the value we place on God's creation. God, who has given us His son and His Spirit has chosen to reside in our bodies. We are His temple! How important it is for us to be aware of the picture we are presenting to the world. But what Jesus doesn't intend is for us to be caught up in the all-consuming comparison game based on appearance. This sport does nothing but accentuate our insecurities and leave us totally self-centered.

In Psalm 139:13 we discover that our appearance is not a surprise to the creator God. God is responsible for making us. Our responsibility lies in what we do with what God has fashioned. It is terribly important to our spiritual and emotional development that we believe God knew what He was doing when He made us. It is also important that we pause to thank Him for His fabulous creation.

Our Creator's perspective is quite different from ours.

In 1 Samuel 16:7, *NIV* we read, "The Lord does not look at the things man [or woman] looks at. Man looks at the outward appearance, but the Lord looks at the heart." It is important to remember that indeed "man does look at the outward appearance." But it is more important to remember that God focuses on the beauty of our thoughts and motivations.

It's a Fantasy

When we contrast our appearance, our accomplishments, our friends or our possessions to others we are making a comparison based in large part on fantasy. We have never walked in the shoes of those women to whom we compare ourselves so we fantasize what it would be like. When we do this we compare our worst, of which we are most aware, to their best. And we're really comparing ourselves to a fantasy. Perhaps this is one of the reasons why soap operas and romance novels are so popular today. We are basically dissatisfied with our existence so we vicariously live our lives through other people.

When we believe we are only worthwhile if we are beautiful, if we use the right products, if we know the right people, if we are successful or if we are financially comfortable, we are building our self-image on faulty foundations. Subtly we find ourselves looking to other "significant" people to define for us what it means to be beautiful, what are the right products to use, who are the right people to associate with, and what it takes to be financially comfortable. One of the nation's top financiers was once asked how much money he would need to be truly happy. His reply was, "just a little bit more."

When we swallow these faddish opinions, society loves us because we fit its mold. But what happens when the mold changes? Once again we experience rejection based on our performance because it is measured against someone else's standard. What insecurity results! This is a disastrously self-defeating process. We feel great external pressure to achieve and when we don't succeed we are immobilized by a crushing burden of failure and guilt.

One of the most ostentatious builders of faulty foundations is the secular media. Producers bombard women with the belief that their sense of fulfillment can only come outside of the home and that her brain is in neutral while she is at home. How do we respond to that indoctrination? The secular women's magazines tell us how very easy it is to be completely fulfilled. All we need is a little organization and efficiency and a highly competent housekeeper to run our homes while we pursue a career.

Picture this model mother of the media. Her alarm rings at 5:30 A.M. and she leaps out of bed, ready for another meaningful day. She feeds and dresses the baby, puts a load of laundry in the machine and enjoys a leisurely bubble bath while her toddler sleeps a little longer. (The authors of these motivational articles never tell you what the baby is doing while mother is having a leisurely soak!)

While the clothes are in the dryer, the model mother prepares a marvelous new recipe for breakfast which she clipped from a magazine the day before. When the toddler awakens she somehow manages to bathe and dress him, make the beds, read the morning paper, get herself dressed in her classic blue lint-free business suit, and serve a nourishing and appetizing breakfast for her family who has allowed her to work with no interruption.

At precisely 7:45 the housekeeper arrives. Mother has 15 minutes to give her directions for the day, play with the children and kiss them good-bye before leaving the house. She looks well put together and ready to face the business world.

The challenges of the day are faced with enthusiasm

and competence because she knows that things are being handled well at home. Before she leaves the office at night she takes time to redo her makeup and dab on a little fragrance. She's had a busy day but she arrives home peaceful and fulfilled in a relaxed frame of mind, anxious to have quality time with her children and her husband. After a beautiful, candlelit dinner together and story time with the children she puts her contented, happy, sweet-smelling offspring to bed. Then she changes into "a little something" and prepares for an exciting, intimate exchange with her husband. They relax together and then go to bed feeling sexy and oh, so fulfilled.

The articles tell us it is quite possible to juggle motherhood, marriage, a career and your own sense of autonomy. Only after we have been bombarded with this fantasy long enough do we realize the impact it has had on us: we have extreme difficulty hearing what God is really saying. We fail to realize that we have value apart from whether we stay at home or work outside the home, apart from the wardrobe or finances we have, apart from who we know and how we look.

We're Not Alone

Our struggle in this area is not such a unique one. Thousands of years ago, a woman was formed by the hand of God Himself so absolutely perfect that God was satisfied. She was created in the image of her creator, equal to her husband and gifted with the ability to reason. She was placed with the man in a garden paradise. We can only imagine its perfection and beauty. But that was not all. She and her husband could fellowship daily with their Creator and everything was made for their own enjoyment.

There was only one stipulation—the tree that was in the middle of the garden was not to be eaten of. The rest of the story is familiar, isn't it! God's Word was twisted by the serpent. He placed a doubt in Eve's mind about God's love for her. The deceitful words of the serpent were: "You will not surely die. For God knows that in the day you eat of it your eyes will be opened, and you will be like God, knowing good and evil" (Gen. 3:4-5, *NKJV*).

Eve's desire was aroused and she asked herself if God was hiding something from her. Eve didn't have to choose to listen to a lie. She didn't have to choose to doubt God's love for her. She didn't have to believe a lie—but she did. The end results we are all too familiar with—a loss of innocence, a broken relationship with her God, an inhibited marital relationship and God's judgment. Eve left the freedom of truth and experienced the bondage resulting from believing a lie. As a result Eve knew fear for the first time in her life. This didn't have to be the case because in 2 Timothy 1:7, *KJV* we read, "For God has not given us a spirit of fear, but of power and of love and of a sound mind."

Eve experienced the spirit of fear because she questioned God's love, believed a lie and acted on the basis of that deception. Prior to this time Eve had based her life on God's spoken word and freedom had been the result. How different it had been.

When God created us as women, He created us with a need to feel worthwhile. He also lovingly created a way that need could be met. If we choose to listen religiously to the voices we hear in our society, the voices that yell "you're only of value if . . . ," our need to feel worthwhile will never be met.

I really believe that in no other area are we, as Christian women, faced so obviously with an encounter similar to the one faced by Eve. Just like our ancestor we often question God's love: If He really loves me why is my nose crooked? Why am I in this predicament? Why do I have to work? Why am I single? Why am I divorced? Why am I poor? Why am I confined to home? Why don't I know the right people? We don't take fruit off the tree as Eve did but we do act on society's belief system. As a result we are sucked into a vicious cycle just as if we were being sucked into a whirlpool.

Why Do I Feel Like I'm on Quicksand?

The Consequences of Choosing a Faulty Foundation

So you say you're a Christian. You have asked the Lord Jesus Christ to be your personal Saviour. That delights me. But I want you to be aware that just because you are a Christian does not mean you are immune from basing your self-esteem on faulty foundations. It is possible, after inviting Christ into your heart, to build your life not on the new foundation of Jesus Christ and His Word, but instead on the familiar mentality that surrounds you. The familiar, even if counterfeit to Christianity, feels much more secure.

Here in California we often experience torrential rain storms during the winter months. At least 20 coastal homes went crashing into the sea during one particular storm in 1984. What a tragedy! This serves as a vivid illustration of our lives when built on ever-shifting sands.

When storms hit our lives we find ourselves demolished. Perhaps we are even led to reject Christianity because it didn't seem to work for us. Of course it didn't work! Our Christianity must be founded on the solid rock of Christ Jesus, not on anything else.

In the Western culture there is status in certain jobs and not in others. Jesus Christ tells us to do all jobs to the best of our ability as unto Him. Society tells us our worth is tied to our possessions. Our Lord tells us to use our possessions for His honor and glory. Contemporary thinking tells us some people are more valuable to us than others. Jesus Christ tells us we are all in need of the Saviour. We're also told our value is based on how we look. Our Lord puts His Holy Spirit inside us so we can become beautiful loving people. God's foundation is solid rock. Contemporary thought is like ever-shifting sand.

In this chapter I will introduce you to two women who have committed their lives to Christ but who have built their lives on faulty foundations. They are both in bondage even though each woman's bondage is revealed in a very different way. You will meet Gloria, who is in bondage to others and Jasmine, who is in bondage to herself. Do you recognize either of these women?

The Dependent Woman

In an attractive, two-story home in a small Nebraska town lives Gloria, her husband, two children and two dogs. Gloria, who is in her early forties, works as a dental assistant at one of the offices on Main Street. Often, when she is not at work, you will find her serving in some capacity in her church. She has a good marriage, beautiful and healthy children, a career and avenues of ministry. She is also absolutely miserable. Few people know this because Gloria is a master of disguises. Most of the time she is attractively dressed with a smile on her face, moving quickly from one activity to another. People just assume she's fulfilled by these activities. Well, they couldn't be further from the truth.

Gloria's Incomplete Scriptural Understanding

Gloria accepted Christ as her personal Saviour five years ago and thought this would end her feelings of insecurity. But she's been miserable. She accepted Jesus by faith and for a short time grasped the idea that because of Calvary, she had been set free from the necessity of trying to please God. But soon she slipped into a trap. Through the eyes of new-found love Gloria read about Christ's life in Scripture. She decided that if Jesus had lived a life pleasing to God, it was possible for her to imitate His pattern. How quickly she accepted the myth that she could make herself acceptable to God by meeting a perceived standard.

From that premise it took very little effort for Gloria to decide that if she kept to her standard, God would be pleased with her. If God was pleased with her, she reasoned, all would go well for her, for hadn't He said that "all things work together for good to those who love God . . . ?" Likewise, she reasoned that if God was not pleased with her He would strike her with sickness, death and failure. As you can imagine, Gloria developed a real fear of God. She was terrified of Him. She was convinced that He would zap her if she didn't live up to those perfect standards she pulled out of the pages of Scripture.

Let's call Gloria's theology the "worm theology," for she has just enough religion to make her absolutely miserable. As she faces over and over again her inability to live up to her self-imposed standards, she focuses *only* on the sections of Scripture which tell her she is deeply fallen, such as Jeremiah 17:9 *(NIV):* "The heart is deceitful above all things and beyond cure. Who can understand it?" It *is* necessary for us to confront the truth of those words. The tragedy lies in Gloria's inability to see beyond them.

Gloria has grasped only partial truth. When she looks at Calvary she sees the awfulness of her personal sin that put Christ there. She has no eyes to see that because of Calvary she is greatly loved. She only sees her personal inadequacy and feels worthless, sinful and guilty. Even the church she and her family attend spends most of its energy teaching about sin. Very little is mentioned about the freedom Christ offers.

Due to the Fall, Gloria believes she has no value. She believes the image of God was completely wiped out when Adam and Eve sinned. Today there is nothing of God left in any of us. Jesus is everything and she is nothing. Her total emphasis is found in Galatians 2:20 *(NKJV):* "I have been crucified with Christ." She views herself as worthless and God as one who takes sin very seriously and who constantly reminds us of our failures. Because of this viewpoint it is impossible for Gloria to see or accept God's grace and unconditional love.

Faulty Foundation 1: Identity = Performance

There are several negative results from Gloria's incomplete scriptural understanding. First, Gloria works very hard to earn God's favor—along with everyone else's. To accomplish this goal she demands from herself a perfect performance.

Gloria's sense of value is tied to her performance. She sets tremendously unreasonable goals for herself and exerts all her energy to see those goals become a reality. Prayer, worship, study, church activities and traditions become goals she must reach in order to please God.

When she is successful in reaching her goals she feels good about herself. When Gloria fails she feels she is less than nothing. Her emotional pattern resembles a roller coaster.

But Gloria is not content to impose these standards on just herself. She also puts a lot of pressure on those around her. Since she doesn't see God at work in people and circumstances, she lives with the belief that everything depends on her. Gloria has to have the perfect house, the perfect children, the perfect husband and the perfect friends. Everyone and everything she touches gets caught in her stranglehold of expectation. This stranglehold is most evident in Gloria's emphasis on the "outer wrappings." When you are with Gloria it is difficult not to feel judged as to whether or not you are living up to her version of the scriptural standard. Because Gloria is not aware of how a loving heavenly Father has forgiven her and because she isn't able to release herself from her self-condemnation, she finds it difficult to forgive others. She gets great joy in sharing with you an experience of victory (usually as a result of meeting her own standard) but she will not confess personal needs or defeats. In fact, in times of real personal need she will remain aloof and withdrawn because she doesn't want you to know there is failure in her life. But when she finally crashes into reality, the conflict between what *is* and what she believes *should be* leads her straight to frustration and depression. Recently Gloria spent a week in bed because life got to be too much for her. When her performance doesn't match her expectations it is difficult for Gloria to forgive herself.

Gloria needs to confess her self-defeating pattern to a loving heavenly Father. Instead she spends a great deal of time copying other Christians who appear to be more successful at meeting the standards similar to those she has set for herself. Gloria is viewed as a very pleasing, easy-to-get-along-with person who never rocks the boat. Fellow church members see her as a highly spiritual and submissive Christian woman. Her pastor, the dentist she works for and her husband all think extremely well of her—and their opinion is tremendously important to her.

Faulty Foundation 2: Identity = Possessions

Possessions, whether they be for personal use or for her family members, are tremendously important to Gloria. Her home is a showpiece but she rarely entertains because she worries about spills and messes. The family boat is their latest purchase and they store it on the side of the house with pride, for it is the best on the block. Finances are often a source of irritation between she and her husband but Gloria continues to spend to the limits of their credit out of compulsion. Whenever stress rises at work she finds solace in a shopping trip.

Faulty Foundation 3: Identity = Relationships

Who she knows is equally important to Gloria because other people set her standards for her. Because of her failure to meet self-imposed standards she has lost all sense of personal wholeness and value. It is due to these negative feelings of worthlessness that she latches on to other significant people. Constantly she watches the non-verbal and verbal cues of these people to get clues as to what she must do to be accepted. How she longs for approval and acceptance. These significant other people always determine Gloria's sense of self and she has no idea of who she is apart from them. She has never really gotten in touch with what she thinks. John Powell describes the dependent woman's fear so well: "You ask me who I am and I'm afraid to tell you because if I tell you who I am you may not like who I am and it's all that I've got."[1]

When entering a new situation Gloria will test the waters and then fall in line with the opinions of the significant leaders of the group. Gloria has become a cheap imitator of those who have made it, those who seem to have God's approval more than she.

Gloria is quick to point out that her roles as wife, mother and career woman are comfortable for her. The shallowness and lack of originality with which she plays her roles leads one to wonder if they were chosen for her, however. Let's look at the way she chooses to act as a wife. Gloria and her husband are inseparable. She appears to believe everything he believes, like everything he likes and do everything he wants her to do. Gloria has no sense of who she is apart from him. It is as if Gloria has abdicated all responsibility of thinking to her husband and the significant others in her world.

Faulty Foundation 4: Identity = Appearance

This external motivation carries over into Gloria's appearance. It is terribly important to her that she look as successful as she possibly can. She pours over the latest women's magazines to catch up on the very latest fashions. In her search for perfection she has swallowed the lie that she must have the very latest wardrobe and hairstyle, no matter what the cost. Gloria never feels she measures up to the model on the front of the magazine, however. Most of her conversations consist of a stream of negativity and comdemnation about herself and her appearance. Beautiful Gloria is a constant drag when anyone compliments her—she has no respect for herself. She either looks like a clone or hides behind a smokescreen of inferiority based on her perception that she doesn't meet other people's standards.

Misplaced Sense of Self

Gloria's life is one of external duty rather than internal delight, of external motivation rather than internal motivation, of "other centeredness" rather than "Christ centeredness." She has built her life on the shaky foundation of comparisons and has lost all personal sense of self. She mimics the beliefs, thoughts and standards assumed by those she considers successful. She has become an insecure, frustrated and internally negative Christian woman. The irony is this: it might take you a long time to detect the internal struggle.

One of the positive accomplishments of the Women's Liberation Movement has been to question the wisdom of a woman who builds her life around others. But in their attempts to free us from the expectations of others, the liberationists have moved us into another kind of bondage—the bondage of self-centeredness. Women find no fulfillment there, either.

The Independent Woman

By contrast, the independent woman has more status in our society than does the dependent woman. The woman who "does her own thing" is the prime example of a fulfilled human being—to a great number of people. Listen to any talk show on television, watch any movie or soap opera, read any novel or pick up any newspaper and you'll see her. The independent woman, just like the dependent woman, comes in many shapes and sizes and from many different environments. I want to introduce you to an independent woman I know.

My friend Jasmine is an articulate, attractive, well-educated woman who is a journalist by profession. The day I went to visit her she was working in her oak office, located in a New York high-rise complex.

Jasmine's Incomplete Scriptural Understanding

Jasmine accepted Jesus Christ as her personal Saviour 20 years ago. She still attends church to worship fairly regularly and she still believes in Jesus but she sees Him as not terribly accessible to her. He created her with everything she needs and now it's up to her to develop all she has been given. She knows what she wants out of life and she occasionally looks up, expecting to see God give His nod of approval. In fact, Jasmine's main thrust in life is her own self-actualization. She is going to be all she can possibly be, regardless of what that will take. She is willing to risk everything.

Faulty Foundation 1: Identity = Performance

Jasmine is well versed in the standards society holds up as successful. She has adopted these standards and made them her own. As she talks I am overwhelmed at how she manages to juggle her work schedule with exercise classes, weekend business trips and dinner parties. As long as she is busy she feels worthwhile, so she runs a very tight schedule.

Not only is it important to her identity that she perform well on the job, it is equally important to Jasmine that she perform well sexually. She must keep on her toes because there is always someone younger coming along who might be able to outperform her in either of these areas.

As these thoughts are forming in my mind I am whisked into Jasmine's marvelous library. What an avid reader she is! The written word has always held a fascination for her. On one wall she displays the books and articles she has written and for which she has achieved notoriety. It is an overwhelming sight to see the determination and creativity of a friend displayed so beautifully. She has adopted a basic belief that her fulfillment will happen only as she finds success. And successful she is in several areas. She is a world traveler, an art collector and an accomplished tennis player. Believing as she does that life is to be enjoyed, she tirelessly pursues all life has to offer, grasping all that will bring her happiness.

Faulty Foundation 2: Identity = Possessions

Jasmine's career is flourishing and the financial remuneration it brings to her is evident in her surroundings. One window of her penthouse looks out to the ocean and another window catches the twinkling lights of the city, glistening in the distance. Her penthouse looks as if it has been taken right off the pages of *Architectural Digest.* Gathering possessions has been a method by which Jasmine has found temporary happiness. Once the possession is acquired, she searches for another magnificent plaything which will prove to her how successful she is. It seems to me that she has some of the most beautiful treasures the world has to offer. If ever depression starts to creep darkly into Jasmine's soul, she finds that one of three things will "cure" her blahs—a new male flirtation, a shopping spree or a vacation in some exotic paradise.

Yet even as my eyes take in her treasures I sense a restlessness in my friend. It's as if Jasmine is ever comparing her possessions to others and always coming up wanting. This depression leads her straight to another shopping spree which temporarily stops the pain.

Faulty Foundation 3: Identity = Relationships

Jasmine has been married to the same man for nearly 38 years. Theirs is an open marriage. Believing as they do that one person can't possibly meet all their personal needs, sexually or otherwise, they pursue intimacy in other relationships. But Jasmine doesn't want to get encumbered in relationships, so she leaves at the first sign of a stranglehold. Their marriage has been childless, by choice. Neither was willing to bring children into "such a hate-filled world," nor were they willing to abandon their individual pursuits to raise children. They both felt children were too much of an inconvenience.

Self-gratification is Jasmine's password. She is inclined to change her standard of morality depending on the group with which she finds herself. Meeting all the right people has become a necessary tool as she climbs the ladder of success.

Jasmine worships individuality and delights in uniqueness. Because of this I feel very accepted and free while I am with her. But I am also aware that if I was ever to offend her she would find it very difficult to forgive me.

Once I suggested that we do some volunteer work together but found that she was less than enthusiastic in her response. After all, she couldn't see how she would benefit personally from the activity. I question her very self-centered focus and I wonder if Jasmine will not find herself lonely in the future.

There is no remorse for using others because of her basic philosophy, which she has placed on the wall of her bedroom. It is the "Gestalt Prayer," written by Frederick S. Perls. Framed and attractively displayed, it gives her a boost of energy every time she reads it. To this day she is totally oblivious to its clash with Christianity:

> I do my thing and you do your thing.
> I am not in this world to live up to your expectations
> And you are not in this world to live up to mine.

You are you and I am I;
If by chance we find each other
   it's beautiful
If not, it can't be helped. [2]

As I read this prayer yet another time I can't help wondering about the second line: "I am not in this world to live up to your expectations." The dependent woman exists only as she lives up to someone else's expectations. Is Jasmine, my independent friend, afraid? Is she terrified of becoming a dependent woman or has she once been dependent? Is my friend, who feels she only needs herself and her intellect, tied to the dependent woman in ways she wouldn't care to admit? Is this total pursuit of her own happiness motivated by the fear that if she doesn't use people to fulfill her needs, they will use her to fulfill theirs?

Faulty Foundation 4: Identity = Appearance

Jasmine finds it necessary to have the latest fashions and avidly exercises to keep in top share. But she not only follows the latest fads, she creates them. Jasmine dresses for success and depends on her appearance to speak for her.

In a few moments I leave Jasmine, wondering about my friend who not only succeeds in the competition game, but who comes out a winner in the eyes of our society. Has she *really* found the fulfillment about which she talks so freely?

Only Two Choices?

In today's society we often fall into the trap of believing there are only two roles available to Christian women. It seems we can be dependent women who seek fulfillment through other people or we can be independent women who seek fulfillment only through ourselves. Both are dead-end options to women who seriously search for fulfillment because the foundational basis for each option is similar and faulty.

Our Lord talks much about building on the right foundation in Matthew 7:24-27. We need to stop periodically to reexamine on what foundation we have been building our lives. Have we been swallowing the lie that we are only valuable if we do certain things, if we have adequate financial resources, if we know and have been accepted by the "right" people or if we look a certain way? What happens when the rain comes, if our career crumbles, when our health fails, if significant people in our life walk out on us, when we grow older, when our children rebel or when we make a mistake?

If our identity has been built on foundations of shifting sand, the storms that invariably come will leave us with nothing but collapsed buildings. We will be left muddy, negative, angry, frustrated, depressed, fearful and alone. That's the bad news. But there is good news ahead!

_____3
Is There a Better Way to Live?

Defining Interdependence

In the last chapter I introduced you to two women who both base their identity on misinterpreted Scripture and the standards of secular society. Even though the foundations upon which they have built their lives are the same, the results produced in their lives are as different as night and day. Gloria is terribly dependent while Jasmine has chosen extreme independence. Because of the arguments of both Christians and non-Christians who espouse these two alternatives, many Christian women consider these their only options. And more often than not if they do have a choice they choose dependency because somehow it seems more Christian. But they are left depressed and insecure. Choosing independence can be equally disastrous, however. Many of those women end up critical and alone.

Don't give up! There is another tremendously exciting

option available to those who want to base their lives solidly on the Word of God. Your options are not limited to dependence or independence. You can choose to be an "interdependent" woman whose fulfillment comes through loving.

Elizabeth: A Role Model to Remember

In contrast to Gloria and Jasmine, let me introduce you to a woman named Elizabeth. Her hair is turning white. You often see her standing in the doorway of the church talking to a teenager. Elizabeth's laughter and obvious joy from living speaks a message young people seem to be drawn to. It would be just as normal to see that white head bowed in prayer or bent over the bed of a sick friend. There is nothing stale about this woman. She is kept young by the Holy Spirit and by relationships with younger people. In fact, just this past week she entertained our church's newly married couples class in her home.

How they love her as I do. There is a smile on her face and a positivity that exudes from her, in spite of the fact that she is now a widow and living alone.

What we so deeply value about Elizabeth is her ability to allow each one of us to be ourselves. There is a freedom that comes from being with her and an almost unwritten expectation on her part that we will be questioning, changing individuals. If we don't question our beliefs and opinions you can be sure she'll question them for us.

She would be repulsed if she thought we felt any pressure to be a revised standard version of herself. She has seen the Holy Spirit work in her life over the years and feels no compulsion to be your Holy Spirit and run your life. She trusts her Lord to work out His perfect plan in your life. She believes her part is to love you.

All who spend time with Elizabeth come away affirmed

as a person of value—an equal. They come away motivated and uplifted, changed, as it were, by her hopeful attitude and faith.

But this woman is no phoney. She has very real needs and it doesn't threaten her to let you know about them. After all, she had been happily married for 30 years to an active husband when he was suddenly stricken with a fatal heart attack. Their marriage can be characterized by companionship and mutual respect, and their kitchen table was not only the place where many differences were worked out but where people from all walks of life and cultures had been entertained. It was her husband who encouraged her to go back to college after the children were both in school—during a time when it was an unusual choice for a mother. You can understand why Elizabeth didn't recover overnight from the pain felt when death severed the relationship. She told me one time that as precious as her Lord is to her, He doesn't have arms. How she misses being held.

Through the years Elizabeth has come to realize that honestly sharing her needs and beliefs is the only way those around her can know who she is as a person. But she certainly hasn't fallen into the trap of being so focused on her own needs that her hearing is blocked when you share your needs. There is an honesty about Elizabeth and it is appreciated by all who know her intimately. She doesn't waste any time pretending she isn't human. When she makes a mistake or loses her temper she is the first person to tell you so. When you share a temptation you are experiencing you don't come away feeling put down or condemned. She lets you know her frailties and then carries you straight to the arms of her loving, strong Lord.

What a wealth of experiences Elizabeth has had. How fascinating it is to listen to her talk. She has worn many labels—wife, mother, businesswoman, teacher, widow, grandmother—just to mention a few. But through it all she has been deeply aware that she is God's highly valuable and significant child. These labels have never affected her self-esteem. Instead they have been worn like hats that have been put on and taken off to meet needs and add texture to her life. She was telling me the other day that she is enrolled in a course on computers. "The world is changing, you know. We've got to keep learning." How I treasure this precious woman of God and remain ever thankful that she is willing to share her life with me. It is a thrill to have a living, breathing, walking example of an interdependent woman in my life.

In the remainder of this chapter I will highlight dimensions of interdependency which I pray will clarify in your mind how it is played out in a woman's life.

Defining Interdependency

The Interdependent Woman Has a Strong Sense of Personhood

Many women have been affected by the Equal Rights Movement to such a degree that they believe, as do many staunch liberationists, that women have lost their personhood. The interdependent woman is not one of these women. She affirms her personhood.

Jesus Christ, the creator God, left the glory of heaven to willingly live and die on this earth because of His great love for people—male and female, slave and master, Jew and Greek. The culture he entered differentiated between male and female to such an extent that males were really the only sex granted a sense of personhood. Females were less than people—things—to be used by men for their pleasure.

Into that arrogant world came a radically different Man

who treated women as valued persons. He took them seriously. He affirmed their intellectual capabilities by teaching them the Scriptures. He met their social needs by being their friend. He ministered to their emotional needs by meeting them where they were and never demanding that they place themselves in His position. He used everyday examples of women in His teaching, He listened to them, fellowshipped in their company and trusted women to be the first witnesses of the Resurrection. He offered salvation and healing to women as well as men.

Our personhood has been affirmed by our Saviour. We are people who have been freed by Jesus Christ our Lord and we play a vital role in our world. Since our Saviour treats us as people with dignity, can we treat ourselves as anything less?

The Interdependent Woman Views Others As Her Equal

Only in Jesus Christ do we find true equality. Galatians 3:28 *(RSV)* puts it this way: "There is neither Jew nor Greek, there is neither slave nor free, there is neither male nor female; for you are all one in Christ Jesus." There is no need to get an ulcer trying to prove that we are not inferior as women.

In our society we face a standard which says our value can be earned. The consequence of building our self-esteem on this foundation is that some women achieve the standard and feel superior while others fail to make the mark and feel inferior. This superiority/inferiority teeter-totter keeps us slightly off balance at all times.

There are four options available to us as we examine our views of equality. The first might be chosen by someone lacking any self-esteem—possibly a dependent woman.

"I am nothing and you are nothing."

That is true equality but not the type to which Jesus was referring. If we believe that denying ourselves means we are nothing, we are, as it were, worms. As a worm we have nothing to offer God and nothing to offer a relationship. The final result will be a withdrawal from service, relationships and eventually even life. This is the option that leads people to commit suicide.

Another option often chosen by the dependent woman is:

"I am nothing but you are a person of
worth and dignity."

Acting on this belief leads a woman to total dependence on others. She needs them for security, for hope, for identity and for faith and blames others for her lack of growth. She manipulates the situations around her and chooses to be a victim if things don't go her way. This woman has assigned a role to other people that only belongs to the Lord. She is a clinging octopus. In the beginning, perhaps, there are some men or women who find this flattering, but in the end they find it suffocating.

The independent woman's chosen option is:

"I am a person of worth and dignity but you are
expendable."

This is a disastrous option which leads us to use others, almost as one would use a thing or commodity to fulfill our needs. We become exploiters. We are bound by the smallness of ourselves and the end result is a bitter, selfish, critical, unhappy and lonely woman.

If we are sincere about desiring genuine change in our

lives then we will choose the option of the interdependent woman:

> "I am a person of worth and dignity and you are a person of worth and dignity."

This woman is free to reinforce and intensify another's sense of personhood. She is also aware that each one of us is in need of a Saviour. "For all have sinned, and come short of the glory of God" (Rom. 3:23, *KJV*). She takes personal responsibility for her growth or lack of it; all of us are "heirs together of the grace of life" (1 Pet. 3:7 *KJV*). Her salvation is not dependent on any other person but on her personal relationship with Jesus Christ. She will reject any suggestion that you must be a carbon copy of her or that she must be a carbon copy of you.

How exciting and life changing to realize, as the interdependent woman has, that Jesus Christ's powerful presence is in each of us in the form of the Holy Spirit. Christ is in you and Christ is in me. Therefore the cookie cutter Christianity is neither Christ's desire nor the interdependent woman's goal. Each of us reflects God's image in the context of our own personality and we each play a vital role in the Body of Christ (see 1 Cor. 12). She believes that she is in this world to become all that God intends her to be and that you are here to become all that God intends you to be. If she can reinforce your growth her own will be renewed. Competition is out, equality is in!

The Interdependent Woman Allows Herself and Others the Freedom to Be in Process

This is the woman who accepts herself as an ever-growing, changing and becoming individual. Because she sees herself in process she also views others through those eyes rather than expecting them to be finished products. Nothing is static or fixed about our lives.

Have your goals, talents or roles changed in the last 10 years? I would wager to say they have. And so have the goals and dreams of those around you. But have you ever met a woman who felt her way of doing things was right and everyone else's way was wrong? The interdependent woman opposes such expectations and uses biblical women to influence her attitudes toward diversity.

There is no rigid picture of a Christian woman presented in the Scriptures; the women who followed Christ were free to be themselves. Mary and Martha had a special friendship with Jesus (see Luke 10:38-42), Dorcas's gift of mercy was well known in her area (see Acts 9:36) as was Mary's hospitality (see Acts 12:12). Lydia was a successful businesswoman (see Acts 16:14-15) and Priscilla felt free to talk with Apollos about his erroneous teaching and correct him.

Not only can we choose various roles (and appreciate the roles chosen by the women in our lives) but we can experience them at various times in our life. When we are in our early twenties, for example, we often feel we must do everything and be excellent in all of it right then. Thank goodness this is not true. We may find ourselves pursuing one career or many all our lives. We may choose to stay at home and raise our children for a certain period of time. Life is composed of stages or seasons, as some have termed it, and today you will no doubt find yourself in a different season than the one you were in 10 years ago.

The Proverbs 31 woman is an example of a woman using her gifts and abilities wisely and in season. She has been wrongly accused of being a Super Woman, an ideal that none of us can expect to attain, nor would want to. She has been misunderstood, and we have missed a source of strength if we have tossed out her model. Nowhere are we told that she accomplished all those feats in a day or even a year. She did it in her seasons and according to her needs and her gifts and her energies. She has herself, her family, her roles and her spiritual life in good balance.[1]

What have your seasons looked like? Pause right now and make a line graph illustrating the seasons in your life.

As an example, I will graph my seasons for you. As you can see, my husband has experienced seasons right along with me! I also encourage you to focus on the changes rather than the order in which I have presented them.

My seasons:

single	student	junior college teacher	university instructor	home-maker	author
student	home-maker			mother of 2	director of women's seminars
		home-maker	mother of 1		
	married to a graduate student	pastor's wife	home-maker	Bible study teacher	home-maker
			college dean's wife	graduate student's wife	mother of 2
					psychologist's wife

Now list your seasons:

_____

As you look at your chart, make a separate list of all the abilities and gifts that have been developed in you as a result of the seasons you have experienced.

_____

We are in process and we should be free to prayerfully define our own roles and careers as well as accept the differing decisions made by those around us.

Please don't let the role expectations that others have for you threaten your confidence in the roles you have prayerfully worked out for yourself. Your parents, in-laws, pastors, friends and neighbors all may hold completely different ideas of what is "right" for you. Love those dear, precious ones and listen to their opinions. Then stick to what you believe and are comfortable with unless the Lord shows you differently.

The Interdependent Woman Neither Intimidates Knowingly Nor Is Intimidated

Because the interdependent woman believes she is a person of significance and value and you are also a person of significance and value, regardless of your sex, she does not knowingly intimidate you. She does not try to prove that she is superior or that you are inferior because she believes we are all worth the same sacrifice—the death of God's only begotten Son. She has rejected the lie of our society that it is possible to earn a sense of worth. Her Lord rejected that lie before her.

Jesus was also free from His world's standard. He knew that earning a sense of value was an impossible dream. In the Old Testament God tells us that "all our righteous acts are like filthy rags" (Isa. 64:6, *NIV*). Compared to the holiness of God the Father any action on our part to earn God's favor is insignificant until we have asked Jesus Christ to be our Saviour and Lord.

If identity through success had been important to our Lord, why was He born into a simple carpenter's family in the village of Nazareth of all places? He could have intimidated more effectively had He come from Jerusalem. Why didn't He write books, earn academic degrees or travel the evangelist's circuit rather than pour His life into 12 men, one of whom betrayed Him? How could He let ignorant men crucify Him on a cross, naked, exposed to staring eyes and belligerent taunts? Jesus Christ was not driven by success. Intimidation was not His game.

He also didn't establish relationships with people for the purpose of proving how fine He was. He was friends with a tax collector, an adulteress, a prostitute, ordinary fishermen, women and those in high places. He shows us there are no sexual or cultural barriers to God's love. All people are viewed as living, redeemable human beings.

We don't know much about the Lord's external appearance but we know a great deal about His character, emotions and dreams. Treasures in heaven were the only ones He was interested in collecting. All the methods secular society has ever used to measure a person's value are rejected by Jesus Christ. In the fourth chapter of Matthew Satan tries to attack Christ's identity, berate His sonship and cater to His humanity. Christ was offered satisfaction of all physical needs, prestige and power if He would just bow down to the evil one. Satan's rewards were not worth the price of His lordship so Jesus refused. He was free.

We are also free in Jesus Christ. We don't look at other people as our inferiors and make them our projects. Let's switch places for a moment. Have you ever had the experience of feeling like you were someone's project? They seemed to take personal responsibility for your growth rather than accepting you as you were or resting in the truth that the Holy Spirit was working inside you. You feel like running as far away from that person as you can. When that person is your spouse your situation is complicated, to say the least. Much prayer and communication (sharing the truth in love about yourself, your feelings and your needs) must be called upon in this situation.

Because of Jesus Christ we can also refuse to look on people as our superiors. They have feet of clay just as we do. Heartache is ours when we make another person our object of worship. Inevitably people will let us down due to their humanness and the result can be personal devastation.

We all have areas where our gifts and talents make it possible for us to do something someone else cannot do, but those acts should in no way lay the groundwork for feelings of superiority. Just as many times we are faced with someone else's ability and our inability in a particular area, but that is no reason to feel inferior. We are each unique and we don't want to be like anyone else, male or female. We want to be like Jesus Christ, and the Holy Spirit will work in us until we "take the shape of Christ" (Gal. 4:19, *NEB*).

Is there someone in your life to whom you feel superior? Write down his/her name on a piece of paper. Confess your feeling to the Lord as sin. Thank Jesus for this person. Seek the wisdom of the Lord concerning how you can serve him/her in a very practical way. Also consider approaching that person with a need of yours.

Is there anyone in your life to whom you feel inferior? Write down that person's name on a piece of paper. Confess your feeling to the Lord as sin. Thank Jesus for this person and for his or her area of strength. Thank Jesus for yourself. Review God's perspective on you. Make a list of your gifts and talents. Thank God for the things He is maturing in you. Seek the Lord's wisdom concerning whether the area that caused your feelings of inferiority is an area where you need to grow. If it is, go for it! Take some classes through your church, the YMCA or community college, read some books, meet some new people, ask some new questions—all the time praising the Lord for leading you into this new adventure of self-discovery.

The Interdependent Woman Is Free to Affirm Herself and Others

Affirmation takes place when I see myself and others as valuable, worthwhile, God-created people and when I communicate this perception by what I do and say. In John 13:34 *(RSV)* we are commanded to "love one another; even as I have loved you, that you also love one another."

How does Jesus love? Jesus values each of us for who we are—human beings, highly significant and of great value apart from whatever we can accomplish. Throughout His ministry Jesus saw each person as a cherished child of God. Because of that perception He focused on their possibilities and potential. He held out hope to them. He affirmed us. Jesus delighted in giving His disciples names they could grow into. Jesus changed Simon's name meaning "reed" to Peter meaning "rock." Instead of focusing on Peter's indecisiveness and impetuousness Jesus focused on what Peter would become.

Have you ever noticed that when you label someone all you can see is the label from that time on? Jane and Sue lose their identity in your mind, becoming lazy and impatient instead of being Jane and Sue, God's cherished children. If you are going to give a new name to anyone please make certain you give them a positive, growth-inducing label, just as Christ did.

Never does Jesus label us as sinners. We are commanded to "go and sin no more" but we are not given a derogatory label. Instead hope is always held up to us with words such as these found in *NIV*:

> "You are the light of the world" (Matt. 5:14).
> "You are the salt (seasoning) of the earth" (Matt. 5:13).
> "Follow me . . . and I will make you fishers of men" (Mark 1:17).
> "Your sins are forgiven" (Matt. 9:2).
> "If you have faith as a grain of mustard seed, you can say to your mountain move and nothing will be impossible to you" (see Matt. 17:20).

Jesus affirms us ahead of schedule with positive descriptions of what we are going to become.

Following Christ's example we need, with the eyes of faith, to see the potential for wholeness and transformation in each person, including ourselves. Jesus never waits for someone else to do it; He takes personal responsibility to be the affirmer. The interdependent woman believes that she is in a place that no one else can fill and one of the reasons she is there is to be God's affirmer to those around her. Honest affirmations can soften hearts of stone. An apple a day may keep the doctor away, but a sincere affirmation each day goes a long way toward keeping depression away. We often stand too close to see ourselves accurately. We focus on our failures. How necessary it is to have affirmers in our lives. Affirmations move our eyes away from our mistakes toward our potential.

As a woman, you hold a unique position. You have the unique opportunity to become the cheering section for the people in your life. Reach out and touch the neighbors beside you and across from you. While you are in that office or job remember there are people around you who need to be honestly affirmed. If you are a mother, paint your children a verbal picture of themselves as beautiful, intelligent, courageous and totally dedicated to the Lord Jesus Christ. Paint that picture when they believe it and when they least believe it, when they are 5, 10, 15, 40, 65 years of age—as long as they are alive. Affirm them for what they do, yes, but also for *who* they are—special children of God.

Pause right now and take stock of how you have been doing as an affirmer. How can you sincerely affirm the people in your life today? Before you put your children to bed this evening, will you take the time to hug them and let them know how thrilled you are to be their mother? What about those teens? Do they need you to paint a verbal picture of what beautiful people they are becoming? When

was the last time you affirmed your parents or parents-in-law?

Are you personally feeling a need to be affirmed? Do you take the time to affirm yourself when you're feeling this way? If this is a foreign thought to you perhaps it would help to pretend you are introducing yourself to a friend of yours. Take the time to make a list of the lovely things you would say about yourself.

At the same time you are growing in your ability to affirm yourself, reach out and affirm a friend. In fact, may I suggest that you sit down right now and jot a note of affirmation to someone who is very special to you. Be specific in your affirmation. Describe the characteristic you most appreciate about that person and back it up with a specific example from his or her life.

It is my personal goal to write one of these letters a week. I pray for divine guidance as to who should receive specific affirmation that week. How precious it is to have the Lord's timing confirmed when a friend tells me my note helped her through a specific crisis. Perhaps you would like to make this your goal, too.

After we have practiced on the Lord, ourselves and our friends, then it is time to practice the art of specific affirmations to those we aren't so naturally drawn to.

> But I say to you that hear, Love your enemies, do good to those who hate you, . . . and as you wish that men would do to you, do so to them. If you love those who love you, what credit is that to you? For even sinners love those who love them (Luke 6:27,31-32, *RSV*).

We are able to affirm others and ourselves because we have accepted, by faith, Christ's affirmation of us. We are growing in our ability to see the good in ourselves so we are not threatened when we see the good in others. We affirm others because we know that God has a very special place in His heart for this child of His, just as He has a spot for us.

As the Holy Spirit is transforming us into interdependent women, let's choose to be affirmers by following our Lord's example. We will discover in the process that affirmation of others is one of the most invigorating ways to keep our relationship with the Lord healthy.

The Interdependent Woman Shares Her Vulnerability with Those Around Her

Have you ever felt safe and secure and absolutely miserable at the same time? We all have, haven't we? We search compulsively for safety and security but when we find it we realize we didn't want it after all.

We worship in our cozy, warm little fellowships where we know everyone and their families, totally ignoring the Lord's command to be salt and light in our world. Our conversations consist of being against that which "the world" stands for. We are constantly on the defensive. How much more fulfilling it would be to dare our relationships, our churches and our businesses to be the bearer of Christ's love, those spiritual warriors intent on fleshing out Christ's word to those around us.

Within each of us a battle rages. We desire to risk and yet we fear the unknown. When we are attracted to someone new, do we approach them or do we find ourselves pulling away and waiting for them to make the first move? When we are approached about a new job, a change of location or just a few new responsibilities, what is our response?

How about your mixed emotions when you discovered you were pregnant for the second time? The first time you were swept up in the anticipation of a sweet-smelling Gerber baby coming to live in your home. The second time you knew what to expect: sleepless nights, the change in schedule and all the other realities.

What about the time in your life when your children are ready to leave the nest? Can you send them off with cheer and lots of honest affirmation about the beautiful person they have become? Or do you cower in fear, sure that they won't ever make it in the real world? Do you find yourself strangling them, as it were, with your emotional hold even though you want to let them be free?

Living is risking! My husband Dave and I have a friend who talks about "new normal." He points out that we often sit around waiting for things to return to normal and they never do. Instead we are moved on to yet another "new normal" stage.

Judy Haralson expresses this struggle so well in her poem "Freedom":

Why don't I take it and run:
This freedom to be myself,
The person who God created me to be?

Why don't I take it and run:
This freedom from the bondage
of sin and guilt and shame?

Why don't I take it and run:
This freedom from powers
And principalities, things now and to come?

Why don't I take it and run:
This freedom to soar with the Spirit of God
To the heights of love and life?

Why don't I take it and run:
This freedom . . . ?
Because I've never really been free
And I'm afraid.[2]

But God doesn't give us that spirit of fear (see 2 Tim. 1:7) does He! Nowhere in Scripture do we find Christ promising us security or an absence of suffering. Rather, we are promised His *presence* in the midst of whatever we face. As followers of Christ we are called to leave the comfortable, the familiar and to get to the place in our walk where Jesus is our only security.

Mary was promised by the angel Gabriel that she would be the mother of the Messiah. In our more romantic moments we ponder how wonderful that would be, what an honor, what an affirmation, without pausing to count the cost. Mary, by accepting God's will, had to be willing to be ridiculed. She had to bear the shame of being an unwed mother, to be willing to be misunderstood and to spend her life watching people reject and ultimately crucify her son.

Bruce Larson puts it this way. "To be saved means to be so secure in God's love, present and future, that one has no need to be safe again."[3]

If we have comprehended the security found in God's accepting and forgiving love, if we can truly grasp that God loves us just as much whether we succeed or fail, if we can believe that God's love is a divine gift which we must receive but are incapable of earning, only then are we free to risk. Trust must precede risk. All obedience to God demands risk. Only when we trust God's love can we risk.

When I face something new in my life I can sure relate to these words. "If I am not certain about God's will, I need to fight against my instinctive need for safety and well-being and trust the fact that God wants to give me life . . . ."[4]

Ultimately, we are God's greatest risk because He has chosen to reach out, love and minister to this world through us. God is still risking. We are not robots; we have each been created as unique human beings with the potential to deny or accept God's will for our lives.

I suppose the greatest risk many of us will ever face will be the risk of being who we are. Many dependent women are utterly terrified by this risk because they cannot bear any conflict or rejection. But if we're honest, each of us takes a deep breath when we enthusiastically approach life, as ourselves. After all, we are giving other people the power to hurt us. So why do we do it? Because our Master did it before us.

Jesus was the initiator in being vulnerable. He was open about His hurts, hopes, dreams and despairs. He was the initiator in our love relationship. In 1 John 4:19, *NASB* we discover that "we love because He first loved us."

There is a transparency to Christ's life. The Gospels are rich with examples of Jesus' willingness to let people get to know Him and understand Him. Perhaps one of the ways this is most evident is through Christ's freedom to express His emotions. Because He owned and expressed numerous emotions we are today able to relate to Him and love Him.

Here are a few examples of Christ's vulnerability. He:

> Wept unashamedly at Lazarus's death (see John 11:35-36).
> Showed surprise when met by lack of faith (see Luke 8:25).
> Expressed displeasure to His disciples (see Mark 10:14).
> Rejoiced (see Luke 10:21).

Angered at the Pharisees' hardness of heart
(see Mark 3:5).
Grieved deeply in spirit over Jerusalem (see
Luke 19:41).
Moved to compassion numerous times (see
John 11:33-38).
Experienced feelings of loneliness (see Matt.
26:40).

Jesus was the initiator of vulnerability because He knew we could never love a God we couldn't relate to. Bruce Larson clearly defines how God loved us.

> He became totally vulnerable, which culminated in His crucifixion and death. He did not protect Himself from us. He allowed us to laugh at Him, to mock Him, to spit upon Him, to humiliate Him and finally to kill Him. He had the power to prevent it but chose not to. And this is the kind of love that He commands us to have one for another.[5]

If we as Christian women are to follow Christ's example we must willingly drop our masks and games. We must be willing to communicate the truth in love about ourselves. We must be willing to be vulnerable, not to satisfy our own egos or for another's satisfaction but to glorify God.

So often our women's gatherings are filled with people who outwardly look as if they've got everything together yet inwardly are crying out for someone to really love them. Other Christians can look so put together and peaceful that it takes real courage to admit one's own deep need. Yet, if we don't admit our need, then neither God's love nor His love expressed through other human beings can touch us where we so desperately need it.

Never are we called to be anything but real human beings who allow ourselves to be known. Any time you feel as if the cost of vulnerability is just too great, remember that the alternative is even more painful.

But how we argue with ourselves. Our self-talk sounds a little like this: "I'm a Christian now." "I'm not supposed to feel bad." "I'm not supposed to hold a grudge." "I'm not supposed to be having difficulty loving." "I'm not supposed to be feeling depressed." "I'd better not let others know what I'm really like or they won't think I'm much of a Christian." So our guilt grows—as does our pride. We build walls between ourselves and others and are incapable of giving love to our heavenly Father and others as well as receiving love from our heavenly Father and others.

What deception! In Romans 5:6 we read that "Christ died for the ungodly." We can do nothing apart from our Saviour. Pretending we are perfect doesn't change a thing, it only robs God of the glory for any growth that is occurring in our lives. When I am willing to reveal my weaknesses to you, and when growth happens in my life, together we can give God praise. I have become a living demonstration of God's goodness.

We often don't want to be around others because they might find out our deception. But if we will share how God is adequate, even when we are inadequate, people will know we understand them. They will know the experiential reality of the Saviour we are introducing. At that point we will become fellow strugglers.

How honest are you being with yourself? William Kinnaird writes, "Ironically enough, people who have come to grips with their own inadequacies and limitations frequently are more effective in caring for and supporting others."[6] In order to be vulnerable with each other we have to take off our rose-colored glasses and admit our selfishness. We have to stop pretending we are perfect. Only God is perfect. We also need to own up to our mistakes. We must not be afraid to say, "I was wrong," "I hurt" and "I love you."

Yes, vulnerability involves risk but we can risk because we are loved. The interdependent woman is aware that Jesus Christ, who knows her better than anyone else does, also loves her the most. That knowledge frees her to risk.

The Interdependent Woman Is Balanced in Her Relationships

Jesus Christ is the ultimate model of interdependence that we need to keep our eyes on. One aspect of His interdependence was His willingness to be involved in relationships. In fact, He left heaven so that He, the creator God, could meet us where we are and get to know us intimately. He made Himself available to us to such an extent that He identified with our needs and even our temptations (see Heb. 2:17-18).

Just as He enthusiastically entered the lives of the disciples at whatever stage they found themselves, so He enters our lives and encourages us to go for more. His love encourages us and sparks growth in us.

When involved in relationships Jesus was able to receive help from others. In fact He was not afraid to verbalize His needs. As a result the Samaritan woman gave Him water to drink, and in Gethsemane, His disciples gave Him companionship until they fell asleep. He received a donkey on which to ride into Jerusalem and the gift of a meal from a repentant Zacchaeus.

In the midst of His relationships, Christ never lost sight of either His identity or purpose. He did not make Himself responsible for those around Him. Never does He make Himself responsible for our actions, either. He communicates clearly His love through His life and His words. Then He leaves our responses to us. Never are we Jesus' puppets.

Another way that our relationships can be restricting is if we make ourselves responsible for someone else. We are only responsible for ourselves. As mothers and grandmothers we are responsible to teach our children, but we cannot do their learning for them. What children do with our guidance is entirely up to them. And they must bear the responsibility of their choices.

Now we, as Christ's followers, find ourselves growing through healthy relationships. In 1 John 4:12 *(NASB)* it says, "No one has beheld God at any time; if we love one another, God abides in us, and His love is perfected in us." The Christian life was not meant to be lived in a vacuum. We are encouraged to be involved in relationships.

As we rub shoulders with each other we see the need to be committed to one another. Only in commitment to imperfect human beings can we follow in our Master's footsteps.

The very word "commitment" grinds on many eardrums today in this independent, self-centered society of ours. Yet it is only after we have committed ourselves to the God of love that we can commit ourselves to care for others and we can identify with others in their various stages of growth. We refuse to make others either our projects or our heroes. Instead we choose to walk, as much as humanly possible, where they have walked, to laugh and weep with them, to be available to them, to be as gentle with them as Jesus Christ is with us and to be vulnerable to them, demonstrated by our willingness to speak the truth in love about ourselves when we are with them. I choose to back up my words with an authentic lifestyle. In relationships I am willing not only to give but also to express my needs honestly and receive from others.

We are one of the best means of getting God's life and love to others. Jesus is our source of strength so never do we purposely choose to have others become dependent on us. In all of our relating, we must remember that the purpose is for Christ to be formed in you and in me (Gal. 4:19). If we find ourselves imitating anyone but Christ or pressuring someone else to imitate us then we need to confess and readjust. We need to honestly share, with no inhibitions, what we see happening and together we need to get our friendship back to its original purpose—that Christ will be formed in both of us.

Love is the evidence that I am Christ's woman. Only through dependence on Christ alone will I find myself freed to be a most courageous lover who will not lose her identity through loving but will find her God-given purpose in loving.

4
What Does God Have to Do with My Struggle?

A Solid Foundation for a Healthy Self-Image

Interdependency is unattainable unless you see God, your heavenly Father, as a loving, Holy God. It is terribly difficult to give love unless you have been the recipient of love. During the next few pages let's uncover, together, the truth about how precious we are to God, and how much He loves us.

Who Is God?

My personal standards of comparison only began to change as I attuned myself to the whole of God's Word. And it was during this time that I read a book by Colleen Townsend Evans titled, *Start Loving the Miracle of Forgiving.* In it the author describes God's reason for Jesus:

It has been snowing for 24 hours. Knowing that
it had been a hard winter I filled the bird feeder
with an extra supply of feed that morning. Since
the feeder was sheltered it held the only food
not hidden by the snow. A short while later a
small bird appeared in the yard obviously weak,
hungry and cold. Searching for food he pecked
at the snow.

How helpless I felt! I wanted to go out and point
to the feeder but if I opened the door to throw
out more food he would have flown away. Then
I realized that only if I were another bird could I
indicate where to find food, could I fly with him,
identify myself with his hunger and cold and let
him know that I understood and cared.

Our God, looking at man, knew He must
become one of us in order that we might know
His forgiveness, in order that we might point
above our heads to the source of nourishment
and eternal life.[1]

Only through Jesus Christ can we as women discover
our sole source of freedom. We are free only when bound
to this loving God, who cared enough about each one of us
to send His only begotten Son so we would have a "fleshed
out" picture of what He is truly like. Let's examine the
Scriptures together to discover what Christ showed us
about God, our heavenly Father.

He is the loving, concerned Father who is interested in the intimate details of our lives
(Matt. 6:25-34).

He is the Father who never gives up on us
(Luke 15:3-32).

He is the God who sent His Son to die for us
though we were undeserving (Rom. 5:8).

He stands with us in the good and bad circumstances (Heb. 13:5).

He is the ever-active Creator of our universe.

He died to heal sickness, pain and our grief
(Isa. 53:3-6).

He has broken the power of death
(Luke 24:6-7).

He gives all races and sexes equal status
(Gal. 3:28).

He is available to us through prayer
(John 14:13-14).

He is aware of our needs (Isa. 65:24).

He has created us for an eternal relationship
with him (John 3:16).

He values us (Luke 7:28).

He doesn't condemn us (Rom. 8:1).

God values and causes our growth (1 Cor. 3:7).

He comforts us (2 Cor. 1:3-5).

He strengthens us through His Spirit
(Eph. 3:16).

He cleanses us (Heb. 10:17-22).

He is for us (Rom. 8:31).

He is always available to us (Rom. 8:38-39).

He is a God of hope (Rom. 15:13).

He provides a way to escape temptations
(1 Cor. 10:13).

He is at work in us (Phil. 2:13).

He helps us in temptation (Heb. 2:17-18).

He wants us to be free (Gal. 5:1).

He is the final Lord of history (Rev. 1:8).

As if that isn't wonderful enough, the writer of the first chapter of Hebrews tells us these things about Jesus Christ:

> He is greater than any human prophet (vv. 1-2).
> He is God's Son (v. 2).
> He is heir of all things (v. 2).
> He created the world (v. 2).
> He is Himself God (v. 3).
> He upholds all things (v. 3).
> He cleanses us from sin (v. 3).
> He sits at the right hand of the Father (v. 3).
> He is greater than the angels (v. 4).
> He has the name of Son (v. 5).
> Angels worship Him (v. 6).
> He is the eternal God (vv. 8-9).
> His throne is forever (v. 8).
> He is the ruler of the coming age (vv. 10-12).

The most important thing for a woman is what she believes about God. Do you find the dependent woman's God in the above verses? Where is the condemning judge ready to zap you if you step out of line? He is a figment of an overactive perfectionistic streak and the result of poor teaching. This is not the picture of God presented through and by Jesus Christ.

Our God is *for* us. Praise His Holy name! The God who is beyond us and above us chooses to live with us in Jesus Christ. The wonder of it all! Henrietta Mears, in *431 Quotes* says:

> Jesus is
> God's mouth speaking God's message
> God's eyes seeing our need
> God's ears hearing our cry
> God's mind knowing our troubles

God Himself in human form come to bring us God.[2]

How Does God See Me?

Now that we have wiped away some of our preconceived opinions about what God is like we need to move on to see how God views us. After taking a comprehensive look at Scripture, the interdependent woman believes three things about how her Creator views her: (1) she is highly significant to God; (2) she is deeply fallen; (3) she is greatly loved. Let's look closely at each of her beliefs.

Highly Significant

The interdependent woman truly understands the value God has placed on her personhood. And we all need to see this truth or we will never be transformed into interdependent women. Scripture teaches that we have been created in the image of the creator God (Gen. 1:27). We are divine originals! Even though we do not totally comprehend the wonder of this fact, we are aware of an inborn need and ability to be creative. We also have an awareness of ourselves, a self-consciousness that is non-existent in the animal kingdom. Our ability to moralize and to think rational thoughts all tie into the reality of what it means to be created in the image of our God.

In Psalm 8 we discover that we, as part of the human race, are the highest of God's created beings. With a sense of awe we realize that we have been made a little lower than the angels and crowned with glory and honor. Without God we would be just dust, for God breathed His very breath into humanity to give us life (Gen. 2:7). Then through reading Genesis 1:26, we are overwhelmed by the tremendous trust God committed to each of us when He gave us dominion over the earth. Finally, the great value God ascribed to each of us was declared at Calvary when He sent His only begotten Son to die for our sins. The Almighty God believed we were worth that much! If the value of something depends on the price paid for it, then our own worth is beyond calculation.

In today's world we are confronted daily with people willing to spend phenomenal amounts of money to buy one-of-a-kind-cars, vintage beverages, designer clothes, stamps—you name it. You and I might find it repulsive to spend so much money for those items, yet their value has absolutely nothing to do with our feelings. Their value is found in the hearts of men and women who are willing to pay such fantastic prices for them. In the same way our value lies not in how we view ourselves but in what God was willing to pay to redeem us. He paid dearly by giving of Himself on Calvary (see John 3:16). Scripture also tells us that God loves us so very much that He desires to spend eternity with us (see John 14:2-3).

It should also be pointed out that God not only sees us as highly significant people, He also affirms our sexuality. According to Josephus, the women of Jesus' day faced terrible conditions. The Jewish men prided themselves with the "spiritual truth" (taught in the Talmud) that women were inferior. Yet these same men used women in polygamous relationships and for prostitution, both in and out of the temple.

Into this sinful, arrogant world came Jesus Christ. Here was a radically different Rabbi who affirmed women. To start, God chose to have His Son be dependent on a woman for His birth, His care and nurture. In the fourth chapter of John we find Christ giving the first revelation to a woman that He was the Messiah. He regularly taught women the Scriptures and was not afraid to hold a conversation in public with a woman. In Jewish tradition a woman was not permitted to bear witness, but Jesus' words after the resurrection to a woman were "go and tell my disciples." Many more examples can be pointed out from the pages of Scripture but suffice it to say, Jesus sees women as highly significant people. He also sees us as deeply fallen people in great need of Him.

Deeply Fallen

Jeremiah 17:9 *(TLB)* states that "the heart is the most deceitful thing there is, and desperately wicked. No one can really know how bad it is!" That's not really a lot of fun to read, is it? But your feelings don't make it less true. I believe that Scripture describes our heart as deceitful because we try to convince ourselves that we really are pretty good. When there is something that needs confessing in our lives, do we rush to the Lord with it or do we pull down our masks? *Well you know me Lord, I've got a few faults. But a sinner? Let's not get too extreme now. Remember Lord, I'm busy serving you.*

When I first accepted Christ as my personal Saviour I really didn't think God would have much work to do. After all, I was a pretty acceptable person by my standards. Was I ever surprised when I was confronted with God's standards!

The potential for every imaginable evil lies within each of us. Judgments should not come quickly from our mouths, for given the same circumstances and temptations that others face, we, too, have the possibility of succumbing. "For from within, out of men's (women's) hearts, come evil thoughts of lust, theft, murder, adultery . . . wickedness, deceit, lewdness, envy, slander, pride and all other folly" (Mark 7:21-22, *TLB*).

There is another reason why I believe Scripture points out the deceitfulness of our hearts. This reason is as old as the story of Creation. It is our tendency to believe that the circumstances around us and other people are responsible for our responses to life. This was illustrated graphically to me a few years ago. It was the day before Halloween and our five-year-old son Christopher and his friend Scotty were sitting on the porch swing. Their masks were pulled up on top of their heads and they called to me, asking for some cookies. Since it was only a few minutes before lunch I refused their request. As boys sometimes do, they helped themselves anyway. But in the process the metal lid of the cookie jar banged shut, giving me every indication of what was happening in the kitchen. (Every mother needs a metal lid on her cookie jar!)

When those two precious boys saw me coming toward them, they pulled their masks down over their eyes as if on signal. When they realized they had been trapped in their crime Christopher blamed Scotty and Scotty blamed Christopher. Needless to say, they both had a few moments to sit quietly and think about what they had done. But I was busy thinking, too. How often do I hide from the truth, believing that circumstances and other people are responsible for what I have done? Bruce Larson puts it this way:

> If we really understand the Bible we have to revise our thoughts about heaven and hell. We think hell is for bad people and heaven is for good people. Actually, hell is for people who think they are good and heaven is for those who know how bad they are.[3]

Indeed we are deeply fallen women. 1 John 1:8 *(TLB)* says, "If we say that we have no sin, we are only fooling ourselves, and refusing to accept the truth."

We need to look long and hard at Calvary to see the awfulness of our personal sin that caused Christ's death.

But Calvary also speaks to us of the great value God put on His self-centered creation. Calvary shows us we are greatly loved.

For some reason we as women find it easier to believe in our deeply fallen nature than to believe in the great value God has ascribed to each of us. It is time for us to view the entire picture.

Greatly Loved

As Christian women we sometimes look at ourselves only as forgiven sinners. But in stressing the forgiven part we neglect to stress as strongly God's promise that we are transformed and accepted women. We are no longer just flesh people, we are now brand new spiritual people. Second Corinthians 5:17 *(NASB)* gives us a radical revelation: "If [anyone] is in Christ, he [or she] is a new creature; the old things pass away; behold, new things have come." We are not just forgiven sinners, we are transformed into new creations and are God's very own children. First John 3:1-2 *(NIV)* rings out: "How great is the love the Father has lavished on us, that we should be called children of God! And that is what we are! . . . Dear friends, now we are children of God."

There is a radical difference between human birth and spiritual birth. When a precious new child enters the world, the life-giving cord joining the mother and child is cut. Never again will the child depend on his mother in the same way. When Christ gives us the umbilical cord of spiritual birth (see 1 John 3:9), that cord is never severed. Not only is God always around us, Christ is *in* us.

Abundant life and freedom comes only as we are dependent on God for everything. So not only are we forgiven sinners we are also "new creatures" with God in us. At the same time we are in God (see John 14:20 and Gal.

2:20). Can we grasp the wonder of God's truth?

A woman who only believes she is forgiven focuses heavily on her performance rather than on her Lord. If we only believe we are forgiven, then we can be easily discouraged after confessing the same area over and over again. What one of us hasn't experienced that? We begin to wonder if God has lost patience with us. And it isn't very long until we question whether He'll accept us any longer.

Security is not discovered in forgiveness alone. Security is only found when we accept what Jesus Christ has done. When you have really understood this truth you will no longer sit in a communion service, focusing on the awfulness of your personal sin. You will focus on God's fantastic grace and love.

There are no risks involved in God's love—none whatsoever. God accepts us in Jesus Christ, not because of our performance, but because of Christ's shed blood. The pressure is off, dear women. If we understand the meaning of grace, our defeats and failures should not cause us to turn away from God. They should cause us to turn towards Him in confession, praise and thanksgiving.

Ephesians 1:6, *KJV* points out that "we are accepted in the beloved." Because God is holy He can only accept perfection. Other than Jesus Christ, none of us is perfect, regardless of how much effort we put into trying to become perfect. Christ alone is acceptable to God. Because we have been covered by Jesus' shed blood (see Gal. 3:27) and He indwells us, we are completely accepted by the Almighty God. We are not *just* forgiven sinners! We are not *merely* forgiven sinners. In God's eyes we are received and treated—accepted—as if we are Jesus, because of Christ's shed blood.

There is a fantastic word picture of this truth found in Exodus 11:4-6. The death angel is going to pass over all the homes in Egypt, killing the firstborn in each home unless blood has been sprinkled over the doorpost of that home. What if some well-meaning, perfectionist woman had posted a list describing what a beautiful person she was, the activities all members of the home were involved in and the kindnesses they had done? The death angel would have struck that home bringing death and terror with him. It was the blood that made them acceptable and so it is today. We gain acceptance in God's eyes only because of Christ's shed blood.

That is why I can confidently write this message: Regardless of your past mistakes or failures, if Jesus Christ is your personal Saviour, God looks at each one of you and says, "You are my beloved daughter and I am pleased with you." It is time to take off the backpack of confessed guilt so many of us allow to weigh us down. We are indeed forgiven, accepted and loved women.

One day I saw a two-sided poster and the potency of its message stopped me in my tracks. One side of the poster said: "World's view: I love you, I love you not." As you can guess there was a picture of a beautiful child picking the petals off a daisy. On the other side of the poster it said: "God's view: I love you, I love you, I love you . . . "

So it is. In God's eyes we are beautiful because of Jesus Christ's shed blood. The interdependent woman realizes it is impossible to love and enjoy herself until she has really learned to know and love her creator. When she loves God she learns to love herself, from His perspective.

She believes three truths about herself—she is highly significant, deeply fallen and greatly loved. Her true sense of worth comes in her awareness that she is loved and accepted unconditionally. This realization changes her focus from her mistakes and performance to the beauty of God's love and grace. She is freed from trying to please God and living her life through others, like the dependent woman does. She is also free to take off her masks and to stop pretending she can make it totally on her own like the independent woman does. The interdependent woman is the only person free to be herself because she is aware of who her wonderful God is.

It's a Process

Let me hasten to tell you that becoming an interdependent woman is a process. One does not go to bed one evening and wake up the next morning a new person. How nice that would be! There is no growth without risk and struggle. So it is in our search for interdependency.

This book hasn't been written by someone who has supposedly made it. I am not a signed, sealed and delivered interdependent woman. Rather, I am in the process of being transformed by the Holy Spirit. I have had to face and experience both the counterfeit options of dependency and independency before I could realize what shams they both are.

I see freedom at the end of my process. Before, all I faced was bondage, either to myself or to someone else. Even though I slip back periodically into both roles it happens less and less as I truly become a new creation. I'm thankful the process has started because I don't want to settle for bondage again. Won't you join me as I pray the Holy Spirit will create us both into interdependent women?

Yes, it is true that when you stand before the
   Lord to ask His forgiveness,
Your dress is ragged and tattered because of
   ugly sins,
Your hair is thickly tangled with the web of
   rebellion,

Your shoes are torn and muddy by your past
    failures.
But God never sees any of that!
He sees you Holy,
He sees you perfect
Because you are dressed in His righteousness
And He has covered you with the full length
    cape of His love.
He sees nothing else!
Even when you explain how you really look
    underneath,
He hears but He forgets forever.
The dimension of His forgetfulness is as far as
    the East is from the West,
And it endures past all eternity.[4]

5
How Can I Love Myself?

Beginning the Process

As we express our willingness to become interdependent, the Holy Spirit will take each of us on a personal journey. With His direction let us begin the process of loving ourselves.

Step 1:
Start a Relationship with the God of Love

Many of us have difficulty understanding or even desiring a relationship with God, the Father, because of a painful relationship we have experienced with our earthly fathers. God is not like our earthly fathers! Who of us has a perfect parent or is a perfect parent? Not one of us!

It is essential to our belief in a loving God that we differentiate between our earthly father and our heavenly Father. It is also necessary to forgive our father of any pain he may have caused us. If we refuse, then any time we hear God referred to as Father, we will be overwhelmed by feelings of bitterness, repulsion, anger and perhaps even hate. When our pain is too intense it is impossible to turn towards our loving, heavenly Father with adoration, worship, obedience and praise. We will have great difficulty believing that God views us as highly significant or greatly loved women. Like the dependent person, we will see our deeply fallen nature.

It is almost impossible to love and enjoy ourselves until we have really learned to love and enjoy our Creator. We can't be a better Christian woman than our perspective of God will allow. When we love God we learn to love ourselves from His perspective. Is it possible we have thoughts, ideas and concepts of God that are unworthy of Him because of our painful associations with the word "father"?

There is a person in my life who was severely beaten as a child and who faced more anger than affection from her father. Rarely, if ever, were words of love or affirmation expressed. It was incomprehensible to my friend that God, who was her heavenly Father, could be anything but an angry and vengeful figure.

My friend's eyes were blinded to God's love, grace and forgiveness until she asked the Holy Spirit to walk back through her past with her. Likewise, it wasn't until she was willing to forgive her father (even though this parent still justifies his behavior) and search the Scriptures for clues as to what God's character is really like, that her life began to change. Over a period of time she was finally able to replace her personal experience with the word "father" with Scripture's definition of God as Father. During this time she found Dick Dickinson's paraphrase of 1 Corinthians 13:4-7 extremely helpful in redefining what God the Father is like:

> Because God loves me, He is slow to lose patience with me.

> Because God loves me, He takes the circumstances of my life and uses them in a constructive way for my growth.

> Because God loves me, He does not treat me as an object to be possessed and manipulated.

> Because God loves me, He has no need to impress me with how great and powerful He is because *He is God.* Nor does He belittle me as His child in order to show me how important He is.

> Because God loves me, He is for me. He wants to see me mature and develop in His love.

> Because God loves me, He does not send down His wrath on every little mistake I make of which there are many.

> Because God loves me, He does not keep score of all my sins and then beat me over the head with them whenever He gets the chance.

> Because God loves me, He is deeply grieved when I do not walk in the ways that please Him because He sees this as evidence that I don't trust Him and love Him as I should.

> Because God loves me, He rejoices when I experience His power and strength and stand

up under the pressures of life for His name's sake.

Because God loves me, He keeps on working patiently with me even when I feel like giving up and can't see why He doesn't give up with me, too.

Because God loves me, He keeps on trusting me when at times I don't even trust myself.

Because God loves me, He never says there is no hope for me, rather, He patiently works with me, loves me and disciplines me in such a way that it is hard for me to understand the depth of His concern for me.

Because God loves me, He never forsakes me even though many of my friends might.[1]

It is this same heavenly Father who invites us to come to Him by faith, believing that He will accept us, as we are, into His family. We don't have to earn His acceptance on the basis of our performance, our acquaintances, our possessions, our beauty or our marital status. In John 3:17 we learn that God didn't come into this world to condemn the world but to save and free the world.

It is this same God who sees us as highly significant and greatly loved even though He knows we are deeply fallen women. If you had been the only person on the face of this earth, God would still have sent His Son to die for you. You are that valuable to Him.

Have you asked this Jesus, the risen Christ, to be your personal Saviour? Have you exchanged your concept of an earthly, imperfect father, for the scriptural description of God as a loving, perfect Father? If you choose to begin with a God of love, God will give you the right to become a child of God (read John 1:12-13). Because of what Jesus did on Calvary, you are loved, accepted and viewed as perfect by the very God of the universe. You are, from this moment on, dressed in Jesus' righteousness. You come from greatness!

Step 2:
Acknowledge that Knowing Jesus Christ Is Foundational to Your Search for Wholeness and Esteem

Maurice Wagner has written a thought-provoking book called *The Sensation of Being Someone*. In it he points out that we all need to feel we belong, we are of value, and that we can achieve, if we are to experience a healthy self-esteem. It was thrilling for me to realize that my relationship with Jesus Christ meets my needs in all three of these areas.

Because of what God the Father did by giving us His only begotten and unique Son, I know the security that is a result of belonging. Based on the Word of God I know I am a child of God (see 1 John 3:1 and John 1:12); I have been accepted in the beloved (see Eph. 1:6) and I am a new creature (see 2 Cor. 5:17). I have become part of a wonderful support group, the Body of Christ (see 1 Cor. 12:27). When anyone in my group is suffering I feel pain and when they rejoice, I rejoice. The people in this Body of Christ are the ones with whom I will spend eternity. I can be confident of this truth because in John 14:2-3, Jesus promises to prepare a place for me. When this life is over I can spend eternity with Him and with the other precious Christians I have learned to love here on earth.

Not only do I experience love, support and acceptance

from God and from the Body, as a result of making Jesus Christ my Saviour, I also have a sense of being a person of value who is cherished and respected. Romans 5:8 *(NASB)* shows me that God's love for me is not based on my performance: "But God demonstrates His own love toward us, in that while we were yet sinners, Christ died for us." I have absolutely no possibility of earning God's favor and yet He sent His only begotten Son to earth to die for me. I know I am valued apart from what I can do! I am now at peace with my God, who views me as His beloved daughter.

As if that isn't wonderful enough, God's love also fulfills my need for achievement. When Jesus was here on earth, willingly imprisoned in our humanity, He acknowledged the impossibility of human beings living the Christian life apart from supernatural intervention. He knew He had dreams to give us that would be absolutely impossible without Him. So the Holy Spirit was sent to do the Father's work in each one of us. We have a confidence, based on Philippians 1:6, that as long as we're willing, the Holy Spirit is going to keep us growing.

Why? In Ephesians 2:10 we discover that God wants us to accomplish good works—that is why He is at work in each one of us. The perfect plan involves women who are full of God Himself and who have the arms to hug the people in their world, the ears to listen to the joys and sorrows of their world, the hands to help those around them, the mind through which Christ thinks and the mouth to speak words of comfort, wisdom and hope.

Accepting Jesus Christ as my personal Saviour means I experience the security that results from knowing I belong and am a valuable and competent human being. Now I achieve, not to get a sense of adequacy, but out of an awareness of adequacy. "I can do all things through Him who strengthens me" (Phil. 4:13, *NASB*).

Step 3:
Affirm that You Are First Class Quality

There are stores in Southern California which make a successful business out of marketing seconds and last year's merchandise. You are not a second, however. You are first quality!

> Let us make man in our image, according to our likeness . . . . And God created man in His own image, in the image of God He created him; male and female He created them (Gen. 1:26-27, *NASB*).

You were created in God's image as a woman. It is true that sin has entered the picture but sin only distorts God's image, it does not wipe it out. In 1 Corinthians 11:7 we read that the Christians at Corinth were referred to as the image and glory of God. Given their quarrelsome, boastful, immoral and immature attitudes and actions, that is an amazing statement!

Have you ever taken a trip on a train, boat or plane? Were you rejected—not allowed on board—because you were feeling depressed, unworthy or unattractive? Of course not. There is only one thing that is essential for your journey and that is the ticket. If you have a ticket you can feel angry, happy, excited or frustrated and you will not be denied admittance aboard. Think of the implications. If God, whose standards are perfect, has accepted us, why do we refuse to accept ourselves?

God accepts us not because of our performance or feelings but because of Christ's shed blood. If you have confessed your inability to run your own life plus your need of a Saviour and Lord, you are accepted in God the Father's eyes. He sees you as holy and perfect and dressed in His righteousness. You don't have to prove that you are valuable anymore. You *are* valuable!

Step 4:
Accept Your Humanity

Are you often aware of your humanity, your frailties? Great! You are earthen and that's the way God meant it when He created you. Second Corinthians 4:7 *(NASB)* explains why: "But we have this treasure in earthen vessels, that the surpassing greatness of the power may be of God and not from ourselves." The beauty of Jesus becomes evident to those around us through our humanity. Is it really okay to be human? Yes! Because Jesus the Creator God of the universe chose to be fully human.

Being human means we have mental and physical weaknesses; it means we experience energy limitations; it means we have needs and it means we have a mixture of emotions. Being human also means we have a need to love and be loved and to feel we are significant persons. We will not be able to do everything we want to do or everything everyone else wants us to do. The great news is that God indwells our humanity so His beauty will show forth in us.

What happens when we forget or deny that we are human? We play God and our perfectionistic and superwoman complex glares us straight in the eye. Like Avis, we try harder. But the reality is this: trying harder can never change us from earthen vessels into deity.

Pause in your reading for a moment and make a list of all the shoulds you put on yourself every day. Perhaps your list starts with "I should lose weight," "I should always be engaged in constructive activity," "I should always be happy," or "I should be a good housekeeper."

After you have made your list, reread it and see if you can remember where each particular "should" originated. Did it come from your family, society, your church, your work, Scripture or your own high expectations for yourself? Now go back over the list and decide which "shoulds" you choose to keep and those that need to be dropped. Work hard in the next few weeks at dropping all the shoulds in your vocabulary, for they push personal guilt buttons when we can't consistently live up to them.

The word "should" causes us to feel as if someone outside is controlling you. Replace the word "should" with the word "choose" and you will assume personal responsibility for your own actions. Your choices will be your own rather than someone else's.

A hypocrite is someone who passes herself off as being perfect. It is not someone who doesn't live up to her own standards or we'd all be either hypocrites or women with extremely low standards. *God* is perfect! *We* are human! Affirm your humanity.

I am loved and accepted by God therefore I don't have to reject my own humanity in order to prove my value. I am human and my greatest desire is that the beauty of Jesus will be seen in me.

Step 5:
Celebrate Your Uniqueness and Stop Asking "What if . . . ?"

Each of us is a divine original! We are the creative expression of a loving God. Think what it would cost to buy an original by a famous dress designer. We often fail to focus on the beauty of our design because we are too busy focusing on why our design isn't like someone else's!

What do you feel when you stand on the beach, watching the beauty, power and immensity of the sea? Do you take the time to meditate on the vastness of our universe? When was the last time you focused on the beauty of a flower? How can we feel awestruck by all the rest of God's creation and still have the nerve to downgrade ourselves?

You and I have unique talents and abilities, personalities, and opportunities. What joy are you missing in life because you aren't using the capabilities and potentials you have been given? Jesus wants you to be your own person. Do you feel that someone else is more attractive than you are, more naturally intelligent or better proportioned physically? Are you using that as your excuse for not appreciating what you have been given? Because others have attributes you don't have is no basis for your feeling inferior or their feeling superior. First Corinthians 4:7 (NIV) puts it this way, "For who makes you different from anyone else? What do you have that you did not receive? And if you did receive it, why do you boast as though you did not?"

All of our natural abilities have come from the hand of a loving God. What matters now is our faithfulness in developing what God has given us, rather than arguing with God about what we don't have or wish we had. The time has come to accept what we've been given. We can then be excited and not threatened when someone else excels.

Have you ever taken a child out to a restaurant with you? You were probably excited about sharing the eating experience with her only to discover that she is upset because she doesn't have a straw! In front of her is a plate of delicious, attractively displayed food. But the only thing that matters is the missing straw!

How do you feel as a parent? Is it just possible we use similar antics when we focus on our deficits, compare them to other people's natural abilities and moan? There's a fabulously exciting world out there waiting to be explored and loved. Yet here we sit in our disbelief, eyes focused on ourselves, comparing ourselves with others and drowning in a pool of self-pity. It's time to refuse to feel second-rate because we are not perfect.

When we begin with what we have, as opposed to

what we don't have, we are often surprised at how very much God has given us with which to work. Take out a pen and paper and take some time to focus on your uniqueness.

1. Make a list of at least 10 things you like about yourself . . . 20 things would be even better. No doubt the Lord has brought special people into your life who have helped you develop these characteristics and have affirmed your growth along the way. Put their names down beside your list.

2. Spend time in prayer. Thank God for the 20 things you like about yourself. Do you realize you are praising God for His creation when you do this? Then thank God for the wonderful, affirming people He has brought into your life. Finally, thank God for creating you.

3. Next, make a list of the things you honestly don't like about yourself. Go back and put a checkmark beside the things you *could* change if it was important to you. Please keep this list. We will refer to it later in the book.

4. The unchecked items on your list are the things about yourself which you cannot change. The time has come to thank the Lord for these and to verbalize to Him your acceptance of this "thorn in your flesh." Write out an acceptance prayer to the Lord.

5. After you have written out your prayer of

acceptance, covenant with the Lord not to ever again bemoan the areas you are incapable of changing.

God is limitless but we definitely are not. By working through this exercise you choose the limitations you cannot change. You have also accepted them. This is a crucial step on your spiritual journey. Let's not waste any more time asking, "what if." If the limits on our ability can't be changed, let's accept them and accept ourselves as God does.

Joni Eareckson Tada has had to come to grips with the reality that she is a quadraplegic. But that doesn't stop her from ministering in word and song, from being an artist, from writing or from encouraging others. Michelle Price came face-to-face with the reality of cancer and had to have a leg amputated. But that hasn't stopped her from competing in winter sports.[2] What is the reality you have just faced by writing out your prayer and covenant? That is part of the beauty of you! Celebrate your uniqueness!

Enjoy the Trip

In this chapter we have begun the process of moving towards interdependence by facing the question "How can I love myself?" The process is far from complete but since, "a journey of a thousand miles begins with a single step," we have taken our first five steps. This is not a magical journey. You will not wake up one morning and find you have arrived at your destination. Rather, you will discover you were put on the face of this earth to enjoy the trip. Serendipities await you. So take time to meditate on, pray over and incorporate these into your life-style. In the next chapter the process of learning to love ourselves, as God loves us, will be continued.

6
Will I See a Difference in Myself?

Questioning Your Motivation

Based on a comprehensive view of Scripture, a woman who is growing toward interdependence believes three things: (1) she is highly significant to God; (2) she is deeply fallen; (3) she is greatly loved. This doesn't mean she simply gives intellectual assent to these truths. She has experienced these truths in the depth of her being.

How Do I Respond to My Mistakes?

I have found a good way to determine whether I have really grasped the reality of God's love for me and belief in me is to look at the way I handle my limitations, my mistakes and my failures. There are three questions I need to ask myself whenever I make a mistake:

1. *Do I make negative value judgments about myself based on my deficiency of my mistakes?*

   Does my self talk say, *I don't know how to play the piano.* Or does it say, *I'm worthless. I'm a flop. Everybody must think I'm a real dummy, a failure.*

2. *Do I run away from my deficiencies and mistakes?*

   Do I pretend the mistakes aren't there?

   Do I put on yet another mask?

   Do I blame my mistakes on other people or circumstances?

   Do I blame God?

   Am I once again running away from anyone or anything that makes me feel bad?

3. *Can I look at my deficiencies and own them without threat?*

   Can I forgive myself of my mistakes as God forgives me?

   Do I realize it is impossible to change lifetime habits overnight?

   Do I refuse to discriminate against myself?

None of us is strong or superior in everything. We are all inferior in some respect. I have always chuckled at Maxwell Maltz's statement that "ninety-five percent of us suffer from feelings of inferiority and the other five percent are liars." It's true, so why do we forget so quickly? If we find ourselves answering the questions above by choosing either the first or second option, we must ask ourselves another question: *Do I want to believe what God says about me or would I rather suffer?*

Why Do I Choose Negativity?

It seems to me there can be a perverse sense of satisfaction in being negative about ourselves. There is even a security in it because if we are negative we only define what we are not. We don't ever have to define who we are. We say things like this:

> "I'm such a failure."
> "I can't do anything."
> "There is no hope for me."
> "I have no talent."
> "My nose is too big" . . . and more.

After reading this list of negatives I want to ask you two questions: Are you any closer to knowing this woman (you!) who says such things about herself? Is she any closer to understanding herself? A resounding no is, of course, the answer to both questions. As a matter of fact, by constantly putting themselves down, many women chose the pathway to withdrawal. They hide behind the smoke screen of inferior feelings rather than face the truth that they don't really know themselves.

This doesn't mean we are never to experience negative thoughts and feelings about ourselves. That belief would make us phonies. Negative thoughts only indicate we are aware of our limitations. It is at that point we can work to change those limitations into areas of strength, if we consider them important enough.

If I want to be able to look at my deficiencies and own

Questioning Your Motivation

	Dependent	Independent	Interdependent
View of God	Afraid of the all powerful God who will punish me if I fail. Deeply spiritual and loves God greatly.	Ignores God. Doesn't need Him. "The sacred exists within me."	Awe and love. God is Holy. God is my friend. He wants what is best for me.
Motivation	Duty, guilt, fear, laziness or a desire to please.	Self.	Love.
Identity found	Through another person.	Ourselves.	Loving God, self and others.
Basic outlook	Negative. Sees problems. Carries crosses. Attempts to earn God's favor.	Fluctuates. If successful— positive. If failure— negative and angry.	Positive. Seizes opportunities. Faces challenges.
View of myself	Negative.	Inflated: "I am all that I need."	Positive. Sees myself as: a. highly significant; b. deeply fallen; c. greatly loved. "God is at work in me."

	Dependent	Independent	Interdependent
	See myself as not living up to "my" standards or "God's" standards. Punitive—condemning of self. Insecure, low or no self-esteem.		Sees possibilities. Can laugh at self. High self-esteem.
View of others	Addictive relationships; needs others. Dependent on others. Life revolves around others. Pushes for uniformity. Finds it difficult to forgive others. Ministers from a position of superiority—shares only when victorious. Feelings of dread or panic at the thought of losing the people she depends on.	Self-centered relationships. Uses others. Independence stemming from dependence. Life revolves around self. Push for diversity. Finds it difficult to forgive others. Why minister? "You do your thing and I'll do mine." Doesn't get tied into relationships where she could be hurt.	Love relationships. Loves others. Dependent on God. Free to serve others. Balanced. Pushes for unity and reconciliation. "I have been forgiven, therefore I can forgive." Free to be vulnerable. Ministers out of love. Shares with you as a sister. Feelings of deep sadness when a relationship ends.

them as my own without threat, if I want to be able to release the hold my mistakes have on me, I must first believe what God has said about me. I must see myself as highly significant, deeply fallen and greatly loved.

One Sunday morning, Dr. Robert Schuller used this illustration. An artist asked a beggar if he could paint the beggar's picture. For lack of something to do, the beggar agreed. A few hours later the artist finished the painting and let the beggar look at it. Astonishment registered all over the beggar's face as he viewed the canvas.

"Who's that?" he asked, for before him was a painting of a tall, dignified gentleman.

The artist's reply came quietly back, "That's the you I see."

"Then" said the beggar, "that's the me I'll be." Jesus sees us, dear women, not as the sinner we indeed *are* but as the saint we *will be*.

If you ask this loving God to illuminate your life and believe what He has said about you, you are going to see some real changes in your outlook on life.

Look now at the comparison chart which illustrates the difference between the dependent woman who is motivated by guilt, the independent woman who is motivated by self and the interdependent woman whose motivation comes from love. Motivation is indeed everything!

What Do I Believe About God?

What a difference our thoughts and beliefs about God make. What is more security-producing than to know that the Creator of the universe is acquainted with me personally? He values me, understands me, infuses me with His life, acccepts me and loves me enough that He would allow His son to die in my place. What freedom comes with the realization that this same God has the power and desire to redeem all the experiences of my life. He longs to fill my emptiness with Himself and He is preparing a place for me in eternity where there will be no feelings of inferiority, no limitations. Philips Brooks has been quoted as saying: "The true way to be humble is not to stoop until you are smaller than yourself, but to stand at your real height against some higher nature that will show you what the real smallness of your greatness is."

The interdependent woman is the only woman who can stand tall and give life all she's got because her God is so much greater. She stands in awe of the love and beauty of God's plan. She is both truly humble and enthusiastically proud that she can have a part in touching a hurting world with God's love.

Unlike the dependent woman, she does not try to create herself into a loving person because that is what is expected of her. She can stop the straining, the super-woman antics, she can trust that since she has given Him the go-ahead, the Holy Spirit is creating God's "agape" love within her. She is indeed becoming a loving person.

Now instead of having her daily devotions so she can alleviate the pangs of guilt with which she is struggling, the interdependent woman realizes her need to be in Scripture so she can cooperate with God in this loving process. Instead of trying to pray a few seconds before she falls off to sleep, because if she doesn't she will feel guilty, prayer now becomes an affirmation of her openness to being changed. Prayer becomes an opportunity to receive Christ's power before she acts.

Prayer is often used to ask God's approval of our plans and to advance our causes. But because the interdependent woman understands God's love for her and His desire for her best, the cause she wants advanced is Christ's, even if that involves a change in her perspective.

Why Are My Relationships the Way They Are?

Dependent Relationships

Sometimes the change in perspective that takes place is almost overwhelming. In no area is this more evident than in our relationships with others. The dependent woman specializes in addictive relationships, for she has lost all sense of wholeness. She needs others and depends on them to determine her sense of self; she has no idea of who she is apart from them. Her life revolves around others and her hold on others could be described as a stranglehold. In the Body of Christ she pushes for "cookie cutter" Christians—for uniformity. If everyone looks the same way, believes the same things and does the same thing, she feels secure.

Often it is the dependent tendency in us which makes us set ourselves up as judges, to see if other people live up to *our* version of the scriptural standard. When people fail in her eyes, the dependent woman finds it very hard to forgive them. After all, she has never learned to forgive herself. The dependent woman may become aloof and withdrawn because she doesn't want you to be aware there are struggles in her life. When she does share with you, *if* she does, she will share with you from a position of superiority. It is only when she is experiencing victory that she will be open.

Independent Relationships

Antagonized by the dependent woman, the independent woman sets out to do her own thing. Yet I see the independent woman as dependent on others. She is just like the adolescent who is in rebellion against her parents as a matter of principle. She has to know what her parents' stand is on every issue so she can take the opposite position. That adolescent is not free! She is still dependent on her parents and tied to them, even though she believes she is independent. So it is with the dependent woman.

I discovered a column in a woman's magazine today called "Swap the Old Lady for a New Woman." The old lady column (a derogatory view of old, by the way) stresses dependence while the new lady column stresses independence. It seems to me the independent woman is reacting to the dependent woman, who she either used to be or is terrified of becoming. She does not want to have to live up to anyone's expectations but her own, so she pursues self-centered relationships. If you can meet some of her needs you will be her friend. If not, she doesn't have time for you.

There is one basic problem with such a self-centered existence. When we build our lives around ourselves and insist on filling all of our own needs, we find ourselves bound by the smallness of our lives. A sense of superiority is often a cover for feelings of inferiority. Instead of knocking herself down and condemning herself as the dependent woman might, the independent woman builds herself up. Oftentimes she knocks other people down in the process—be they women or men—to gain her sense of selfhood.

Interdependent Relationships

There is no freedom in either dependency or independence. We need to be a new creation, a woman who is not afraid of losing her identity if she loves. Walter Tubbs answers the *Gestalt Prayer,* mentioned in chapter two, and in the process defines the meaning of interdependence:

If I just do my thing and you do yours,
We stand in danger of losing each other and our-
    selves.

I am not in this world to live up to your expecta-
    tions;
But I am in this world to confirm you
As a unique human being
And to be confirmed by you.

We are fully ourselves only in relation to each
    other;
The I detached from a Thou
Disintegrates.

I do not find you by chance;
I find you by an active life of reaching out.
Rather than passively letting things happen to
    me,
I can act intentionally to make them happen.

I must begin with myself, true;
But I must not end with myself:
The truth begins with two. [1]

Only the interdependent woman achieves the balance
of freedom to be with others without being inhibited or
restricted by those relationships. This is the woman who
is free to be a wife and mother because her identity is not
found in the labels she wears. She is free to love and she is
free to serve, not out of duty but out of loving concern.

The interdependent woman pushes not for uniformity
but for unity and reconciliation. She realizes her personal
responsibility to be all she can be but she does not take it

upon herself to make you into her image. One of her goals in her relationships is to be the first one to make positive, concrete steps towards reconciliation whenever necessary. Because she realizes she is "in process" she makes an effort to view other people as in process also. A realization of how much Jesus Christ has forgiven her helps her when she is tempted to be judgmental and unforgiving.

This is the woman who wants you to be aware of her loving heavenly Father. Therefore she is free to share even in her weakness and need so you will be aware of God's creative activity in her life. She has nothing to prove to you, for she is secure in the love, acceptance and forgiveness offered to her by a loving God. She is able to let God love her and is free to be a loving human being.

Motivation Is Everything!

Indeed, our motivation makes an astounding difference. The dependent woman, bound as she is by guilt, duty and fear, faces life negatively. She is frustrated with God, herself and others most of the time. She seems to continually carry what she refers to as a cross. Because of her motivation, she sees problems when she looks at life.

By contrast, the independent woman's outlook on life is a fluctuating one. When she feels successful in achieving her personal goals she is positively inclined, but when she does not realize those goals she becomes negative and angry. You might even find yourself being blamed for her inability to reach her goal.

It is only the interdependent woman whose basic outlook on life can be positive. This is the woman who, when faced with problems, seizes opportunities to love and faces challenges head-on because Christ is her helper and guide. Instead of life becoming a condition for approval, this woman's life becomes a song of praise.

7
Why Again, Lord?

Dealing with Your Past

Why Look Back?

Proverbs 23:7 states that "As a [man] thinketh in his heart, so is he." I say, "As a woman thinketh so is she!" We act on the basis of our belief system and the truth of this statement makes it necessary for us to not only examine our beliefs but also the origins of our belief system. Even though we are not solely the product of our past it is a necessary first step, in becoming interdependent, to examine whether our thought patterns about ourselves are based on hearsay, from parents and peers, or on reality, as we see it.

Do you question the necessity of facing the past? Is it painful? The first major reason why healing memories is a necessity is because we aren't free to love others in our *present* when we're carrying so many scars from the *past*. How often do we run into people who remind us of people in our past who have hurt us?

The second marvelous reason for facing the past involves the emotional release one experiences when facing and forgiving. In Scripture we read that the truth sets us free. Let us go on record by saying the truth about ourselves can make us miserable. Only when it is confessed and forgiven are we set free. For years many of us have barricaded a part of ourselves and have refused to let God's love reach inside. What freedom comes to us when we do what we most fear and face our pain. We find a loving Saviour who is eager to hear our willingness to forgive as well as "cast our sins into the depth of the sea" (see Mic. 7:19).

A third amazing thing happens. When we forgive someone who has hurt us deeply, *they* seem to experience a new freedom. One can only imagine what would have happened in young Saul's life if Stephen hadn't uttered these words to the Lord as he was being stoned to death: "Lord, do not hold this sin again them" (Acts 7:60). This was, beyond a doubt, one of the tools used by the Holy Spirit as He transformed young, intelligent, well-bred Saul into the Apostle Paul. *Am I blocking a freedom the Holy Spirit desires someone to have?*

The Lord has made *our* forgiveness dependent on our willingness to forgive, even if no one has asked us, and this is the last reason we need to face our past. Mark 11:25-26 *(NASB)* states it clearly: "And whenever you stand praying, forgive, if you have anything against anyone; so that your Father also who is in heaven may forgive you your transgressions. But if you do not forgive, neither will your Father who is in heaven forgive your transgressions "

It is a well-known fact that we act not on the basis of reality but on the basis of our perception of reality. I may see an attractive middle-aged woman approaching me on the street. You also see her and based on the warm, accepting relationships you have experienced in your past with women of this age group, you will find yourself anticipating meeting this stranger. On the other hand, if I have felt rejection from my mother, from my aunt or from a middle-aged teacher in my past, I might be extraordinarily leery of coming face-to-face with her. Our past affects our perception of the present.

As a child we learn who we are and who we are not from the people around us. This doesn't change as we mature. A teenager's peer group is extremely important to their search for identity. As an adult we choose the people we have around us and that group will also be an extremely important indicator of who we are. What we believe others think of us is crucial to our feelings and understanding of ourselves.

Where did those negative feelings you have about yourself originate? When did your negative self-talk originate? Where did your fear of leaving the familiar, your lack of direction in your life and your frustration with your limitations come from? Facing our discontent is necessary to the healing of our many childhood memories.

It is also necessary to establish, before we begin to recall our childhood, that the purpose of this exercise is not to tear our parents apart limb by limb. They did the best they could do given the emotional, spiritual and financial resources they had at the time. The purpose of taking the time to remember is to discover where our positive and negative ideas about ourselves have come from. Perhaps we will also unearth how our concept of God has evolved, since many of us have difficulty understanding God as Father because of painful relationships we have experienced with our earthly fathers. Lastly, this journey backwards will give us new insights into the relationship or lack of relationship our parents shared. Many of us, even today, are affected by that relationship which seemed so very normal to us for so long.

Be Real About Your Past

What do you remember about your life between the ages of birth to five years? Six years to 10? 11 years to 14? 15 years to 20? Take the time to get comfortable and to really let your mind wander into your past. Perhaps you will find it helpful to play some soft orchestration, to close your eyes and be still. Ask your heavenly Father to take this journey backwards with you and ask the Holy Spirit to bring those memories to your mind which will aid you in your understanding of why you feel the way you do about yourself.

Remembering Family Relationships

Do you remember much about your parents? How would you describe your mother—your father—your sisters—your brothers? What kind of a relationship did you have with your sisters or brothers? How would you describe your relationship with your parents? What upset your parents about you and how did they express their frustration to you? What feelings did you pick up from them about the way you looked—about the accomplishments you made at school? How were you compared to your brothers and sisters? Were your feelings accepted and considered by your parents or did you grow up learning to distrust your own feelings?

Your Parents and Their God

Did your father have a personal relationship with Jesus Christ? How would you describe this relationship? How do you think your father viewed God? Did your father ever discuss his faith with you? What was your emotional reaction to these discussions? Did your mother have a personal relationship with Jesus Christ? How would you describe this relationship? How do you think your mother viewed God? Did your mother ever discuss her faith with you? What was your emotional reactions to these discussions?

Your Parents' Relationship

How did your family view relationships with other people? Would you say your family put a greater emphasis on relationships or accomplishments? Did you feel valued by your parents? Did you feel your parents valued each other? What was your mother's style of relating to others—dependent, independent or interdependent? What was your father's style of relating to others—dependent, independent or interdependent? What feelings did you pick up about the concept of submission?

Your Parents and You

What did you have to do to win your parents' approval? How did they express their approval and disapproval of you? Do you feel close to both of your parents? Do you feel closer to your mother or to your father? Are you similar to your mother? In what ways are you similar to your father? How are you different from your mother? How are you different from your father? What do you appreciate most about your mother? What do you appreciate most about your father? How did your parents handle your developing sexuality? How did they deal with your steps toward independence? What was their attitude about your leaving the nest? Are your growing up years a joyful experience to remember or have these questions stirred up emotions of sadness, despair, bitterness, anger or even hate?

Acknowledging the Wounded Child

Just this past week I came in contact with a beautiful young woman. Maria was adopted as a child and throughout her 28 years of life has been carrying around deep feelings of rejection. Maria cannot understand the desire her adoptive parents had for her, the heartache they felt as the legalities increased their time of waiting, the sacrifice they made financially to get her and the fear they experienced until they knew she was really going to be allowed to stay in their family. Her vision is clouded and she cannot focus on how very much she was wanted. Rejection is all she can see. Her new husband is doing all he can to fill her need for acceptance, as did her adoptive family before him, but to no avail. Maria is continually searching for acceptance. She wants to be held on an extremely high pedestal and worshiped, as it were, to prove that she is acceptable. In fact, this need is making her a prime candidate for an affair. Why is all of this happening to such a beautiful, competent woman? It is occurring because there is a rejected and deeply-wounded child inside the very competent adult Maria—a child who is certain no one really wants her.

Are you carrying a deeply wounded little child within you? If you are, this child will affect every area of your life. It will affect whether you choose marriage or singleness. It will affect your career, your friendships, your attitudes, your capacity to change, your actions and reactions, your values, your happiness (or lack of it) and finally, your style of relating to God, yourself and others.

Perhaps as a child your parents mirrored non-acceptance to you. Perhaps your grades were the issue, your athletic ability or just your overall prowess. Perhaps you constantly found yourself being compared to your sister and you felt like the bottom of a totem pole. It didn't take you long as a child to decide that you were not as good as other people. Then you took your negative value system into the cruel world. At school your peers were unmerciful, they labeled you "stupid" and this reinforced your fragile, negative belief system. You told yourself others felt the same way your parents did so therefore, the harsh criticism must be true. Somewhere along the line you decided to talk to yourself in this negative, derogatory way. It wasn't long before you believed that other people in the world, people you hadn't even met yet, felt the same way about you. They saw you as incompetent, too.

Does the Child Still Hurt?

If you now happen to attend a church which focuses heavily on your unworthiness, sin and guilt, you must constantly go away knowing nothing but condemnation and never experiencing the freedom Jesus wants to give you. The burden of this condemnation is so phenomenally overwhelming you decide to prove to the world that you *are* acceptable by being spunky, getting even or withdrawing behind a mask and eventually behind closed doors. Perhaps you've become the clown or little miss spirituality. Maybe you've lowered your standards to prove you were acceptable. Perhaps you've rejected your parents' lifestyle and joined a peer group where you found acceptance. Perhaps you choose to be so busy you don't have to think about the issue at all. Perhaps you've retreated behind a box of chocolates in front of the television set.

What happens when criticism comes from the people you're trying so hard to impress? Anywhere we find ourselves in the world, there will be criticism. We *all* fail and have to face our failures. But each time you are faced with a failure, is it proof positive, to your hurt inner child, that you are incapable, unacceptable and stupid? As your self-image becomes severely malformed by the blows life deals, do you reject even the positive pieces of information coming your way? How do you respond to a compliment? Can you say thank-you and accept it or are your uncomfortable when faced with affirmations?

If you are involved in a relationship, do you find yourself clinging to your very special person, afraid that he too is going to find out the truth about you, criticize you and abandon you? Do you find yourself smothering the life out of him? If you are in a position of power, do you find yourself giving in to the internal tendency to criticize and condemn others before they can do it to you? Do you come unglued when an employee finds fault with some facet of your business?

Where did this germ of self-hate, which has spread into a cancerous disease, come from? It began in so many of our pasts when we were severely and harshly criticized, compared, labelled and even abused.

Won't the Pain Go Away?

I can almost hear some of you precious readers now, sharing Paul's writing from Philippians 3:13-14 *(NASB)* with me: " . . . but one thing I do: forgetting what lies behind and reaching forward to what lies ahead. I press on toward the goal for the prize of the upward call of God in Christ Jesus." It seems to me that there is only one way to forget the past; we must deal with it. The past needs to be faced before it can be filed under "forgiven and reprogrammed." If we are full of fear, hate and prejudice, these will dictate our behavior. If we think we can just shove the past under the surface and walk away from it, one day we will find ourself in a new situation or in front of a stranger who will trigger a memory button. For no explainable reason we might find ourselves intensely disliking the stranger or dealing with a surge of negative emotions that threaten to overwhelm us. If we assume the ostrich stance with our head in the sand, ignoring the past, we are limiting the healing the Holy Spirit so desires to bring into our lives. The past must be dealt with before we can begin to love ourselves, our God and our neighbors. Proverbs bears repeating, "As a [woman] thinketh in her heart so is [she]." Denis Waitley puts it this way:

> All individuals are born without a sense of self. We are like tape recorders without the key message—with some prerecorded facts and background music, but no central theme. We are like mirrors with no reflections. First through our senses, during infancy—then through language and observation—we tape record, build and photograph our video, audio and sensory cassettes of ourselves. This recorded self-concept or self-image—this mental picture of self—when nourished and cultivated, is a primary field in which happiness and success grow and flourish. But this same mental self-concept, when undernourished or neglected, becomes a spawning pond for low achievement, defiant behavior, and unhappiness.[1]

Yanking Out Your Elephant Stake

As a child I remember sitting in church when my father told this story of an elephant. Did you know that an adult elephant, weighing 10 tons, can be tied to the same size stake that a 300-pound baby elephant is tied to and never pull it out? When the large elephant was a baby he was secured by this stake. Try as he might, he found it impossible to escape. For the rest of his life, even as a 10-ton elephant, the animal remembers he cannot get away from that stake.

Are we a little like that elephant? Did someone in our past tell us we weren't pretty, we wouldn't amount to much or we were stupid? When did we start believing them? When did we drive an elephant stake into our subconscious mind? As adult women, are we being held back by some erroneous stake from our past?

My sixth grade teacher, who also happened to be my first male instructor, told me (no doubt in desperation) in a physical education class one day that I was the clumsiest person he had ever seen. That comment hurt and it has stuck with me all these years. To this day when I walk in front of a group, especially of men, that stake wants to hold me down. I was also the adolescent with the purple acne. It cleared up long ago but when a pimple appears now it is easy to overreact and recall those adolescent feelings. A dear friend who has lost a great deal of weight shared with me the other day that her inner tape needs to be reprogrammed because it is very easy for her to still feel tremendously overweight. What inaccurate tape is playing in your mind? What "elephant stakes" have you driven deep in your subconscious? Do you desire to be healed, to cooperate with the spirit of our Lord by pulling the stakes out? Or do you want to continue the pattern you have established?

Deal with Your Past

If the ache is excruciating enough, the pain so intense that you desire the Holy Spirit's healing touch on your memories, there are five steps you must first take to deal effectively with your past.

1. Invite the Holy Spirit to Take Part in Your Journey

This is not a journey for us to embark on alone. This is not to be a solo flight. For this voyage we need to be dependent on our Lord and on His Holy Spirit. But this same Spirit needs a personal invitation to take this journey with us. Never will God barge in and force Himself on us. He needs to be invited in. "Behold, I stand at the door and knock; if any one hears my voice and opens the door, I will come in to [her] and will dine with [her] and [she] with me" (Rev. 3:20, *RSV*). Every aspect of God is available to us all but we must extend the invitation, we must turn the tap on as it were. Imagine a narrow pipe coming straight down from heaven. This pipe carries all of God's grace, love, power and healing to each one of us. In the center of this pipe there is a tap. What power we have! By turning the tap off we can shut off the flow of God to us. We can go thirsty if we choose to. Or we can turn the knob and open up the pipe so all the power of God is available to each one of us. Our inner self is God's terrain but we must take an active part in the exploration of that newfound land.

By choosing to be an ostrich, by refusing to face our painful memories and our hurts, we have turned off the tap. We have refused to allow God's cooling waters of forgiveness and healing to touch our pain and we will continue to find ourselves parched, cracked, dry and oh, so thirsty. Let's lay down our reading for a moment and let's together invite the Holy Spirit to accompany us on our journey backwards. A written invitation is always a thrill to receive. Let's extend a written invitation to our precious Lord:

> Holy Spirit, today I invite you to walk down the corridors of my past with me. I ask you to bring to my mind incidents that have brought me pain, people who I would just as soon forget because they have hurt me or I have hurt them. Bring to my consciousness attitudes which are unhealthy and delusions under which I have been living. Today I turn on the tap so all of you can flow freely to all of my pain and need. Thank you for coming Holy Spirit. I don't want to stop the flow of your Spirit ever again.
>
> Signed,
>
> (Name)_____
>
> (Date)_____

Praise God! He is nearer to us than any problem, any conflict, any pain. Our Lord is in us and with us. The next helpful step after extending our written invitation to the Holy Spirit is—

2. Listen to Yourself.

What have our bodies been telling us lately? Our marvelously created bodies are in many ways alarm systems, designed to go off when things are not right. Have you found yourself overwhelmingly fatigued for no apparent reason? Have you been furiously angry and amazed at the depth of anger within your being? What about depression?

Do you find yourself depressed most of the time or do you only get depressed in certain situations. Are there roots of deep-seated negativity, jealousy, bitterness and competition within you? What have you been dreaming about lately? Would you classify yourself as healthy or have you been physically ill a great deal in the past few months? When was the last time you had a physical? What is your body saying to you? If we are to love ourselves we must learn to listen.

3. Face the Master Openly

When we make Jesus our Lord and Saviour we give this Redeemer our lives. With all His graciousness our Lord lovingly takes our gift and thanks us for it. We've given Jesus the gift of ourselves, or have we? Often what we've done is give the Lord the wrapping paper and the beautifully colored bow on our package. We've given Him a superficial gift.

Jesus desires that we get to know ourselves deeply and give Him whatever is real—not just the shiny, pretty, sweet-smelling, competent parts. Prior to making Jesus our Lord there is a lot of clutter, garbage and pain in our lives. Perhaps we have a prick of conscience periodically but that prick certainly fades away as the years pass. Then we invite this light of the world to be our Lord and suddenly all the garbage, clutter, pain that has been festering is exposed. Whatever is inside us is totally known to Jesus—the hurt, pain, anger, fear, whatever. He is never shocked by it. He is never repulsed by it. Why, that's what He died for. He came to this earth to redeem it. But what do we do? Often we slam the door on it, pretend it isn't there, act as if everything is fine and wonderful and assume the stance of an ostrich. Just like the ostrich, if it doesn't work well to put our head in the sand we will run faster than anyone else and get busier and busier. If we are hiding our hurt inner child from anyone, it certainly isn't God. Most likely we are hiding it from ourselves.

4. Drop Your Masks

Over and over again we hear committed Christian teachers tell us to do what is right even if the feelings aren't there and to act as if something is true and eventually the emotions will follow. Never would I deny the truth of this statement—but in the area of the healing memories it has to be applied very carefully. Taken to its extreme, this advice can lead us into acting spiritual while we're developing an ulcer as a result of our internal gymnastics. God is deeply concerned about our relationship with ourself. He wants those of us who are divided to be reconciled to Him *and* to ourselves. This is never accomplished by wearing a mask.

I love Paul's writings, for Paul was free to share himself with people. The more I read the epistles the more I become aware of his willingness to share his deep emotions with fellow believers. "For we do not want you to be ignorant, brethren, of the affliction we experienced in Asia; for we were so utterly, unbearably crushed that we despaired of life itself" (2 Cor. 1:8, *RSV*). Never does he set himself up as "Mr. Perfect" in order to help people. But sometimes we, as Christians, even use our faith as an excuse for failing to be honest with each other. Our logic goes something like this. "I'm a Christian now. I'm not supposed to be depressed or have an uncontrollable temper. I'm supposed to have overcome these things. I better not let others know what I'm really like or they won't think I'm much of a Christian." So we put on a mask and our pride gets entangled in the mask. We're phonies and we know it, but we must keep others from guessing the truth.

We end up lonely and cut off from others. The longer we pretend the deeper grows the gnawing fear that sometime we'll let the mask slip.

We are in need of a Saviour. After all, isn't that why we asked Jesus to be our Lord in the first place? It is only pride that tells us we must minister as the strong one to the weak. In reality we are called to minister as one needy human being to another needy human being. When we minister in this way others come away seeing the magnificence of our Lord. They desire Him, they praise Him and they see their need of Him rather than thinking, "I can't possibly be as good a Christian as she is." It's the difference between seeing grace or being faced with our inability to be perfect and leaving guilty and put down.

Pause right now and ask the Holy Spirit to make you aware of the masks you have been wearing. Spend some quiet time waiting on the Lord about this matter. As the masks and the phoniness are brought to your mind, confess and ask the Lord for His forgiveness. Confess that once again, you've tried to be the all-perfect one instead of letting God be the all knowing, all wise, holy, perfect, loving Father. Ask the Holy Spirit to make you aware the next time you start to hide behind another mask. Enjoy the healing as it comes straight from the hand of God. Be refreshed in Him! Praise and thank Him for His all encompassing forgiveness, acceptance and love.

5. Understand the Source of Your Pain

Questions have been provided throughout this chapter which I pray have been helpful to you in reviewing the stages of your past and in attempting to unearth any memories that still cause you pain. As that pain, which has been festering for years, is exposed to the Light it becomes evident that three things can be traced to the source. First,

*perhaps we locked the doors in our life because of sin—
something we have done or neglected to do.* Perhaps we
haven't used the gifts our Lord has given us for healing and
love. Perhaps they have only been used to build the kingdom of ourselves and the result has been pain.

Second, *it is also possible that our pain is caused by
something that someone has done to us.* This pain is the
result of another's sin against us. This pain can exist on
either a conscious level or on a subconscious level. I have
a dear friend who had a recurring problem which centered
around an inability to trust men. As she sought the Holy
Spirit's assistance in walking through her past, a picture
flashed into her mind of an uncle sexually molesting her.
Perhaps you were abused as a child or raped as an adult.
You especially know the excruciating pain of having someone sin against you. Perhaps you have been the victim of
withheld love. Others can cause us much pain and if it
hurts too much and we feel incapable of doing anything to
stop their sin against us, we often shove that hurt under
the surface and into our subconscious.

*Lastly, there may be festering sores in our emotional
lives because of something that has happened to someone else
we care deeply for.* We pick up someone else's pain and
carry it for them. But did you know that often, they're not
carrying it at all? To this day I find it easier to be criticized
myself, which still is not a lot of fun, than to hear my family
criticized, especially my husband. Perhaps this is an area
that we who have been or are pastors' wives are particularly susceptible. In our very first pastorate I had a lady
turn to me during the Sunday morning worship service
with these words, "Doesn't your husband have anything
else to wear? I'm so tired of seeing him in that one suit."
Believe me, this is a mild example of what happens to pastors' wives and children. But whatever the situation, perhaps there is pain in your life because you have been car-

rying someone else's pain all these years.

Now Let Him Heal Your Past

As women eager to be created into interdependent women by the Holy Spirit, there are six choices we need to be willing to make in order to find inner healing.

1. I Choose to Focus on God's Forgiveness and Acceptance of Me

"I have wiped out your transgressions like a thick cloud, and your sins like a heavy mist. Return to Me, for I have redeemed you" (Isa. 44:22, *NASB*).

"As far as the east is from the west, so far has He removed their transgressions from us" (Ps. 103:12, *NASB*).

"And their sins and their lawless deeds I will remember no more" (Heb. 10:17, *NASB*).

Our God is never shocked. He knows the parts of us we aren't even aware of. Satan is the condemner, Jesus Christ is not. It would be extremely helpful to commit the above verses to memory. Meditate on them and get to know your Lord in a new way. Often I discover that God has accepted in me what I am having difficulty forgiving another person for. It is a worthwhile exercise to make a list of 10 things Christ has forgiven you for. Then write forgiven and accepted over your list. When you believe this you have really come to terms with how much God loves you. Then ask yourself, "Who has hurt me the very most." Retreat for a time of extended prayer to love that person with God's type of love.

I have found it helpful in my own life to hear a trusted friend speak Jesus' promise of forgiveness to me. We are just like Lazarus who when physically dead was raised to new life by Jesus' word. Even though he was to live, Lazarus had to be unbound by the hands of his close friends, who willingly took the grave clothes off of him and put up with the stench. In many ways we have been dead to a portion of our emotional self. We come to a new awareness of God's love, forgiveness and acceptance through Jesus' word. Then we find we need to be unbound by the hands of a close loving friend or by the hands of a trained Christian psychologist or pastor who is willing to face the garbage, the hurt, the pain with us and point us again to a forgiving Lord. We often feel God's forgiveness more when spoken in audible terms by the voice of a friend. It is one of the ways we can be God's voice to those around us.

2. I Choose to Change My Habit Pattern of Rehearsing Past Hurts

In the past, when we have experienced deep hurt, it is likely that we responded one of two ways. We either rehearsed the hurt so faithfully we hated the person who hurt us or we withdrew from the situation. Both responses are dangerous. In the first instance we end up being controlled by the person we are cursing. In the second case we have erased the possibility of a positive message overriding the hurt. We have closed out God's love and the human love that others want to give us. Let's change our habit pattern. Let's stop flogging others and flogging ourselves. Let's focus on God's forgiveness and acceptance of us. Let's stop waiting for some magical time when all of our unrealistic standards for ourselves and others have been met. Judas focused on his guilt and hung himself. Peter focused on our Lord's forgiveness and he hung up the guilt. Let's do likewise.

3. I Choose to Confess Immediately and to Forgive without Being Asked

I have found in my own life that confession must be immediate. The longer I nurse my hurt or rehearse my guilt, the harder it is to let it go. I keep a prayer journal and I find it extremely helpful to write out my prayers of confession. After them I often write the words of 1 John 1:9 *(NASB)*, "If we confess our sins, He is faithful and righteous to forgive us our sins and to cleanse us from all unrighteousness."

Since God's hands of forgiveness are tied until we are willing to forgive those who have hurt us, I choose to forgive. I do this because of my Lord's example. As I write this, Easter is one week away. I have been meditating on the day prior to and following Christ's death and resurrection. Christ was rejected by those into which He had poured His life and love. He was jeered and He was publicly humiliated. He was hung naked and exposed to the stares of men, women and children. He was hung between two common criminals. Not one of the jeering mob sought His pardon at Calvary. What was His response? He was willing to forgive people who had no comprehension of their need to be forgiven: "Father, forgive them for they know not what they do."

Peter once asked Christ how often he would need to forgive someone who had offended him. Jesus' reply was "as many as seven times seventy." On Calvary, the creator God of our universe lived out the truth of His words. We are often called to repeatedly forgive—especially after family gatherings held during the major holidays! I choose to forgive. I choose to obey. It's up to God to release my emotions. I will know I have been forgiven when I can face the cause of my pain and not feel turmoil.

4. I Choose to Be Dependent on God's Resources

Building the kingdom of "me" will not release the inner hurts and tapes of my past. My highest aim in life must be to know Christ. Often in this process we need to be willing to wait, the very thing many of us find most difficult. There are so many Scriptures referring to waiting.

> In repentance and rest you shall be saved, in quietness and trust is your strength (Isa. 30:15, *NASB*).

> Yet those who wait for the Lord will gain new strength; they will mount up with wings like eagles, they will run and not get tired, they will walk and not become weary (Isa. 40:31, *NASB*).

> I am the vine, you are the branches; he who abides in Me, and I in him, he bears much fruit; for apart from Me you can do nothing (John 15:5, *NASB*).

There is no shortcut to cooperating with God in changing ourselves. It involves waiting silently; it involves filling our minds with God's Word; it involves meditation.

When we try to love independently of God's resources we often do it to get something back, to manipulate or to impress. Let's ask God for the love and compassion we need to love ourselves and others.

5. I Choose to Love Unconditionally and Creatively the Person I Am Struggling Against

Jesus Christ offers us an unconditional, initiating love. How many times we put "ifs" on our loving. We tell ourselves that *if* she will do such and such *then* I will love her. God's love isn't dependent on what we do or what others do. Thank goodness! It's as if we have a giant magnifying glass within our heads; a glass that enlarges the negative in ourselves and others out of proportion. Our love isn't dependent on other people meeting our expectations. Our love is only dependent on God. Then in faith we act.

Have you thought of asking God for His creativity in loving someone you've been struggling against? Have you asked God to help you see that precious person through His eyes? Sometimes it is necessary to provide a time when we can mourn the relationship we never had. After we have worked through that process, with the Holy Spirit's guidance, it is easier to go on with reality-based expectations concerning that person.

There is a person in my life whom I have mourned. She is incapable of giving me the type of relationship I desire. This relationship has taught me many valuable lessons, including one on love: you learn to love by giving away *all* you have to give. In prayer one day the Holy Spirit convinced me that I needed to make it a point of doing one affirming thing for my friend each week, even while I was going through this mourning process. It's been fascinating to watch the relationship slowly, oh so slowly, take a turn for the better. A real moment of truth came when I received my contract for this book. Guess who I shared the good news with? That's right! I chose to unconditionally and creatively love the person I had been struggling against and the Holy Spirit did a loving work in me.

6. I Choose to Be Grateful for the Growth Resulting from the Hurt

At this stage we choose to ask ourselves, *How can I grow from this pain?* rather than using the condemning words, *I should have.* This is the time when we pray, *Lord help me to learn positive lessons from the hurtful things I will encounter in life* rather than praying, *Lord, don't let me be hurt anymore.* In our world it takes people who have experienced and worked through pain to be able to minister. These women will be less likely to throw out pat, unthinking answers. They will be less likely to clout you over the head with Scripture verses. They will be less likely to be Job's comforters. They will listen, love and lead you to the resources of the Lord Jesus Christ.

The choices we make enable us, with the Holy Spirit's guidance, to reprogram our thoughts and our habits when reacting against anyone or anything that hurts us. As women moving toward interdependence, we have valuable choices when dealing with pools of pain in our lives. The first step towards interdependence is a step backwards. It opens the locked doors of our lives where we have not felt the warmth of Jesus' accepting and forgiving love for years. How warm the Son feels!

Do I Have to Be All Things to All People

Beating the Superwoman Myth

Interdependent women are continually in process and I choose the word "process" because it points out an important truth—we will never arrive. When you were a child perhaps you collected butterflies and made a display plaque onto which they were mounted. Interdependence isn't like that. We can't collect it. We can only celebrate it.

Our individual process begins with a personal relationship with Jesus Christ. Because of Calvary He gives each of us the opportunity to view ourselves as a highly valuable person. It then becomes necessary to balance the acceptance of our humanity, and the needs and limitations that come with it, with our affirmation that we are first-class quality. Trying harder, as the superwoman does, will never change us into deity.

The superwoman spends every waking moment comparing herself with a fantasy. She compares everyone else's best with her worst. She pressures herself with a vision of perfection. She cannot, of course, live up to the expectations she has set for herself but she feels like a total failure anyway. In fact, if she continues she is well on her way to being a *totalled* woman.

Pull Out of the Competition

How do we grow as Christian women? Certainly not through competition. Do you find yourself involved in activities in which you are competing with those around you? Do you feel a pressure to be a superwoman? Perhaps it would be wise to consider pulling away and using the time to evaluate and focus on what God wants to do in your life.

The Christian woman has been freed from the necessity to compete. Her assignment is to cooperate with the Holy Spirit and what He wants to do in her life. So this becomes the key question:

Am I willing to embark on a joint adventure with the Holy Spirit?

In Philippians 2:12-13 *(RSV)* we read, "work out your own salvation with fear and trembling; for God is at work in you, both to will and to work for his good pleasure."

This doesn't mean we can save ourselves or can work our way into a right relationship with God by our own efforts. If this were possible it would be most appealing to the independent superwoman in each one of us. It does mean we are to join God in working out those things He is most effectively working on. Our assignment is to cooperate with the Holy Spirit and there are three very practical ways we can do this.

Be in the Word (see 1 Tim. 2:15)

Why? Not for the reason *I* used to read Scripture, which was to alleviate my feelings of guilt. You see, I knew it was something I was supposed to do if I was going to be a good Christian, so most nights I mechanically read a few verses, wondering all the while why so many people made so much of it. Personally, I found it quite a bore.

It wasn't until my guilt-motivation was replaced by a love-motivation that I discovered I *wanted* to be in cooperation with this Saviour who loved me so very much. I wanted to learn more about this holy, loving, forgiving, accepting Lord so when my mind was centered on Him, the Holy Spirit would transform me into a loving, forgiving, accepting person.

We must be in the Word so we can discover where we need to grow to achieve our full potential. Just as electricity must run through a conductor, so must the Holy Spirit work through the means God has provided—His Word. Have you asked the Lord to make you enthusiastic about meeting with Him daily? It's a daily battle for all of us, isn't it! Just as we don't get food for our bodies by looking at the unopened packages in our pantry, neither do we get spiritual food from an unopened Bible. We can attend three Bible studies a week, two seminars a month, all the church services available to us and hear others talk about the Word, but it won't nourish our spirits unless we personally take in the Word of God on a regular basis. We are limiting what the Holy Spirit can do in our lives otherwise.

The story is told of a husband whose wife died suddenly. He was left alone and broken to father their precious little girl. When the first Christmas holiday arrived he decided to take the week off and spend it with his daughter. How he was anticipating that shared time. When the first morning finally came the father rose excitedly, only to find that his daughter had shut herself in her room and would not come out until suppertime. The distraught father didn't know what to do.

Finally Christmas morning arrived and under the tree was a package wrapped in newspaper, tape and layers of ribbons. Triumphantly the little girl offered it to her beloved daddy. Upon opening it he discovered a pair of socks she had knitted for him. "Daddy, this is what I was working on each day for you!" she exclaimed. The daddy gathered her up in his arms, hugged her and with tears rolling down his cheeks said, "Honey, I love the socks, they're beautiful. But all I wanted was time with you."

I wonder how often Jesus weeps over our busyness, our independence, our service for Him—longing to say to us. "My child, I just want time with you." Moffatt's translation of Isaiah 65:1 goes like this: "Ready was I to answer [women] who never . . . sought me. I cried out, 'Here am I,' to folk who never called to me."

Pause now and spend a moment centering all your thoughts on Jesus. Talk to Him about your desire to know Him better. Now ask Him to make you enthusiastic about time alone with Him. He desires time with you, not to make you feel guilty, but rather so He can love you into your full potential as an interdependent woman. But beware. It could be habit forming!

Be in Prayer (see 1 Thess. 5:17)

The duty-motivated person reads this suggestion for cooperating with the Holy Spirit and asks, "Haven't you laid enough guilt trips on us?" After all, when we're guilt-motivated we *do* pray. But we often ask God to put His okay on our plans and causes just before we fall into bed at night, exhausted. Then we fall off to sleep, relieved that we've done our duty.

The woman who is deeply touched by God's love for her prays because she is open to being changed. She admits her need for Christ's power to act. She prays in order to get a new perspective and to advance the cause of Jesus Christ.

We are in an exhilarating, creative partnership with the God of the universe when we pray. Prayer is not just a one-way communication with God where we tell Him all our needs and problems. It is also a time to adore, confess and thank our loving heavenly Father. It is a time to be completely honest with God. Are you angry with God? Confess it! He won't faint. He knows it already. Prayer is a time to ask questions and wait for His ideas and answers.

It is also a time to be silent and to open your mind so God's thoughts will flow in to you. The psalmist writes,

> Make me know Thy ways, O Lord;
> Teach me Thy paths.
> Lead me in Thy truth and teach me,
> For Thou art the God of my salvation;
> For Thee I wait all the day. (Ps. 25:4-5 *NASB*).

God wants to shape our will and direct our steps. He will enlarge our vision through prayer and give each of us a dream which would be impossible without Him. Prayer will open up new possibilities in our world. Anne Ortlund uses an illustration comparing life to a funnel. The non-Christian woman enters at the wide end and finds that as she progresses through life, her options are narrowed until she finally finds herself at a deadend with no hope in sight. By contrast the Christian woman enters at the narrow end of the funnel, through belief in Jesus Christ as her Saviour, and then finds all of life in its fullness opening up to her as she travels on through.

Do you feel a need to enlarge your vision or to change your perspective? Then cultivate your prayer life. Dream

God's dreams for your life and your situation.

Be Your Own Best Friend (see Mark 12:31)

One of the cruelest things we can possibly do to another person is to withdraw our hope from them. Is it possible you have done this to yourself? What kind of an opinion do you have of yourself? Do you look for the best in yourself?

There isn't any opinion more important to your well-being than the opinion you hold of yourself. Do you treat yourself as if you were a beloved friend? In the last week, what did you do just for yourself? I'm aware that as a woman you are probably called on to do many things for others, but what have you done for yourself? Have you even allowed yourself the joy of stopping and smelling the flowers?

It doesn't glorify God when you nag one of God's children. Remember, you are one of God's precious children! How have you been talking to yourself? Some people are cursed with a computer in their brain, programmed to find the worst in everything and everyone, including themselves. Are you one of these people?

One word of destructive self-criticism does about 10 times as much damage to your self-esteem as a word of criticism from someone else.[1] Women who verbally downgrade themselves with consistency will eventually come to the point of believing what they hear. Once they believe, they automatically act on their beliefs.

It becomes obvious then, that our words program our spirit either to success or defeat. How do you talk to yourself? How do you talk about yourself? Do you build your own set of limitations by the words you say? Are your words faith words or slave words? Does your vocabulary consist more of "I can," "I choose," "I will" or "I'm not,"

"I can't" and "I won't." One of the surest ways to lose our sense of self-worth is by persecuting ourselves with unreasonable, unscriptural, illogical and negative thoughts.

Years ago, my husband and I house sat for a couple who were often called away on weekend business trips. Five high school through college-age boys came with the house! We'd move in, cook the meals, attempt to keep the schedules straight and try to maintain order. How indebted we are for the lessons we learned from that wonderful family. One of the best lessons was the "no knock" policy in their home. Criticism of other people or of one another was not tolerated at a meal or any other time.

Isn't it time we adopt the no knock policy for ourselves? What do we gain through criticizing ourselves? We gain a self-centered perspective, we adopt no personal responsibility for change and we fill ourselves full-to-overflowing with self-pity. Is that what the Holy Spirit desires for us? It's almost as if we're tempting God by saying, "I dare you to do anything with this negative, depressed and discouraged lump of humanity."

Philippians 4:8 tells us to *dwell* on things that are true, honorable, right, pure, lovely, excellent and of good report. Are these the things on which you have been dwelling? In John 10:10 we learn that it is Satan's purpose to steal, kill, destroy and tear down. Whose side are you on? Have you been cooperating with the Holy Spirit or with the devil?

From this point on let's make it a habit to affirm ourselves. Let's be sure that our self-talk is consistent with God's Word. Now stop for a moment and repeat these statements out loud:

"I am highly significant to God."
"I am of great value to God."

"I am loved by God."
"I am unique."
"I am special."
"I'm glad that I am me."
"I'm glad I am alive."
"I am glad I am a woman."
"I am glad I am single/married."
"I am God's precious child."
"I am a loving and gentle person."
"I am a joyful person."
"I am a patient person."
"I am a trustworthy friend."
"I am a thankful person."

Add some of your own affirmations to this list.

Saying words like these is like watering seeds. Don't underestimate the power of positive affirmations.

Follow Christ's example by prayerfully exchanging your negative names for yourself with positive ones. This isn't looking at the world through rose-colored glasses. This is faith! Giving yourself a positive, scriptural affirmation will also be one of the best ways of fighting off those superwoman tendencies. A positive self-concept must take place in your imagination before it will ever be useful in the skirmishes of life. This is cooperating with God's view of us. This is being our own best friend and not a superwoman!

9

How Can I Value Myself?

Choosing to Be Positive

You will feel slightly uneasy making personal affirmations if this has not been your habit pattern. A part of your mind may even be suggesting that this isn't in line with Scripture and you are just becoming arrogant. Any new habit feels awkward until it becomes integrated into your life-style.

It is my belief that we need to align our lives with the positive affirmations and promises of Scripture. Never is God glorified or His people helped as a result of negativity and a critical spirit.

The Holy Spirit seeks positive women who are cooperating with the changes and growth He desires in their lives. He wants women who are in communion with Him through prayer, who through their study of the Word are growing in awareness of their freedoms and possibilities and who are committed to adopting His view of themselves and others. These are women who acknowledge that the cross of Jesus Christ is the ultimate plus sign and who are committed toward growing into positive believers rather than negative ones. Have you ever had the courage to ask a close friend whether she felt you were basically positive or negative in your reactions to life?

I believe there are 10 reasons why we need to choose to be positive.

Positive Christian Women Are Christ-Centered, Not Sin- or Guilt-Centered. Do you often carry around with you a fuzzy feeling of guilt that is impossible to define? Do you find it easier to focus on guilt than on Jesus Christ's love and forgiveness? If you struggle with guilt, there is a marvelous verse I would like to introduce you to: "There is therefore now no condemnation for those who are in Christ Jesus" (Rom. 8:1, *RSV*). Self-inflicted guilt and anger must be dropped if we are going to choose to believe God. Because we have confessed our need for the Saviour and have asked Jesus Christ to be our Lord we are free from divine punishment.

The Holy Spirit does use guilt to convict us. We are pointed, however, to specific areas that need to be changed and can be changed. But God doesn't act as a sledgehammer, as we so often do to ourselves. Through Scripture we are introduced to a fatherly, loving corrector. After our sin is confessed the Lord desires us to change our feelings of guilt for a sense of cleansing and freedom.

Self-punishment and condemnation are *not* to be viewed as God-given feelings. But you aren't the only person who has experienced those unspecific guilt feelings or John wouldn't have written 1 John 3:19-20 *(NASB)*: "We shall know by this that we are of the truth, and shall assure our heart before Him, in whatever our heart condemns us; for God is greater than our hearts, and knows all things."

Through this verse we are assured that even though we may feel condemnation we can positively assure our hearts that God, who has forgiven our sins and cast them into the deepest ocean, is greater than our hearts. If we claim this as truth we will be Christ-centered women.

Positive Christian Women Refuse to Lose Hope. Why? Because where God is, there is always hope. Do you believe that "all things work together for good to those who love God?" If you do the result will be a positive belief, affirming that everything happening in life occurs for your benefit. Learning to accept your realities and working with them is the outward sign of your inward hope. Do you demand that people or circumstances must change in order for you to be happy? There is a heavenly reason for everything in life: may we always learn and grow from our experiences.

This doesn't mean we should say we don't have any problems. Neither does it mean we should expect to be happy in the midst of difficult circumstances. It does mean we can positively affirm that there are no circumstances in our lives which we, as believers in Jesus Christ, cannot use to help our growth. This is our basis for refusing to lose hope.

Positive Christians Accept the Scriptural Truth that Whatever We Sow We Will Also Reap. Proverbs 23:7 *(NKJV)* states "as [a woman] thinks in [her] heart, so is [she]." Positive thoughts lead to positive acts which in turn lead to a positive life-style. What we put into our minds is soon displayed in our lives.

If we dwell on inadequacies we decrease our self-assurance and we destroy a part of ourselves. It may be a small self-criticism to begin with but it often grows into a monstrous, controlling habit. We criticize ourselves first so someone else won't have to. Sometimes we fantasize other people taking pity on us. If this happens we've really got something to be unhappy about. These habits invite even greater negativity into our lives.

There are pay-offs for being negative which we must learn to reject. A person steeped in negativity often lives out the script of a martyr overflowing with self-pity or lives in such a way as if to prove she really is unlovable.

What I Gain Through Self-Rejection

A. Self-rejection is an excuse for not accepting responsibility for my own happiness.

B. I can hide behind a smokescreen of inferiority rather than admitting that I don't know who I am. I only know who I am not.

C. I can avoid the risk of sharing my honest feeings.

D. I can be lazy about maximizing my growth.

E. I can hold on to a bag of self-condemnations in an effort to endear myself to others.

F. I have a perfect justification for continuing to be dependent on others rather than facing life on my own.

G. I have an excellent justification for failure.

H. I have a valuable reason for indulging in self-pity.

I. Satan's off my back. After all, I'm doing his work for him.

Is that the abundant life that Jesus Christ desires for us? Thoreau refers to us as sculptors who have the ability to create the person we want to be. What food are you feeding your thoughts? Whatever you sow you will also reap. Being positive means more than just casting out negative thoughts, although that *is* an important aspect of it. Pause for a moment and answer these questions:

Are you actively looking for the good in yourself, in others and in situations? (See Phil. 4:8.)

Think back on your activities of last week. What
magazines and/or books did you read? What TV
programs did you watch? What functions did
you attend?

What we watch and think has a direct effect on us. Are we
suffering from emotional malnutrition because of the diet
we have been feeding our eyes, ears and souls? Denis
Waitley asks a profound question in his book *Seeds of
Greatness:* "If a 60 second commercial, by repeated viewing, can sell us a product, then isn't it possible for a 60 minute soap opera or 'smut-com' by repeated viewing to sell
us a life-style?"[1] The Holy Spirit is necessarily limited in
His effectiveness in our lives by the choices we make.
Whatever we sow we will also reap!
   *Positive Christian Women Choose the Positive Over the
Negative.* Our God is a positive God. The Bible is good
news. What is your personal focus?

> Religion or relationship?
> Doubt or faith?
> Fear or hope?
> Sin or salvation?
> Regret or discipline?
> Yesterday or today?
> Negative or positive?
> Crisis or challenge?
> Reacting or responding?
> Taking chances or making choices?
> Impossibilities or possibilities?
> Failures or successes?
> Blaming or blooming?
> Criticizing or creating?
> Nightmares or dreams?
> Analyzing or affirmation?

When you look in the mirror do you focus on what is wrong or do you notice the things you like? Do you view yourself and others as people who are in the process of becoming all that God wants us to be?

Choose to focus on what the Lord has done in your life rather than on the part not yet finished. Praise and thanksgiving will spring from your lips.

Before reading any further, take the time to chart your spiritual journey to this point in your life. At what age did you commit your life to Christ? How have your relationships affected your faith? Did your educational experience affect your beliefs? Don't just mark the failures. Star the successes that your loving and encouraging Lord has brought into your life.

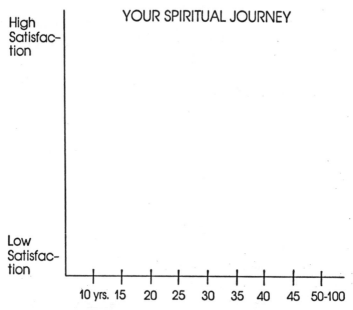

Positive Christian Women Look at the Events in Their Lives As Opportunities to Grow. We often let the events in our lives define for us who we are. If we are divorced we look on our situation as a confirmation that we are a failure; if we are single we assume we are undesirable; if we are happily married we choose to believe we must be acceptable; and if we are unhappily married we feel there is something wrong with us.

The events in our lives only provide opportunities to grow and to learn. They do not determine our identity. God has declared us significant and of value because of Jesus Christ's shed blood, not on the basis of the events in our lives or based on someone else's opinion of them.

It's true, past failures cannot be changed but they can be forgiven. Mistakes as well as successes are learning experiences and stepping-stones in life if we allow them to be. There is no experience in life that we, with the Holy Spirit's assistance, cannot grow from if we choose this perspective.

My family experienced a real tragedy a few years ago. My father is a Presbyterian pastor in Toronto, Canada, and an arsonist broke into his study, taking all the books off Daddy's shelves. He then broke into the file cabinets and removed messages and research from 30 years of study. Next he found all the church hymnals and choir music. After creating a giant pyramid in front of the church altar he set fire to it all. Daddy was wiped out! His comment to me was, "I feel absolutely naked."

After an extraordinarily painful period of shock and denial, my father decided to act on his dream to get his doctorate. He applied to Fuller Theological Seminary in Pasadena, California, and was accepted. With his dream ahead of him and my mother's loving affirmation surrounding him, he began to study as well as maintain his full-time pastoral duties. In June of 1984 at the age of 63, my father received his doctorate. He is living proof that for those who commit themselves to the faithful Lord who gives dreams, beauty does come from ashes. Are you willing for growth to be the result of every event, no matter how hurtful, in your life?

Positive Christian Women Move Out Even When Their Knees are Shaking. Why? Because they have been kneeling on those knees that are shaking. Not only do they know *who* they are they know *whose* they are. Faith is not the absence of fear. Faith involves facing your fears and moving out in God's Power, despite those fears.

Positive Christian women know they accomplish things not because of their fabulous potential but because they are willing to be vessels used by the Lord. They are willing to risk failure and criticism. They are also aware that failure and success are only temporary.

I had to face my personal fear of failure when the Lord first gave me the dream to put my thoughts on self-esteem into book form. Would you believe I fought the dream for six months? I finally asked myself, "What is the worst thing that could happen to you if you failed at writing this book?" When I put the cold hard realities down on paper I decided I could live through possible failure far better than I could live with not carrying out my dream because of the fear of failure. Risking is terrifying, yet the option to shrivel up and die is far worse.

> To laugh is to risk appearing the fool.
> To weep is to risk appearing sentimental.
> To reach out for another is to risk involvement.
> To expose feelings is to risk exposing your true self.
> To place your ideas, your dreams before the crowd is to risk their loss.
> To love is to risk not being loved in return.
> To live is to risk dying.
> To hope is to risk despair.
> To try is to risk failure.

But risks must be taken, because the greatest
    hazard in life is to risk nothing.
The person who risks nothing, does nothing,
    has nothing and is nothing.
He may avoid suffering and sorrow.
But simply cannot learn, feel, change, grow,
    love and live.
Chained by his certitudes, he is a slave.
He has forfeited freedom.
Only a person who risks is free![2]

How we need to understand that not trying is the only
failure in life. The only way to keep from making mistakes
is to do nothing and that's the biggest mistake of all. We
are willing to risk because we are not trying to prove ourselves. Our significance and value has been declared,
apart from what we do, by Jesus Christ. That allows us to
formulate God's dreams for our world and to act on those
dreams, until with the Holy Spirit's assistance, they
become reality.

God delights in using human beings with their limitations and inadequacies who are willing to be used. He used
Mary, an obscure young girl, to be the mother of His only
begotten Son. It becomes evident why Mary was chosen
when we read her response to Gabriel: "Behold, I am the
handmaid of the Lord; may it be done to me according to
your word" (Luke 1:38, *RSV*). She could have argued with
the angel and let her negative self-concept be an excuse
for not allowing herself to be used. It must have been
something to hear an angel say to her, "Hail, favored one!
The Lord is with you . . . you have found favor with God."
I am so glad that Mary accepted his affirmation and didn't
deny it. I'm glad she believed that with God nothing was
impossible. I'm glad she was willing to risk. The question

to ask yourself now is this: How do your attitudes compare to those of Mary?

Positive Christian Women Don't Stand in Line Waiting for Approval. They Move Beyond by Giving Out Honest Affirmations. We are approved women! The King of Kings and the Lord of Lords has declared it to be so. No longer do we have to stand in line waiting for others to affirm our value. One woman describes it this way in the book *Love* by Dr. Leo Buscaglia:

> Now I know why I am so miserable all the time. It's because I expect to be loved by everyone and that's not possible. I can make myself the most wondrous, the most delectable, the most magical, the most juicy plum in all the world and then there are people out there who are allergic to plums. Then you know what—You make yourself over as a banana because you just met a banana lover. But you'll always be a second-rate banana where you could have been a first-rate plum and just waited for a plum lover to come along.
>
> If you stopped being a plum and concentrated on being a banana then that person thinks that a banana should split and you don't know who you are.[3]

Rather than continually seeking approval the positive Christian woman uses her energy to look for the good in others. Her God-given mission becomes the builder of self-worth in others. She can look for the good in others and tell them about it. This neither threatens her or does she use it as a tool for manipulation because she is free to see the good in herself, too. Likewise, her affirmations are focused not only on what other people do but also on who they are as individuals. They are significant and of great value in God's eyes, and because of that they are significant in her eyes apart from what they accomplish.

Positive Christian Women Make Goals Not Excuses. An interesting exercise for each of us is periodically to keep a running journal of all the excuses we make in any given week for not risking something new or for not achieving some goal. I've discovered through keeping a record of my excuses that my attitude is really what holds me back from being all God and I want me to be. It's yet another illustration of an important truth: What happens *in* us is far more important than what happens *to* us.

One day after reading over all my excuses for not accomplishing things, I grouped my excuses under the topics of negative attitude, procrastination, pettiness, inflexibility, self-pity, worry, laziness, lack of discipline, bad habits and denial. I then went to Scripture to see what God had to say about each one. What an eye-opener! It became crystal clear that God did not want me to limit myself in these ways. Listed below are the excuses I came up with based on my personal experience. Perhaps you have used one or two of these yourself. Are you curious about what Scripture has to say about each of these attitudes?

Attitudes	What God Says
Negative Attitudes	Colossians 3:17 _____
	Philippians 4:8 _____
Excuses	Genesis 3:11-13 _____
	Exodus 4:10-12 _____

Procrastination	Ephesians 5:16	_____
Pettiness	Colossians 3:13	_____
Inflexibility	1 Samuel 15:23	_____
	Proverbs 29:1	_____
Anger	Proverbs 27:4	_____
	Proverbs 27:15	_____
Worry	Philippians 4:6-7	_____
Laziness	Proverbs 24:30-34	_____
Lack of Discipline	Proverbs 25:28	_____
	Galatians 5:22-23	_____
Bad Habits	Hebrews 12:1	_____
Denies Mistakes	Proverbs 28:13	_____

The positive, spirit-filled woman knows it isn't in God's will for her to limit herself. In obedience she stops making excuses and sets goals instead.

Positive Christian Women Assume Personal Responsibility for Their Own Happiness and Self-Esteem. No woman wants to spend the majority of her time being or feeling out of control. Yet many of us have allowed ourselves to slip into this habitual pattern. We are:

- bullied by our emotions
- conned by our circumstances
- whipped by our guilt and "if only's" and

- manipulated by our fantasies about the future.[4]

Often we don't even want to think about the future because we foresee having even less control than we have now. But that is negative imagining.

There are many things positive women acknowledge having control over. We are, for example, responsible for our conversation. A beautiful definition of healthy communication is sharing the truth about ourselves in love. We need to realize that as women we are also responsible, when involved in a relationship, for defining who we are. In addition we need to come to grips with what our needs are, what we think and how we feel. When those things are communicated our conversation is deep and precious.

This type of communication only happens if we take personal responsibility for it. Rather than spending our time trying to control other people by telling them what they should or should not do, we need to learn, through practice, how to communicate the truth about ourselves in love.

There is something we are *not* responsible for, however. We are not responsible for how others act. If your spouse has left you, your children are angry with you, you're divorced, you've been demoted, your friends avoid you or your child is in trouble with the authorities, you cannot conclude that you must be unlovable, a bad parent or a failure who destroys everything she touches. You are only responsible for your actions. You and I are free to choose how we will act but once we have made our choices we are responsible for them.

In Betty Coble's worthwhile seminar and book entitled, *Women Aware and Choosing,* she points out that we are often the happiest when we are doing something we consider to be worthwhile. Our fulfillment often comes as a result of being in charge of our time. A large part of feeling worthwhile is tied into how you feel about the dull, mundane realities of life.

Are you doing something each day you consider worthwhile or are you only doing what everyone else demands that you do? Do you feel as if you are in charge of your time? Certainly there will be days when it seems to get away from you but on the whole, are you in charge? How do you feel about the dull and mundane necessities in your life? Do you ever dream up silly little games to help you get them done faster?

I must confess to allowing myself only 20 minutes to accomplish any given task. If it is necessary I break larger tasks into smaller units. Why? Because then my sense of accomplishment grows as items are checked off my list. Remember, we aren't accomplishing tasks so we can affirm our value. We do these tasks, no matter how mundane, out of a sense of value. Do you tackle the toughest, perhaps least enjoyed assignments, first? May I recommend you do this because you will derive a sense of gratification from having made the effort to do the job. You'll also have additional energy for the remaining tasks.

As Spirit-filled women, we acknowledge that our sense of peace and joy results from our relationship with the Lord Jesus Christ. We also affirm that we, moment-by-moment, choose whether or not to be women who believe God's view of ourselves. Do you remember how you thought you would find happiness as a result of such and such a relationship, or as a result of being married? It is fantasy to believe anyone can make us happy. Rather, we choose to be happy women who share our happiness in each relationship of which we are a part.

If you feel you have no control over your life, look at the Seven C's of Self-Control by Denis Waitley:

1. We Control the Clock. Yes we do. Although it always

runs, we can use it as we choose.

2. We Control Our Concepts. We control our thoughts and creative imaginations.

3. We Control Our Contacts. We can't select all the people we'd like to work with and be with; but we control whom we spend most of our time with and we can meet new people.

4. We Control Our Communication. We are in charge of what we say and how we say it.

5. We Control Our Commitments. We choose which concepts, contacts and communications warrant the most attention and effort.

6. We Control Our Causes. We set our long-range goals in life, which become our causes, and the things we are most identified with by others.

7. We Control Our Concerns. Most people react emotionally to everything they interpret as a threat to their self-worth. Because you and I have a "God-given self-image" (my term) and a deep-down inside feeling of self-worth, regardless of what's going on around us—we respond, rather than react.[5]

I pray each of you will grow in your awareness of your personal responsibility for your own happiness and self-esteem. You make the final decision about whether you will have a positive self-concept or whether you will downgrade yourself with negative, unscriptural and illogical self-talk. You also have the final word to say about your happiness or lack of it. Take the time to ponder the choices you have been making.

Positive Christian Women Seek Out an Affirming Support Group. The Christian woman may choose to affirm the good she sees in others, but she also needs to be affirmed. One woman expressed her need for an affirming support group with these words, "People can't fight my battles nor make my decisions but they can hold me up. They can comfort me, reassure me, cheer me on. So many of our battles have to be fought essentially alone. But it is nice to know that there is a cheering section close by believing in me."[6]

We all need a positive cheering section. My daughter Amy was born at four in the afternoon on the day my support group met. These precious people arrived at the hospital at 6:30 P.M. and prayed over our little girl. Another time someone in our group was going through a season of intense pain. Each member provided food for her and brought little homemade gifts all wrapped up. When the pain was terribly intense she had the joy of opening one of the presents and feeling loved and cared for.

Then there are the goals we share with each other. In our particular group we split up into groups of twos. We exchange our goals, agree to pray over each other's goals daily, phone each other at least once a week and hold one another accountable for personal growth. One can't help but see growth, given that kind of support!

It is such fun to celebrate each other's special days, to pray for each other, to send or receive a surprise postcard of loving affirmation and to be handed a small package to open later as you board a plane for some distant destination. The depth of benefit experienced from receiving and giving such support is tremendously meaningful and can only be measured in the heart.

You've no doubt heard the story of the woman who was about to jump off a high bridge and commit suicide. Another woman came along and the two of them sat down to talk. After an hour, both of them jumped off the bridge. None of us can survive indefinitely if all the voices coming our way are degrading, negative and judgmental. Make it a specific prayer request that the Lord will give you a cheering section and will allow you to be the cheering section for someone else.

Cooperation Is the Key

As a Christian woman you are freed from the necessity to compete. Your assignment is to cooperate with the Holy Spirit and what He wants to do in your life. Christ is present in you in all of His power. This power is waiting to be unleashed in your life if you will cooperate by spending time in God's Word and drinking deeply of God's love, forgiveness and acceptance. You must also spend time praying, praising and choosing to be positive. The question becomes, Am I cooperating with the Holy Spirit's working in my life rather than competing with some perfect standard to prove my worth? In her impatience, the superwoman completely overlooks the truth that growth is a process and processes take time. Think of the years it takes for a seed planted in the earth to blossom into a fruit-producing tree. Christ wants us to go through this process using His strength, not our own. It is so much more satisfying to go through each day aware of God's forgiveness, acceptance, joy, peace, power and love than it is to go through each day competing, failing, and despairing. It is my prayer that on your personal journey towards interdependence you will allow yourself to be transformed from society's superwoman into God's woman. The choice is yours!

10
Will Others Notice a Difference in Me?

A Call to Serve Others

Throughout the pages of this book the dependent woman, the independent woman and the interdependent woman have been examined. Together we have discovered that we fluctuate in our self-discovery by switching from one mode to another mode, depending on our circumstances. As we seek the Holy Spirit's maturing influences we find ourselves moving more and more towards interdependence and rejecting either dependency or independency as viable options.

The interdependent woman finds her identity first through Jesus Christ's loving sacrifice for her and next through loving God and others. Her self-fulfillment comes as a by-product of loving service. The woman who accepts this as her life's direction will find she is walking a holy walk, not always easy or popular but always growth-producing. She will discover she is walking in her Saviour's footsteps. In Philippians 2:5-8 *(NASB)*, Paul exhorts us to "Have this attitude in yourselves which was also in Christ Jesus, who, although He existed in the form of God, did not regard equality with God a thing to be grasped, but emptied Himself, taking the form of a bondservant, and being made in the likeness of men. And being found in appearance as a man, He humbled Himself by becoming obedient to the point of death, even death on a cross."

Our minds, so often self-centered, can hardly comprehend the fact that the Creator God of our universe would be willing to take on the form of a servant. But that is exactly what He did. He was willing to leave the comfort and honor of heaven to walk through the dust of this earth, to serve the disciples by washing their feet and to rub shoulders with religious and irreligious humanity—who not only didn't believe He was God, but who contemptuously ridiculed Him. He, our God, chose to walk straight to His death on a tree at the hands of mankind which He had created.

Our Lord was also a serving Lord after His resurrection. Recall Christ was on the shore of Lake Galilee, cooking breakfast for seven exhausted disciples who had toiled all night trying to catch fish? A change in His status did not mean a change in His service. Truly Jesus Christ was among us as one who serves (see Luke 22:27). In chapters one through three in the book of Revelation we discover that the risen Lord is the sovereign servant of the Church even today.

As we begin to follow in our Master's footsteps we learn that a commitment to servanthood has to be preceded by a strong sense of identity. Jesus was sure of His identity. He was God! John 10:30 records Christ's words, "I and the Father are one." He didn't have to grasp for deity, He was God. Because He was sure of His identity, He laid aside His position and willingly became human. Only human beings can serve God.

We, as interdependent Christian women, also have a strong sense of identity. We know we are highly significant to God and deeply loved by God. We know we are forgiven and accepted by God because of Jesus Christ's sacrifice and the Holy Spirit's power in us. We don't have to grasp for deity as Satan and Adam and Eve did—we face that tendency in ourselves. We know who we are as God's children and never lose sight of that. Because we are sure of this identity, we can choose to lay aside our rights and willingly become a servant of God and of others.

Apart from the Holy Spirit within us, we give in order to receive, we love in order to be loved and we forgive in order to be forgiven. Servanthood must be the result of the fullness of Christ within us. The story of Mary and Martha serves as a reminder that our service must be because of the fullness of God within us. Otherwise it will be nothing but a duty, an obligation and a real pain.

Service in Worship

We've all been there, haven't we? We've served because we felt it was expected of us, because we wanted to be loved and appreciated, because we wanted to be served in return. It wasn't exactly a joy, was it? We didn't find any fulfillment in it, did we? Fulfillment never comes when our loving and serving is motivated by self. Rather, fulfillment is the result of worshiping our Lord through our service. Peter must have encountered this begrudging attitude because in 1 Peter 4:9 *(NASB)* he admonishes the Christians to "be hospitable to one another without complaint."

If servanthood is indeed our calling, we need to be constantly asking God to fill all of us with all of Him. We need to be filling our minds and spirits with our own Scripture search, with prayer and meditation. We also need times to focus on the wonder of God. Worship releases us from self-centeredness and shows us that freedom comes from dependence on Jesus Christ. Joy is found there. As we spend quality time worshiping the risen Christ and delving deeper into the truth of God's Word we will adopt a servant life-style. We resemble the people we spend most of our time with, don't we?!

Servanthood is the way we identify with our Christ. In Ephesians 5:1-2 *(NASB)* we read this command: "Therefore be imitators of God, as beloved children, and walk in love, just as Christ also loved you, and gave Himself up for us, an offering and a sacrifice to God as a fragrant aroma." In Christ's value system "the greatest among you shall be your servant" (Matt. 23:11, *NASB*). We are called to be imitators of our servant Lord rather than status seekers in the world's system. As we give precedence to God's plan and words in our lives we will discover the truth of finding ourselves through losing ourselves.

Love Knows No Equal Rights

Even though we affirm, as interdependent women, that others are our equals as we are their equals, we acknowledge that as Christ's servants we set aside our equal rights. We willingly, voluntarily, become servants to one another in the Body of Christ because we are identifying with our Lord.

Jesus was equal with God but He didn't cling to His rights. He was willing to risk servanthood so our needs would be met as a result of His sacrifice. He loved us enough to serve us. Can that statement be truly comprehended? Rather than pouting over what He was giving up, Christ chose to concentrate on the people to whom He was giving. Can we do less? So He laid aside His rights and submitted to His Father God's plan. The result came to life when Jesus, the Creator God, knelt in front of mere humans and washed their feet.

One time an admirer asked Leonard Bernstein which instrument was the most difficult to play. Bernstein's answer is classic. "Second fiddle. I can get plenty of first violinists but to find one who plays second violin with as much enthusiasm or second french horn or second flute, now that's a problem. And yet if no one plays second we have no harmony."[1] This illustration hits home because I know how often I find myself building the kingdom of Jan, how often I like the front-row seats, how often I enjoy being center stage and how often I am self-conscious as opposed to God-conscious. The Holy Spirit is actively teaching me lessons about enthusiastically playing second violin. How's the harmony in your home, office and life-style?

Weigh Your Words

Yet another way Christ demonstrated His servanthood was through His verbal availability. We must recognize that our servanthood is demonstrated in the same way. Our words do much to let the people in our lives know if we really are available.

Our words can draw someone near or they can drive them away. They can undergird or undercut, bolster or belittle, demonstrate our respect or disrespect. Words indicate whether we are more concerned with kindness or with always being correct; whether we are more interested in a ministry of reconciliation or in keeping a record of wrongs; whether we are more interested in lecturing or listening; whether we consider it necessary to be responsible for another person's actions or responsible for loving another person; whether our children, husbands or friends are our friends or our foes. Words can encourage or enrage, affirm or attack, betray excitement or exhaustion, demonstrate concern or criticism. They can welcome or wound. Words betray our availability.

When an acquaintance arrives unexpectedly, your husband arrives home or when your children come home from school, what attitudes do your words convey? When you are in the middle of an errand, what do your words and attitude indicate to other people about your availability? Our words betray, as little else does, the value we put on availability. Our attitudes are also highly contagious. Like the measles they reproduce themselves a hundredfold in our lives and they spread into the world around us.

Be a Lover of Life

You've heard the saying that the darker the night is the brighter the stars shine. We are called to be the bright shining stars in our homes, communities and churches and love is the evidence that we are Christ's women, called to be in partnership with our Lord in loving and serving our world.

Even though Christ is the initiator of love while we are the responders, this does not give us license to be passive responders to life. Dependence on our Saviour alone frees us to be the most courageous lovers and servants of our world. In Romans 12:10-13, *(NASB)* we read these words: "Be devoted to one another in brotherly love; give preference to one another in honor; not lagging behind in diligence, fervent in spirit, serving the Lord; rejoicing in hope, persevering in tribulation, devoted to prayer, contributing to the needs of the saints, practicing hospitality."

Service in Hospitality

Servanthood will also be demonstrated through the adventure of hospitality. When I use the word hospitality, do you immediately think of a beautifully set table with a full set of matching china, crystal and sterling silver? I appreciate the beauty of those things but that is not what I am referring to when I use the word "hospitality." I am referring to an *attitude* of being receptive and open to people including my family, friends and even strangers. It involves a willingness to see others from God's point of view as highly significant, deeply loved and valuable in spite of what they do, how they act or what they look like. It involves acknowledging that everything I have, own and am comes from God's hands. It becomes a willingness to share God's blessings with others. Obedience is involved and Paul challenges us to "accept one another, just as Christ also accepted us to the glory of God" (Rom. 15:7, *NASB*).

A very wise person once pointed out that the world is full of either guests or hosts. It seems to me the difference between the two is our willingness to make the world a beautiful place, both physically and emotionally, for other people.

I once experienced some people who felt they were guests in life. It was a Thanksgiving Day, and in accordance with our tradition, we invited people who don't have family close by to our home for dinner. Although each one in attendance was a special person, not one of them was willing to be responsible for initiating conversation, helping to serve the food or clean up afterwards.

When they left I fell into a chair exhausted and asked the Holy Spirit what He was trying to show me. He asked me if I hadn't slipped back into being a guest rather than a host with the people in my life. Without the cross of Jesus

Christ we would all be guests. That cross can transform us into hosts.

How gentle the Holy Spirit has been with this goal-oriented woman, in molding me into a hospitable woman. I certainly was not always willing to be part of the process. When I was a new bride I really wanted to spend all my time with this new husband of mine. He had come from a home that was constantly full of people. I, on the other hand, had come from a home that entertained only a few times a year because of my mother's career plus the responsibility of being a pastor's wife and mother. Well, since Dave was used to a house full of people he thought it was a little quiet with just the two of us. So with my husband as a motivator I started to entertain. What a spread I put on! What a table I set! Trouble was, by the time our friends arrived I was not only exhausted but had usually experienced one or two blow-ups with my hubby. I was not very interested in my guests' emotional state when they arrived. But I certainly wanted their compliments.

Would you believe the next year the Lord placed us in a pastorate? There I was—a minister's wife who viewed people as interruptions. You see, I had a college teaching job for the first time and I wanted to be good at it. At the same time we entertained mostly young people and I found myself doing it a great deal. It couldn't be spectacular because we just couldn't afford to feed myriads of young people that way. I was miserable. I was lonely. I resented the time I didn't have with my husband because of all his church responsibilities. It got so bad I felt I was wasting my time if I spent time talking on the phone.

Eventually we moved on to another position and God in His goodness sent an angel. The woman's name was Irene and she helped the selfish, angry child in me. Dear Irene. Such a gift of hospitality you rarely see. Irene always had time. If you arrived at her home first thing in the morning or late at night she was genuinely glad to see you. If you surprised her, after an initial comment about the state of affairs in her home, she would focus on you as if you were the most important person in her world. She entertained creatively but simply and she wasn't afraid to let you help. People were her main focus.

I was mightily impressed by the fact that Irene was as hospitable to her own family as she was to others. This was not a lady who had nothing to do. In fact, what she accomplished often made my head spin. But people were her focus and she loved us with an accepting, affirming, servant love. As you can guess, Christians and non-Christians alike flocked to her and the Holy Spirit used her to begin a work in me.

Slowly I began to change one thing at a time. The first thing I did was change my menus. Every experience didn't have to be gourmet. Whatever I prepared I attempted to have it completed 20 minutes ahead of the time our guests were to arrive so Dave and I could pray for our friends and the evening. The result of those two decisions was miraculous.

That was the turning point in my life and no longer am I guilty about time spent with others. I now believe that relationships are the most important thing in my world. In fact, I've been told I have the gift of hospitality and I think I do. But I know it's a gift that's been created in me by a loving heavenly Father who cares desperately about His children's relationships.

Perhaps you are naturally a people person. What a wonderful characteristic to have! A people person likes to be around people much of the time and she chooses when she will be alone. A non-people person likes to be alone and chooses when she will be with people. Regardless of our natural inclination, we are all called to serve through the vehicle of hospitality.

One summer we worshiped with a precious group of Christians in Fort Collins, Colorado. On the wall of their multi-purpose auditorium hung a huge banner. The words caught my attention and pulled on my heartstrings: "This is a healing place where inspiration, rest, the love of Christ and the praise of God will lift men's hearts and save their souls."

Dear Lord Jesus, in my attitudes, in my home, through my words, make me a healing place for people to come to. What I serve will be an extension of my creativity but that is really beside the point. Fundamentally important is whether the people in my life have found a healing place of inspiration and rest, where Christ is held up and because of it people are lifted and meet my precious Lord face-to-face. That is hospitality. That is servanthood. Amen.

> For your Holy Spirit, God,
> I'm thankful!
> Without Him, I'm nervous, anxious,
> fearful—too often thinking of me:
>
> What will she think of me?
> How will I impress him?
> Will they think I'm weird?
> What if they don't like my idea?
>
> But oh, how happy I am with your Holy Spirit!
> He focuses my thoughts on You:
> How may I best represent Jesus?
> Will I be careful of His reputation?
> What will be their response
> to His love
> through me?
>
> Release! Support! Affirmation!
> And then comes His serendipity!

In each person He shares with me
He reveals His Son.
He enables me to enjoy their differences!
Because of what He paid for them;
Because of what He's doing within them;
Because He's promised to finish
what He's started in each who chooses Him,
I can love them—
actually enjoy them—
each unique, special creation.

Thanks much, Lord,
for replacing my fear
with your love,
my anxiety
    with enjoyment,
my doubt
    with hope.

Your Spirit is my stronghold!
He is my treasure, my precious friend.[2]

Is It Okay to Be Me?

Examining Mutual Submission

The only woman who is free to submit is the interdependent woman. And when she uses the word "submission" she is referring to the concept of mutual submission in all her relationships, even her marriage. In her mind mutual submission is not involuntary subjection, a "tradeoff in domination,"[1] or self-negation. Neither is it a fifty-fifty relationship, in which she only contributes 50 percent and the other party does the same, or a relationship which allows one party to be used as a doormat.

Rather, mutual submission is the result of being filled with the Holy Spirit. Elaine Stedman defines it in a way I find personally meaningful:

> Authentic submission is not reluctant nor grudging, nor is it the result of imposed author-

ity. It is rather a chosen, deliberate, voluntary, love-initiated response to another's need. It is an act of worship to God, whom we serve in serving others. In no way, then, is authentic submission a violation of our humanity. It is appropriate to the purpose for which we were created, since in serving his creatures we are serving and worshipping our Creator. And it acknowledges the dignity of our humanity because it is service freely rendered from a will surrendered to the loving purpose of God.[2]

Submission is voluntary—a personal choice—and is only possible for those women and men who have a strong understanding of who they are. Mutual submission is only possible between two people who are aware of their equality before God and each other. The need for mutual submission is clear, for it is impossible to share our faith in Jesus Christ by word and by example with someone we are treating as a doormat or with someone we have placed on a pedestal.

Mutual submission results from our awareness that in serving others, we are really serving and worshiping our God. It is possible only when we believe the command "Be ye . . . perfect, [whole, complete, fulfilled] even as your Father which is in heaven is perfect [whole, fulfilled, complete]" (Matt. 5:48, *KJV*) was given to both men and women. Therefore both members in the relationship will do their best to develop and affirm each other's gifts, talents, wholeness and completeness. They are also willing to improve their communication skills—the ultimate tool of mutual submission.

It is not my purpose in this book to delve into the biblical and historical arguments about submission. If you desire a thorough study from a biblical perspective, may I recommend the book, *Heirs Together* by Patricia Gundry. My purpose is to show how dependent and independent women misunderstand and misuse God's plan of submission. And, although this chapter carefully analyzes submission in the marital relationship, the information can be applied to our friendships and family relationships.

The Dependent Woman

The dependent woman has lost her sense of wholeness. She specializes in addictive relationships as a result. Her only sense of identity, apart from her relationships, is negative and inferior. Therefore she defines herself in relation to others, depending on *them* to determine her sense of self. She is the little girl always trying to earn someone's approval and pushes for uniformity in her relationships because that makes her feel secure.

The dependent woman is all too happy to turn over the controls of her life to a man—or so it seems. Since throughout her dating years she has repressed her true self, it appears she will submit to the man in a marital relationship, becoming what he wants her to be and repressing her true self.

In his book *How to Become Super-Spiritual or Kill Yourself Trying* John Sterner describes a woman who has opted for dependency:

> Suzy Submissive is totally dedicated to the care and feeding of her husband's ego. Each day of Suzy's life is filled with plans: She plans food that Fred will enjoy, sex that will excite him, and conversation that will be stimulating to him. She plans a fulfilling life for Fred.
>
> Suzy read somewhere that wives are supposed

to submit to their husbands (Eph. 6) and she has been doing it ever since. The trouble is, Suzy is rapidly losing her personality, her friends and her cool. Her conversation is loaded with "Fred says" and "Fred thinks." Suzy has stopped thinking. She has also stopped going to church because Fred thought she was becoming too religious. She watches only the T.V. programs Fred likes and she has stopped seeing any friends Fred does not care for. She has for all practical purposes, stopped living.[3]

Does submission mean destroying our individuality and never rocking the boat? The dependent woman believes that is exactly what it means. After all, this is how she lives.

May I introduce you to three dependent women who are submissive.

June met and married her husband while she was in her late teens. She put him through school by working in a department store—a job she continued to hold until he became fairly established in a new business. She then stopped working altogether due to an insistent and very persuasive Bible teacher who was certain the woman's place was in the home. Eventually two little children came along and now at the age of 45 June doesn't know who she is or what she wants out of life. All she knows is this: she wants more than she's got. Absolutely nothing makes her content, even though she keeps quite a frantic schedule teaching home Bible studies.

June's reactions to her life are drastic and debilitating. The loneliness caused by her ever-absent husband is wearing on June and she feels unappreciated and unloved most of the time. Her husband has not lived up to her expectations and she is deeply depressed. In fact, she is spending more and more time in bed due to one "illness" or another. Her house is in a shambles and she is developing an ulcer from all the inner turmoil and anger she feels. On top of all this she has a gnawing fear in her heart that her husband is going to leave her. This thought almost suffocates her so she clings tighter and tighter to her man— even though the life she clings to makes her miserable.

Monica is single and hates every second of it. All of her life, her mother has told her she is nothing without a man and Monica has swallowed her mother's philosophy hook, line and sinker. Monica believes in her heart of hearts that men are superior so she doesn't live her own life. Instead she gives her life to any available man, always hoping this will be the one to complete her. Since she doesn't enjoy her own company nor trust her own judgments or intellect, she latches onto someone who will provide the goals, rules and orders for her life. She spends her life being someone else's person, with no self-identity. Needless to say, Monica is miserable. Because she considers herself to be only half a person she is continually attracted to men who are only half-men. Her latest romance was with a traveling salesman whom she later learned was married.

Carol is a beautiful woman who also happens to be a talented musician. Carol was headed toward a masters degree in music when she first met her future husband, Dave. He was threatened by her gifts and she responded by erasing *her* academic goals and nurturing *his* dream—to become a pastor.

The concept of oneness has always appealed to Carol. She believed she not only took her husband's name but also his identity. In Carol's case this means being a pastor's wife!

If Carol is really honest there is a part of her that has never really wanted to grow up. When she first met Dave she was looking for a man who would care for her. She still wants this today. In her own words, "I need a man to lean on, to tell me I'm okay."

Rather than accepting God's approval as well as searching internally for her own approval, she needs her husband's affirmation to prove her self-worth. Being a busy, preoccupied and often threatened pastor, Dave has little affirmation to give. Nevertheless Carol waits like a small child for his nod of approval.

Carol is increasingly afraid to stand up for what she believes because her husband might be threatened and she might become unacceptable in his eyes. Out of this fear she refuses to communicate the truth in love about herself. She is so terrified of rejection she can't say no to anything her husband wants and is at his beck and call 24 hours a day. She consoles herself by saying, "It could be worse. I could be single."

The Payoffs

June, Monica and Carol are dependent in their relationships with the men in their life. But there are payoffs from dependency and don't let anyone tell you there are not. First, the dependent woman feels cared for and safe. She doesn't have to grow up. Since she is familiar with what it means to be taken care of by parents she is quite content to let a man take care of her, too.

Second, it is possible for her to feel more spiritual when she uses self-blame and self-punishment. This is the height of arrogance because Jesus Christ has already bled and died as a sacrifice for our sin. The dependent woman somehow believes she can add to Christ's sacrifice.

Staying dependent also involves laziness and this is the third payoff for dependent women and Satan alike. He will either persuade you you're fine as you are or you're so very rotten you can't possibly change. It is then easier and safer for the dependent woman to stay the same. The hard work of setting goals to change attitudes, thoughts, feelings and actions can be avoided. This woman is certainly no threat to Satan, is she!

As long as these women are able to blame others, they won't have to change. They will also get a great deal of sympathy from people which promotes continual denying, repressing and suppressing of the issues. She chooses to live in a personal fantasyland, never *really* desiring to change.

Women who believe that dependency and submission are one and the same have often learned this style of submission at their church. Therefore they believe dependency to be the Lord's pattern for their life.

The Dependent Woman's Lethal Weapons of Control

But here is a trap and how easy it is to fall into it. A woman can *pretend* submission. How often have you heard a woman say something like, "He may be the head of this home but I'm the neck that moves the head"? These women affirm their husbands by saying, "Whatever he says is right, after all he is the leader." But how they dishonor their husbands and themselves through their actions.

The dependent woman's lethal weapons of control are manipulation and retaliation. Notice the small step separating *being controlled* from *being controlling*. These women are the pussycat manipulators who resent their own lack of control so much they get back at their man—any way they can.

One manipulative method involves suffocating their men with kindness by babying them. By refusing to be honest about any issue or conflict, the dependent woman protects her man from self-understanding. She picks out everything from his suits to his deodorant and how she delights in making excuses for him. The children, for example, are not to bother their father with their problems because he is exhausted and works much too hard. She babies him because she is terrified of change. This can be avoided if he remains the same.

She can be dishonest with her words and actions. While claiming to be submissive and a follower she can destroy her husband's financial base by wasting their money with unwise purchases. She can talk disparagingly to him by reminding him of every irresponsibility—every way he hasn't shaped up to fit her expectations. She can also choose to be disrespectful and divisive—like the pastor's wife I knew as a child, who refused to go anywhere her husband was preaching. She can subtly shame him, use sex to manipulate him, silence to frustrate him, use guilt trips to condemn him, self-pity and nagging to overwhelm him and a poor state of health to blackmail him. She often waits until her man gives an opinion before subtly opposing him.

These women are dependent on their men but their need for men is unhealthy. They seek personal security in their man but indulge, flatter and attempt to buy them any way they can. In other words, they become masters of manipulation. It almost happens in self-defense, for no woman or man can experience emotional health when their sense of self is defined by someone else.

The Independent Woman

This is the woman who reacts with horror to the concept of submission. Antagonized as she is about the misuse of submission, she "throws out the baby with the bathwater" and isolates herself.

Although the dependent woman receives some payoffs from manipulating her partner within a submissive relationship, the independent woman experiences a temporary payoff by rejecting submission altogether. She feels in touch with herself and believes she is in control of her life by accepting relationships on her own terms and doing things her way. She ignores 1 Corinthians 11:11, *NASB* which says, "However, in the Lord, neither is woman independent of man, nor is man independent of woman."

A middle-aged woman recently shared with me how she had decided to nurture her career rather than intimate relationships. She sold out to the business establishment and rose quickly up the corporate ladder—at the expense of healthy intimacy, however. Two relationships had been important to her at one time but not so precious that she would make any concessions for them after her decision to make business her life. Eventually her personal relationships faded away. There she sat, beautifully groomed and financially comfortable but absolutely alone. She certainly had offers but only, it seemed to her, from people who wanted to use her for their pleasure or to further their career. She was absolutely miserable. There are no payoffs ultimately for total independence!

The Interdependent Woman

Friendship with the interdependent woman may not always be as easy as a relationship with the "yes, whatever you want" or dependent type of woman. Because both people in a relationship happen to be Christians does not insure that their values will always be similar. There may also be wide differences between husbands and wives. But it is in the face of conflict, which is inevitable when two thinking people are involved in a relationship, that the principle of mutual submission shines. How fascinating it is to find out what each other is like.

James Fairfield has created a diagram illustrating five fairly normal styles of relating.[4]

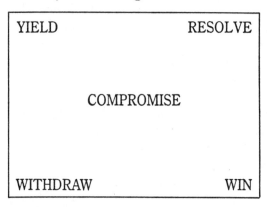

When one person in the relationship constantly WINS and the other one YIELDS it shows a low concern for the relationship and each other. The person who consistently yields is repressing his or her thoughts, feelings and opinions. This is unbiblical and unhealthy.

If one person or both people WITHDRAW from the conflict, that also shows a low regard for the relationship. They are just not willing to stick in there and communicate. They may also be terribly afraid.

The COMPROMISE position, or what I call the "horse-trading" position ("If you do this, I will do this . . . ") shows a slightly higher regard for the relationship—but it is not the ideal.

It is the RESOLVE position we are headed for. If an issue is to be resolved, both people must be willing to hear what the other person feels and thinks along with the reason he or she holds that opinion. Both individuals then examine the positives and negatives of each position and finally settle on a resolve which both find satisfying. This is a verbal picture of mutual submission.

I am nothing but you are a person of worth and dignity. (dependent) (unhealthy submission)	YIELD RESOLVE COMPROMISE	I am a person of worth and dignity and you are a person of worth and dignity. (mutual submission) (interdependent)
I am nothing and you are nothing. (No regard for a relationship, self or other).	WITHDRAW WIN	I am a person of worth and dignity but you are expendable. (independent) (authoritarian)

The ultimate goal is to work each conflict through to the resolve position. It often takes time to get there. Waiting until each side can get more facts and a more educated solution might be the best move. If that seems to be impossible the couple must compromise, change direction or work it through together until they come to a mutually agreeable solution. If one person has greater expertise in one area, by all means call on that knowledge and agree together to use it. Free that person up to make decisions in their area of expertise.

As Christian women we need to be willing to take the first step toward reconciliation. Never is our motivation for reconciliation to establish a position of superiority or to acknowledge inferiority. We choose reconciliation as our goal out of obedience to our Lord and because we value ourselves, the other person and the relationship.

Benefits and Blessings

This type of relationship, as I have stressed before, will not always be easy but the benefits will be overwhelming. I've included 17—do you have any to add to the list?

1. *It frees us up to be ourselves.* If we are married, our husbands fell in love with a spunky, interesting woman. Mutual submission gives us the freedom to be that woman for a lifetime. "It allows both husband and wife to contribute to the union from the richness of all that they are. It allows both mates to contribute all their abilities and attributes."[5]

2. *We become real in each situation.* It forces us to get in touch with ourselves. Our feelings, thoughts, dreams and questions suddenly take on a new importance.

3. *We become much better listeners.* We genuinely care about other people's feelings, thoughts, dreams and questions. This makes us a more effective communicator.

4. *We acknowledge equal rights in a relationship.* David Augsburger and John Faul comprehensively define what this means:

   I am free to choose my words and acts;
   Therefore free to change and grow.

   I am free to be spontaneous;
   Therefore free to make mistakes.

   I am free to trust my hunches;
   Therefore free to be illogical.

   I am free to be flexible;
   Therefore free to change my mind.

   I am free to live by my own supports;

Therefore free to refuse help and kindness.

I am free to take the consequences for my acts;
Therefore free to offer no justification for my choices.

I am free to love and care for others;
Therefore free to tell you without permission.

I am free to want relationships;
Therefore free to reach out for contact.[6]

5. *We become affirmers to others just as our Lord is to us.* We learn to help other people believe that their dreams can become reality. Each person is helped to find, cherish and develop all that they are. Luke 6:31 (*TLB*) puts it this way, "Treat others as you would want them to treat you."

6. *Mutual growth is a result.* As long as one person is not free to grow the other partner won't achieve his full potential either. Both partners are helped to deepen, grow and change.

"When husbands and wives live the way Jesus did, they do not play out roles in which one or the other hides away a part of himself or herself in order not to be upset or displease the other. They trust God will be in their every move and then they move—even if it rocks the boat."[7]

7. *We value each other equally as persons.* We acknowledge we are both equally important to God, to each other and to the relationship. We mirror that belief through our actions.

8. *Unity rather than conformity becomes an important value to each person.* Harmony is considered far healthier than being a revised standard version of someone else.

9. *Each partner owns his own emotions, expressions, experiences, actions and happiness or lack of it.* As a result he is not emotionally controlled by the other person or absorbed with the other person.

10. *Both partners treat each other with equal respect for they are "heirs together" of God's grace.* Both people are valuable, therefore they will refuse to take advantage of each other nor will they be possessive of each other. Feelings of intimacy and trust are heightened.

11. *We become equal in opportunity.* Both partners are free to be involved in ministries. Christ's world is in front of both of us and He cheers us on while we cheer each other on.

12. *Together we assume personal responsibility for the style of our marriage.* There is no longer a need to live by someone else's formula.

13. *Our children become God's children,* entrusted into our keeping for only a short time. One person is not solely responsible

for the raising of them. Neither is one partner cheated of the joy of really knowing his
children as people.

14. *We will gain increased feelings of self-confi-
    dence* as a result of accepting our God-
    given identity and maturing as the Holy
    Spirit directs. We will no longer be domi-
    nated by others.

15. *We will be increasingly dependent on the
    Lord Jesus Christ* because we refuse to be
    dependent on someone else for our spiri-
    tual growth and personal development.

16. *The manipulation comes to a swift halt.*
    Instead, I give you the very best I have to
    give. I lift you up because we are equals. I
    serve you with joy because I love. We are
    free. Ponder these words by Nancy R.
    Smith:

"For every woman who is tired of acting
weak
    when she knows she is strong,
there is a man who is tired of appearing
strong
    when he feels vulnerable;

"For every woman who is tired of acting
dumb,
there is a man who is burdened with the
constant
    expectation of 'knowing everything;'

"For every woman who is tired of being
called
    an 'emotional female,'

there is a man who is denied the right to weep
   and to be gentle;

"For every woman who is called unfeminine
   when she competes,
there is a man for whom competition is
   the only way to prove his masculinity;

"For every woman who is tired of being a sex object,
   there is a man who must worry about his potency;

"For every woman who feels 'tied down' by her
      children,
There is a man who is denied the full pleasure of
      shared parenthood;

"For every woman who is denied meaningful employment
   or equal pay,
there is a man who must bear full financial
   responsibility for another human being;

"For every woman who was not taught the intricacies
   of an automobile,
there is a man who was not taught the satisfaction
   of cooking;

"For every woman who takes a step toward her own
      liberation,[8]

there is a man who finds the way to freedom has
been made a little easier."⁹

17. *Each partner takes responsibility for the
home.* No longer is it only the wife's
responsibility to keep house, hold an outside job, raise the children and be a respon-
sive mate. Therefore, she is freed from the
necessity to be a superwoman. Rather,
each partner takes personal responsibility
for some of the mundane chores that need
to be done in any home.

Dave and I find that Sunday evening, after our children
have been put to bed, is a good time for us to make mutual
submission a reality in our marriage. First, we share our
individual calendars for the next week. We share our feelings about the week and the pressures that lie ahead of us.
Next, we examine each other's commitments and review
our list of the mundane chores that need to be accomplished around our home. I know you face some of the
same things each week in your home: laundry that needs
to be done, floors that need to be vacuumed and scrubbed
and furniture that must be dusted—along with the grass
and flowers that never take into account how busy you
are! We divide up these necessities, making certain that
there are a few items on our individual lists we enjoy
doing. If your children are old enough, I suggest you
include them during part of your planning time. It is their
home, too.

We also find this a helpful time to check the goals we
have created for ourselves, our *marital* relationship, our
spiritual growth and our children's development. This is
the time to check up on how we feel we did during the last

week. It is necessary to examine whether our goals are realistic and if they aren't, to re-evaluate them. Then we spend a precious time in prayer, committing each other and our week to the Lord and thanking the Lord for the gift of each other.

Lest you think that we have always done this, let me hasten to point out that this tradition in our marriage came out of total failure and frustration. At first this meeting time provided us with a way of coping with an unhealthy situation. It was in the process we discovered, with the Lord's leading, that we had stumbled onto something valuable. Feel free to use our idea or modify it to fit your personal situation.

Before we progress any further let's examine the habit patterns you have established in your relationship.

My Style of Relating

Dependent Life-style
What percentage of the
time do you:

	95%	75%	50%	25%	5%
1. Deny yourself the joy of knowing yourself?					
2. Deny others the joy of knowing you and growing with you?					
3. Own your feelings, thoughts and dreams?					

	95%	75%	50%	25%	5%
4. Hesitate to express opinions leading to conflict?					
5. Find that your need to be liked is greater than your need to be honest?					
6. Allow others to manipulate you?					
7. Have a difficult time saying no?					
8. Feel other people are more important than you are?					
9. Feel powerless to change yourself or situations?					
10. Find yourself comparing yourself with others and always coming out on the low end of the totem pole?					
11. Talk about yourself in a self-negating way?					

12. Feel used, taken advantage of, resentful and retaliatory?					
13. Feel you would be helpless if something happened to your mate?					
14. Feel you are living someone else's life for them?					
15. Feel you are the caretaker of your husband's emotional needs?					
16. Value conformity over unity?					
17. Feel inhibited by your relationships?					
18. Feel bound by your labels, not knowing who you are apart from what you do?					
19. Feel your partner (or friend) is an authoritarian tyrant?					

	95%	75%	50%	25%	5%
20. Feel you are unusually harsh on yourself?					

Independent Life-style

	95%	75%	50%	25%	5%
1. Find yourself getting your own needs met at any cost?					
2. Find yourself seeking to manipulate and control others?					
3. Feel superior to other people?					
4. Feel judgmental of others? Feel they are finished products?					
5. Own your feelings, thoughts and dreams?					
6. Seek after conflict?					
7. Blame other people or situations for your state of affairs?					

	95%	75%	50%	25%	5%
8. Feel you are more important than other people?					
9. Tell people off?					
10. Expect the worst from others?					
11. Find yourself trying to control others?					
12. Feel hostile?					
13. Communicate the truth in hostility by using "you" statements? (Example: You never . . .)					

Interdependent
Life-style

1. Feel like you are a person who counts?					
2. Own your own feelings, thoughts and dreams?					

	95%	75%	50%	25%	5%
3. Accept yourself as in process?					
4. Accept others as in process?					
5. Feel equal to other people?					
6. Refuse to be intimidating?					
7. Refuse to be intimidated?					
8. Feel honest?					
9. Believe your relationships are based on love rather than guilt, manipulation or fear?					
10. Define your own needs?					
11. Communicate the truth in love by using "I" statements?					
12. Feel your relationships help you to understand yourself?					

	95%	75%	50%	25%	5%
13. Take responsibility for yourself and not someone else?					
14. Confront when necessary?					
15. Feel you are a significant person apart from the labels you wear or what you can accomplish?					
16. Define your own roles?					
17. Respect yourself and others?					
18. Choose to be affirming of yourself and others?					
19. Choose to serve out of love?					
20. Choose to be a participant in mutual submission?					
21. Risk new ideas and growth?					
22. Feel free to be vulnerable?					

	95%	75%	50%	25%	5%
23. Feel spontaneous and real?					
24. Confront in love when appropriate?					
25. Feel like an excellent listener?					
26. Refuse to be a revised standard version of anyone else?					
27. Feel you have equal opportunity to do what you believe the Lord wants you to do?					
28. Feel parenthood is a shared responsibility?					
29. Experience increased feelings of self-confidence?					
30. Experience an increased dependency on the Lord?					

Promoting Change Negatively

I hope you find yourself moving away from the dependent and independent life-style and moving toward the interdependent one. It is in this style of relating that you will discover the beauty of mutual submission. But what if you are locked in a relationship resembling anything but mutual submission? Do you want to bring about change?

First of all, let me point out there are some terribly unhealthy ways to communicate your desire for a change in your relationship. In fact, using these methods shows we are still operating from the dependent or independent mode.

We will never be able to *nag* our mates into changing and my dictionary gives the reason why. Nagging is defined as "persistent petty faultfinding, scolding or urging." Let's take a moment to examine just how clever we have become at the game of nagging. First, by betraying our basic lack of trust in him, we often nag our husbands for not doing something he hasn't had a fair chance to accomplish. A second method is to ask a question we *know* the answer but really don't *like* the answer: "Why aren't you like so and so?" "Why won't you change jobs?" Third, we nag our partner over something that has absolutely nothing to do with what is really upsetting us. Let's establish right now that nagging does not work. A man will never be drawn toward mutual submission if the tool used is nagging.

Nor will he be drawn toward submission if we use *false flattery* to move him in that direction. He may put up with it for a short time because it's certainly better than nagging but he knows you are not speaking the truth to him. This leads to feelings of mistrust—and mutual submission can never be built on that foundation.

The last tool we often delight in using, when the other

two methods have failed, is *outright judgment.* Rather than using the desirable "I" statements like, "I feel . . . ," "I think . . . ," "I need . . . ," "I would enjoy . . . ," we switch into a judgmental attack position. Suddenly everything we say has a dagger in it. Our words and attitudes are accusatory—"You never . . . ," "You always . . . ," "You're such a . . . "—and let him know that we think he's inferior, dull and generally stupid. We usually use this when we are afraid he will never change. Our goal of mutual submission seems blocked and we're furious.

Promoting Change Positively

Does instant success happen very often in your life? It certainly doesn't in mine. Give your partner *time and room* to grow. Allow him his thoughts, feelings, questions and opinions. After all, he was created in the image of God, too. Pray that the Lord will change him. Then acknowledge *your* willingness to grow and change, too.

Use this transition time to really *get in touch with yourself.* Own your feelings, thoughts and beliefs and share these lovingly with your partner. Express why you feel the way you do. If he is open to doing some reading with you, by all means read some books and articles together taking the time to listen to his perspective on the issue. Who knows? You might even grow as a result!

Remind him, in the midst of these times, that you are vitally *concerned with his needs as a man* and as a husband. Even in the midst of conflict, remember to treat him as the highly significant and valuable human being he is. Why? Because that is the way Jesus Christ looks at you.

Sometimes our husbands refuse to be of assistance around the house, for example, because they're unwilling to admit they don't know how to be of help. Perhaps as a child or even as an adult when he did help, someone always criticized the way he assisted. Maybe your husband does help but has such a bad attitude you almost wish that he wasn't part of the work team! Women, who says that either of you has to enjoy everything that needs to be done? He is responsible for his own happiness or unhappiness. You are not. If he chooses to be miserable let him be. Affirm him for his assistance anyway.

Press On Toward the Mark

This will not be an easy stage for you. Growth rarely is easy. Change is not comfortable. The familiar pattern, even if totally destructive and confining, always feels more secure and comfortable. Somehow it feels right even when it is wrong.

Being married is a mutual growing experience. The biblical principle, which frees both partners in the marriage to be all that they can be, is the concept of mutual submission. Rather than suppressing each other, we are free to serve and help each other in love with the Holy Spirit's presence active in our lives. When our marriages begin to move in that direction the road may not always be smooth, but the journey becomes an extremely fulfilling one for both partners.

> I love you
> Not only for what you are,
> But for what I am
> When I am with you.
>
> I love you
> Not only for what
> You have made of yourself,
> But for what
> You are making of me.

I love you because you
Are helping me to make
Of the lumber of my life
Not a tavern,
But a temple;
Out of the works
Of my everyday
Not a reproach,
But a song.

I love you
For the part of me
That you bring out;
I love you
For putting your hand
Into my heaped-up heart
And passing over
All the foolish, weak things
That you can't help
Dimly seeing there,
And for drawing out
All the beautiful belongings
That no one else had looked
Quite far enough to find. [10]

12
We're Free to Be Interdependent Women

Looking Up, Looking In, Moving Out

They came to Bethsaida, and some people brought a blind man and begged Jesus to touch him. He took the blind man by the hand and led him outside the village. When he had spit on the man's eyes and put his hands on him, Jesus asked, "Do you see anything?"

He looked up and said, "I see people; they look like trees walking around."

Once more Jesus put his hands on the man's eyes. Then his eyes were opened, his sight was restored, and he saw everything clearly (Mark 8:22-25, *NIV*).

Looking Up

Although this passage refers to a blind man in Jesus' day I, too, have been that blind man. Years ago my precious family and friends brought a questioning, struggling, intellectualizing young woman to Jesus Christ so she could be touched by His forgiving love and complete acceptance.

Knowing Christ Intimately

Jesus took me away from the familiar and into a land where I was to walk by faith, not by sight. He took me out of myself and confronted me with His reality. He quieted my excessive chatter and replaced it with wonder. He showed me that the search for truth was as important as either the questions or the answers. Christ introduced me to a process of searching for truth rather than giving me a packaged product. He assured me, through the words of the Apostle Paul, that "He who began a good work in you will bring it to completion at the day of Jesus Christ" (Phil. 1:6, *RSV*).

Over the last 15 years of knowing Jesus intimately, I have come to recognize different levels of seeing. When Christ first touched me I became aware of reality as I had never experienced it before. I felt liberated, but I saw only partial truth. The blind man puts it so profoundly, "I see people, they look like trees walking around."

Then as time progressed and I searched the Scriptures, I acknowledged my personal need for a constant filling by the Holy Spirit. I grew as a result of teaching, friendships and circumstances and my vision began to clear. My sight has not been totally restored, nor my perspective made crystal clear. No doubt the place where all the scales will fall from my eyes will be in heaven. But I am at a point in my life where my sight has undergone a transformation. Meeting Christ has made a dramatic difference in my life-style as I pray it will in yours. My view of God, myself and others has changed as a result of knowing Jesus intimately.

When I was first brought to this beautiful Christ I committed what I knew of myself to what I knew of Him. I was still the center of my attention, however. Christ was invited into my life and He accepted my invitation as He will yours: "Here I am! I stand at the door and knock. If anyone hears my voice and opens the door, I will go in and eat with him and he with me" (Rev. 3:20, *NIV*). But I didn't know my new Friend enough to trust Him completely. I had heard much of His love but I had also heard much of His holiness and anger. I knew little of His acceptance. So I added Christ to my already hectic schedule. I thought, *I not only need the time to do all the other things that are a part of my life-style, I am also supposed to have time to read this new Friend's love letter, talk to Him and meet with His Body here on earth. How can I ever fit it all in?*

Needless to say I couldn't. But the Holy Spirit does a work in us, sometimes in spite of us. Here is a picture of the transformation He brought into my view of priorities:

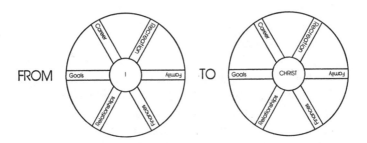

As I experienced the trustworthiness of Christ, the forgiveness of my Saviour and the accepting grace of my Redeemer, I, like Martha, was gently rebuked for having my priorities reversed. As I learned that God views me as deeply fallen but also a highly significant and greatly loved woman, I came to see that God always gives us the very best that He has. Very quickly transformations began in my life.

I began to understand the importance of making Christ central so the other things in my life, as important as they were, didn't become a distraction. Faith and worship and love of God became the hub, as it were, with the other things flowing from it. Everything in my life now has become an opportunity for communion with my Saviour, for He has truly become the unifying, centralizing and cohesive force in my life. My eyes were touched by Christ so my focus would switch away from religious activities and onto a life-style of worship.

When Christ touched my eyes, as He did the blind man's, not only did my view of God and His place in my life change, but so did my view of myself. Because I had swallowed the world's lie that I had no real value unless I earned it, I had let the events of my life define who I was. See diagram on the following page to see how I picture it.

As the Holy Spirit gently but firmly shows me that I am a cherished child of the Living God, I have come to realize what an indestructible support system I have. The God who knows me at the deepest, most intimate levels, even better than I know myself, loves me the most. Because of this awesome knowledge I have come to view the events in my life as opportunities to grow and learn, not as measuring sticks to determine my identity. My identity was settled at the cross.

But not only are my views of God and myself revolutionized as Christ becomes dearer to me, so are my views

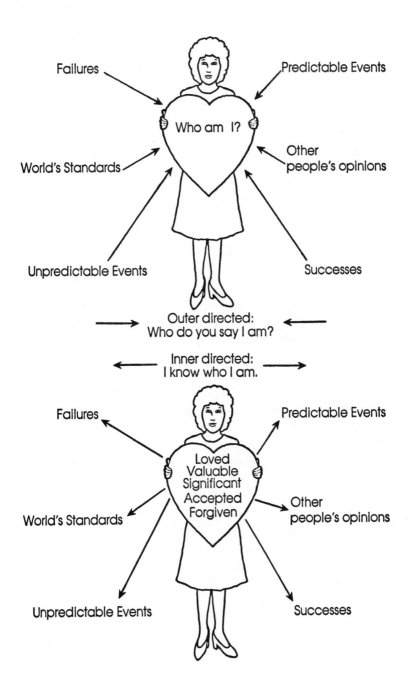

of others. Because I have truly grasped God's forgiveness and acceptance, I can let go of my confessed guilt. Now, with my new support system, I don't have to build my life around other people, be it my husband, friends, children or myself. Because I have been declared equal and adequate, I don't need to prove I am as good as any other man or woman. I don't need to make myself an object of worship because I worship the Christ, the son of the living God.

Just as I am a cherished child of God, so is every other person. I respect God's priceless investment in each and every person. I see the futility of pretending to be better than I am, for mutually we are all God's children. Possessiveness, uniformity, pretense and manipulation are to have no part in my life-style. Rather than seeing through each other, each of us is called to see each other through.

Using people to promote my image, my dreams and my plans is always manipulative. I am to use things, not people. When I truly comprehend that we are all part of one Body, I realize that any damage I choose to do to other Christians not only hurts them, it also hurts Christ and is ultimately self-destructive.

As we *look up,* we experience God's touch on our lives. Just as the blind man's vision and perspective changed, so will ours. With Paul, who had been in the ministry 25 years, we will breathe out our deepest desire: "that I may know him and the power of his resurrection" (Phil. 3:10, *RSV*). The yearning of our hearts is satisfied by Christ alone.

Finally, as I come to know Christ more intimately I am able to see that I am not a victim of the events in my life but a child of God, placed on this earth to love the people in my life. In the process of loving I can affirm their value apart from their performance. I can affirm our equality in Christ. I can warn those involved in dependent and independent relationships and encourage, with the Holy Spirit's filling, interdependent relationships—all as a result of knowing Him.

Looking In

We who are privileged to be Christian women have an excellent God. We who are representatives of the Lord Jesus Christ are involved in a purpose bigger than ourselves. We are His vehicle to provide hope to our hurting world.

Our purpose is vast. We are ordinary women but when we dare to join forces with an extraordinary God, we find ourselves pursuing excellence, shooting for the stars and daring to be the best we can possibly be. In Ecclesiastes 9:10 *(NASB)* we read these words: "Whatever your hand finds to do. . . do it with all your might." A pastor put it this way, "Pray as if it all depends on God and work as if it all depends on you."

During the writing of this chapter the Twenty-third Olympiad was being held in Los Angeles. I was thrilled by the dedication, sometimes in spite of unbelievable odds, the young athletes exercised. The results were evident in their strong, courageous, healthy bodies. We sometimes forget that we, too, are in a race—a race for a goal far more valuable than gold. Are we living our lives as if the Olympic games were an every day reality in our lives?

Are we aware that without Christ we can do nothing (John 15:5) but with Christ we can do all things? Each one of us needs an impossible dream to keep us alive—a dream that will take Christ to make it happen.

Do you have such a dream? Have you dared to get to know yourself well enough that you can define what are the desires of your heart? Or have you denied your personal needs for so long that panic has begun to strike when you read this section?

Remember that God "is able to do exceeding abundantly above all that we ask or think . . . " (Eph. 3:20, *KJV*) if we let Him. So let's join forces with our miracle working God in the pursuit of excellence.

Even when we commit ourselves to a dream it is possible to be sidetracked from our original intention. In order to avoid having this happen, there are 10 things we need to do on a continual basis in our lives.

1. Scrutinize Your Life-style, Gifts and Abilities

God wants you to be your own unique, unrepeatable person, not just a carbon copy of someone else. Since He, as it were, broke the mold when He made you, there is a particular position in His kingdom you can fill.

Take stock of who you are. Pause and reminisce for a short time. What experiences have you had in your lifetime? Take the time to list these no matter how insignificant they seem.

If you had unlimited resources, what types of things would you most enjoy doing? List these interests. What abilities do you have? This is not the time for negative thinking or downgrading yourself. Make a list. If you are having difficulty ask people who love you to help you. What spiritual gifts has the Lord created in you? Ask women whose wisdom you treasure to help you identify your gifts.

What kind of books do you enjoy reading? What new classes might you be interested in taking? What hobbies do you enjoy? What would you like people to say about you if they were summing up your life? What are the opportunities you have at your fingertips? What volunteer work have you done? Make a list.

If, as you are doing this, you are feeling a mounting

pressure to be a superwoman, stop! Each of our lives have seasons, and with the advent of each new season we are able to accomplish different goals. Never do we accomplish all of them at one time, so relax. Remove any of the "shoulds" you are putting on yourself and continue to brainstorm.

Perhaps you have young children and you have chosen to stay at home while they are young. This season of your life may be as short as five years or as long as 18. Either way, it is a relatively short period of time when compared to a lifetime. You are making a major contribution in this generation and the generations to come. There is no need to prove your worth by running out and getting a job. True, there are aspects of being at home that are the pits, but that is also true in a career.

Pearl S. Buck writes beautifully while she affirms your place in society:

> Do I, who am a professional writer, believe that homemaking is the most important work in the world for a woman? Yes I do, and not only for others but for myself. As a writer, I know that it is essential for a woman to be a homemaker, and this is true whatever else she is.

> Woman, the housewife and homemaker creates more than she knows. While she sweeps and cleans and makes beds, while she cooks and washes and puts away, she is creating human beings. She is shaping dispositions and building character and making harmony . . .

> Seldom indeed do men and women rise

above the atmosphere of their childhood homes. They become rich and powerful, they may build houses very different from the one they first knew, but they carry within themselves the atmosphere of that first home . . . "[1]

One would not know that children are highly valued given the way many adults talk today. It is common to hear that they tie us down rather than to hear them called blessings, even if exhausting blessings!

But the question you need to examine, if indeed you are a homemaker, is *why* are you a homemaker? Is it because you have chosen to be? Is it because you feel it is expected of you? Is it because you are afraid and feel it is your only option?

If you are honest enough to admit fear, perhaps you need to use this stage in your life not only to be a homemaker but also as a time to gain new skills and further your education. If you feel you're too old, how old will you be in 10 years or so if you don't do it now?

Unfortunately, husbands die or leave and children grow up. Perhaps you would rather not face reality but that doesn't change the truth. In the Western world it is important for a woman to feel that if worse came to worse, she could care for herself and her family. Even though Jesus Christ settled the question of our value on Calvary, it is virtually impossible for a woman in our society to feel competent if she believes she has no skill by which she could earn a living.

Perhaps the basic issue is faith. Are you willing to affirm the promise that "you can do all things through Christ who strengthens you?" (see Phil. 4:13). Does that promise cover practical areas such as going back to school or trying a new interest?

Whatever you choose, be it homemaking, a career or both, never forget that you are in full-time Christian service. Perhaps you have chosen a career. Why did you make that choice? I sincerely hope you aren't searching for the happiness ever after fantasy. Perhaps your marriage is less than what you expected and so you are pursuing yet another fantasy. Please examine your heart and be sure you are not choosing a career to run away from home.

One of my favorite cartoons pictures a mother furiously paging through the want ads. Everything around her is in shambles and three children are hanging from the chandelier. Her husband's only question is, "Are you sure you want a career?" We've all had days like that, haven't we?

Perhaps you are working part-time to supplement the family income or full-time either by choice or because you are a single parent. Do you feel your career is helping to develop some of your God-given talents? If it is, what talents and gifts are being developed? There can be tremendous satisfaction in a career apart from the financial reward.

If your present career does not develop your gifts and talents, you may need to search for one that will. Perhaps your search will involve further education. Education is not likely to be viewed as an irritation if it is a means to the end of developing and using your gifts.

By this time you have a fairly comprehensive idea of your abilities, gifts, life-style and opportunities. What are you going to do with your lists?

2. Stimulate Your Dreams

A definition I particularly like for dreaming is "creative imagining." In the last few minutes you have focused on the raw material of you. Let's now focus on the person you would like to become. Terry Hershey refers to dreams as "mental images of who we can be as God's children. They allow us to see what God desires to do in and through us. They can be pictures of what God wants to make of us."[2]

What are your hopes for the future? Define them. Have you wanted to go back to school but just not had the courage? What about the dream of going into business for yourself? Have you wanted to learn a new language or perhaps increase your everyday vocabulary? What about those gorgeous goals you've been thinking about for such a long time? Where would you like to go? Dream a lot and get in touch with some of your fantasies. What do you want to do to further the kingdom of God on this planet?

I am not suggesting we all follow Pinocchio's lead and run off to pleasure island. Rather, I want you to get in touch with some of your unmet needs. Perhaps you feel that as a woman you are obligated to deny or repress those needs. Nothing could be further from the truth.

It seems most of us are constantly giving to others without examining some of our own needs. It is both necessary and possible to develop a plan to meet some of your needs without sacrificing the needs of others.

Pause and list some of your personal needs. While you're doing this may I share some of mine? I find a deep need for private, meditative time each day to worship my Lord. I need supportive, positive, intimate adult friends. I need to keep growing and learning. I have a very strong need for organization in my life and I find it necessary to take time away from my responsibilities for recreation. These are just a few of my needs, ones that I believe you can relate to.

Up to this time you have been letting your imagination run away with you. You have been brainstorming. The next step is to take this mass of information about who you are and begin to organize it. What is important to you must become clear in your imagination before it will take place in your life.

3. Start Prioritizing

What are the top three priorities that govern your life? List them below.

Priority 1:

Priority 2:

Priority 3:

Now that you have listed your priorities, go back and check last week's calendar. Did your activities fall under priority one, two or three? What happened?

If you're like I am, you will discover that unless you consistently check up on yourself, your week will consist of many good but rather unimportant activities if judged against your priority system.

Why don't you chart out an imaginary week, making sure that all entries fall under one of your three priorities. Would your life-style be slightly different than it is now?

If you live life without priorities you will find yourself a victim of everyone else's priorities. Is that what you wish?

Let me stress, once again, that we are God's representatives on planet Earth. We have been designed and appointed to live to the glory and praise of God. None of us want to simply fill up empty space with lots of good but misdirected activities. This automatically happens, I'm afraid, if we don't prioritize. Whatever we choose for our priorities eventually sets the framework for what we will become.

Does it seem overwhelming to start? Often it does, but if you dare to begin, you're miles ahead of many. "And who knows but that you have come to royal position for such a time as this?" (Esther 4:14, *NIV*).

4. Set Goals

My faith in Jesus Christ is central. All else flows from this—including my goals. The woman who sets low goals or no goals will achieve little or nothing. She will live on the isle that Denis Waitley refers to in this poem.

> There is an island fantasy
> A 'someday I'll' we'll never see
> When recession stops, inflation ceases
> Our mortgage is paid, our pay increases
> That someday I'll be where problems end
> Where every piece of mail is from a friend
> Where the children are sweet and
> already grown
> Where all the other nations can go it alone
> Where we all retire at forty-one
> Playing backgammon in the island sun
> Most unhappy people look to tomorrow
> To erase this day's heartache and sorrow
> They put happiness on 'lay away'
> And struggle through a blue today
> But happiness cannot be sought
> it can't be earned, it can't be bought
> Life's most important revelation
> is that the journey is more
> Than the destination.[3]

We need to establish goals, not excuses. Our life-style will be a matter of choice not chance. Let's live according to our priorities because Christ has declared us adequate and empowered us to touch our worlds meaningfully in His name. We do not set priorities and then goals because we are trying to prove our adequacy. The cross established that once and for all.

New Beginnings

First, write down three goals under each of your priorities, rating the goals according to their priority in your life. As you do this remember that your goals need to be realistic, attainable, time related and measurable. Perhaps one of your priorities is to deepen your relationship with the Lord. One of your goals could then be to set aside 30 minutes each day of the week, beginning today. Or perhaps one of your priorities is to keep growing. An attainable, measurable goal for you might be to read one book, every two weeks, for the next three months.

As you form some goals I suggest very strongly that you face your fears. What terrifies you the most? Is it returning to school? If it is, make a goal that confronts that fear. Register for one course in your area of interest at the closest college. Robert L. Stevenson encouraged us to fight our greatest fears or perish. Why not? I started to do this a few years ago and I have found it a liberating aspect to my life and my goal setting. The other day I heard a woman refer to herself as the original "chicken of the sea." If you qualify under that classification, make it a goal to enroll for the next swimming session at your local Y.W.C.A.! Remember, "God hath not given us the spirit of fear; but of power, and of love, and of a sound mind" (2 Tim. 1:7, *KJV*).

May I also suggest that you make it one of your goals to build up someone else's self-esteem. Perhaps your husband or your children need to confront an area of fear in their lives and overcome it. Is there something you can do

The Wheel of Choice

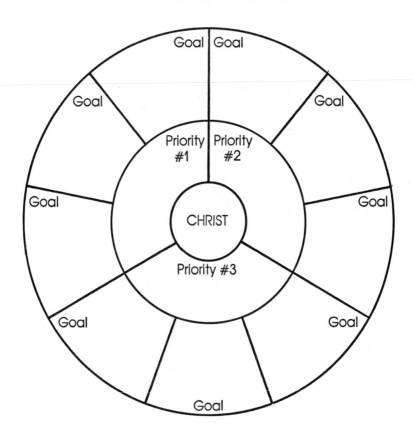

"A wise [woman] thinks ahead . . . it is pleasant to
see plans develop" (Prov. 13, 19, *TLB*).

to facilitate their growth? Is there a phone call of affirmation you could make as part of your daily or weekly lifestyle? How is your letter writing coming?

Do you remember how you responded to the question I posed in chapter seven? What don't you like about yourself that you could change? Perhaps one of your responses can be listed under your goals.

Steps to Make My Goal a Reality

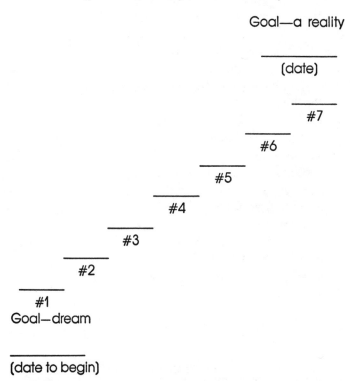

Goal—a reality

_____
(date)

_____
#7

_____
#6

_____
#5

_____
#4

_____
#3

_____
#2

_____
#1
Goal—dream

_____
(date to begin)

Second, choose the priority and goal of greatest importance to you.

Third, list some of the results from accomplishing this goal in your life.

Fourth, list some roadblocks you may encounter on the way to making this a reality in your life. Remember not to wait until all the solutions are obvious because you won't be walking by faith or even have the need to get started.

Fifth, develop a daily and weekly plan so your goal will become a realistic part of your life-style. Be certain you have broken your goal down into small enough steps so it is attainable. Now record your plan.

Happiness is a by-product of being committed to and involved in something you consider worthwhile. Until we acknowledge some of our own dreams and needs, without sacrificing the needs of those dear to us, we will never fully understand personal fulfillment, which is so essential to a healthy self-esteem.

Once your goal has been established, give it all you've got! Your goal is time-dated but if you don't achieve it within the time frame you originally established, revise your schedule rather than giving up your dream. Most people fail to meet their goals because they never set them in the first place.

Don't worry about your other priorities and goals, just work on the one of primary importance to you. When it becomes a reality in your life-style for at least a month, go back and choose another goal you would like to see come to life.

5. Speak Your Goals

Whether you are a homemaker, a career woman or both, home is in many ways the place you will succeed or fail. Home is a place to relax, but not to the extent that all organization goes out the window. Why don't you run your home as if you were self-employed, as if it were a small business?

If you have a full-time career I suggest that you arrange for some help, be it your family members or outside, to run your home efficiently. You are not a superwoman. You certainly don't want to fall into the habit pattern of working 24 hours a day, seven days a week. What jobs can you farm out?

If you are at home with young children, organization can be an immense help. Often your days are full of necessary but mundane chores. Your job description grows to fill the time you have available. Let's not be a victim of our homes. Let's choose to organize.

Over the years I have gained some valuable hints on home organization. I share eight with you here:

a. Make a list of those mundane chores that must be done daily. Divide them up between morning and evening chores. Do some yourself but don't forget to enlist your family's help.

b. Schedule routine weekly, monthly and quarterly activities. For example:

weekly—grocery shopping, write letters to family
monthly—vacuum under the furniture
quarterly—wash windows, shampoo carpets

Put these on your calendar now. Perhaps Friday is the day you vacuum, Thursday the day you shop, Monday and Wednesday the day for laundry. Seasons of your life will vary, of course, so make up a schedule to fit your current life-style.

c. As I mentioned previously, I find it helpful to plan my week's activities all at one time. It is also the time to review my goals and see how I am progressing.

d. Plan your menus all at once. Only shop once a week if at all possible.

e. Have a master plan for your day. If you are a morning person, get up a little earlier to do some of your chores. If you are an owl, do them in the evening before you go to bed.

List the things you have to do and prioritize them. Ask yourself why you feel it is necessary to wash the dishes more than once a day, for example. Check up on your superwoman complex.

Make certain at least one activity you consider fulfilling is on that list. Do the most difficult or tedious activities when you are freshest. Don't use your best hour of the day to read the newspaper or sort through your mail.

f. Pray about interruptions at the beginning of your day so you are confident God has allowed them when they do come.

g. If you normally vacuum on Friday and for various reasons cannot get to it this week, don't add it to Saturday's schedule unless you're unable to ignore it one more day. Wait a week and complete the task the following Friday. Do you know how many years it has taken me to do that? I was the original Mrs. Clean but I used my chores as an excuse for the lack of time I spent on relationships. Please don't fall into that trap. You truly end up a *house*-wife, married to your house.

h. Schedule daily time for personal hygiene. If you are a full-time homemaker it is just as important to you as it is to the career woman to feel you look sharp. Daily exercise can certainly improve your perspective. You will look and feel more beautiful and alive.

7. Stick to It

A primary reason we are tempted to give up is other people. There is a small but significant number of people on this planet whose major goal in life is to encourage others to quit. But we don't have to listen, do we?

Beethoven rewrote his opera Fidelio four times, over-coming terrible failures and poor audience response. Each time he rewrote the opera it improved, until it finally became a masterpiece. Paul Erlich's cure for syphilis is coined 606: the magic bullet, because it was preceded by 605 failures.

There is a story Chuck Swindoll likes to tell about a couple of men who were working alongside the inventor, Thomas Edison. Weary to the point of exhaustion, one man sighed, "What a waste! We have tried no less than 700 experiments and nothing has worked. We are not a bit better off than when we started." With an optimistic twinkle in his eye, Edison quipped, "Oh yes, we are! We now know 700 things that won't work. We're closer than we've ever been before."

Is our Lord persistent? You know it! Does He ever stop loving? Does He ever stop forgiving? Does He ever remove hope from us? Never! If Christ is our Saviour we are promised that "He Who began a good work in you will continue until the day of Jesus Christ—right up to the time of His return—developing [that good work] and perfecting and bringing it to full completion in you" (Phil. 1:6, *AMP*). Since we are called to be "imitators of God" (Eph. 5:1) let's exercise our wills. Let's call on our self-discipline and stick with it.

8. Shun Comparisons

The problem with comparison is this: we always com-pare our worst with the other person's best. And more often than not their best is nothing more than our fantasy.

The first question I am usually asked when requested to do a seminar is, "Do you also sing?" I'll have you know that most of you wonderfully talented women who do both have ruined it for the rest of us!

Jesus calls us to cooperate with one another, not to

compare ourselves to one another. Some of us have been given one talent, some five and some 10. The number isn't the important issue. The questions to ask yourself are, *Am I shooting for the stars? Am I pursuing excellence with what God has given me?*

Jealousy is often a sign we have unmet personal needs. Instead of giving in to those negative emotions, why not reexamine the reasons for feeling the way we do. Instead of envying the trim figure on the girl next door, why don't you enroll in a personal exercise program?

9. Squelch Perfectionism

When perfectionism raises its ugly head in my life, it is a sign that, once again, I'm trying to earn God's favor. I need to remind myself that my adequacy has been declared. I have nothing to prove. May I shoot for the stars out of this sense of adequacy.

10. Shed Negativity

A woman once commented after one of my seminars that damage had resulted from the positive thinking movement. As true as this may be, what is our alternative? Does negativity and a critical spirit honor God? No way!

Your attitude toward life, your family and your job is vitally important because it will affect the atmosphere around you. A positive attitude is conducive to growth, will affect your health, has a predictive power and certainly is contagious. We are called to be facilitators of others' potential, to call forth the ability of others. Paul's goal was to present people to God. Can we do less? This is certainly impossible to accomplish with a negative spirit.

So, you haven't achieved your goal. You had the courage to try, didn't you? Often our biggest enemy is our own inertia. The question is not how you are going to finish but how you are running the race. Because we are human and not divine, we will face failure. A major step in our personal growth happens when we no longer defend our failures but ask the Lord to teach us what He has for us in the face of failure.

So you face a hurt. Why don't you turn it into a hurdle? Are you facing a crisis? Why don't you make it an opportunity? You failed yesterday? Why don't you turn your failure into a commitment to faithfulness? If you're disappointed, why don't you use your disappointment as an opportunity to exercise your self-discipline? Life is the ultimate do-it-to-yourself project in many ways.

If you pursue excellence by taking these 10 steps, a sense of personal satisfaction will result. Surround your priorities and goals with prayer and praise. With the psalmist, David, let's affirm Psalm 71:5-6,8 (*NIV*):

> For you have been my hope, O Sovereign Lord,
> my confidence since my youth.
> From birth I have relied on you;
> you brought me forth from my mother's womb
> I will ever praise you.
> My mouth is filled with your praise,
> Declaring your splendor all day long.

Moving Out

He was born and raised in poverty. He lived on what we would call the wrong side of the tracks. He had neither a wardrobe or a residence to which He could point with pride. He never became the confidant of the big shots of His day. He was the classic example of the common man. He belonged to an oppressed minority group—the Jews. Yet He never returned taunts with belligerency. He knew that insults and injustice could either turn Him into a better person—or a worse person. It all depended on Him. Using a positive attitude, He made negative social situations a way to turn Himself into a more sensitive, understanding, compassionate human being.

His family connection was simple and unpretentious. His father was a carpenter. The family lived in the poorest section of the poorly considered village of Nazareth. Yet He was proud of His family for they were good people.

He held no academic degrees, never travelled more than seventy-five miles from home, published no books, built no marble columned buildings. His only achievement was the building of a personal character and reputation that would be an inspiration to millions yet unborn. How did He become this kind of person? By specializing in the building of self-worth in persons that appeared worthless.

How did He build love in self-condemning people? He never called them sinners. Instead He gave them a new self-image, with words such as "You are the light of the world"—"You are the salt of the earth"—"Follow me and I will

make you fishers of men"—"Your sins are forgiven"—"If you have faith as a grain of mustard
seed, you can say to your mountain move—and
nothing will be impossible to you."

Even His shameful death failed to destroy His
strong self-assurance. To be crucified was to
die the most ignominious death possible—
naked, undraped, exposed in daylight to the
stares of men, women and children. To add further insult and indignity, He was hanged in the
company of two common thieves. Still He died,
as He lived, in dignity. How? By remembering
those around Him had problems. He was first of
all concerned about the executioners: how they
would hate themselves after the bloody deed
was all over. "Father, forgive them, for they
know not what they do," He prayed.

His spirit lives on today. He lives to tell you that
you too are a wonderful person when you allow
yourself to be used by God to save people from
self-degradation and to help raise them to
human dignity.[4]

Have you ever noticed that your own needs and problems seem less threatening when you are busy helping
someone else handle theirs? Have you noticed there is
less time to be critical of others when you are being honest
about yourself and those areas where you need to grow?
No longer is there a need in your life to take others apart
in order to justify your own need for improvement.
Because you are looking for and affirming the good in
yourself, your mission becomes one of building self-worth
in others.

You can now look for the good in others and tell them about it. This neither threatens you nor is used to manipulate them because you can now see the good in yourself, too. Your affirmations will not be focused just on what others do but also on who they are. They are significant and of great value in God's eyes and therefore they are significant in your eyes, too, apart from what they do. It is always possible you may be the closest thing to Jesus any of the people around you will ever see.

There is always something only you can do. If you are married your husband only has one wife—you. You have your neighbors, your children, your business acquaintances or your relatives. If you are single, you have a circle of friends unique to you. What one thing can you do in each of these people's lives to raise their self-dignity?

That's your assignment for the rest of your life. You will discover that loving the Father is done by loving those dear people in your life. You will discover what it means to be a woman, an interdependent woman, whose self-esteem comes as a result of being loved by God and whose self-concept is enhanced after loving and building self-esteem into the precious ones God has given you.

For the first time in many of your lives you will understand what it means to be free as a woman. You are:

> Free to affirm your value but not free to base your value on your performance;

> Free to develop your gifts but not to neglect their use in bettering your world;

> Free to pursue excellence but not to prove your worth;

> Free to soar like an eagle but not free to be puffed up with ego;

Free to define who you are but not to define
who I am;

Free to reach out to others but not to make
yourself responsible for their choices;

Free to love but not to lean;

Free to wear labels but not be defined by those
labels;

Free to be single but not free to be an island;

Free to be married but never to forget you are a
person;

Free to be a homemaker but not because there
are no other options;

Free to establish a career but not to escape to
utopia;

Free to lead but not free to lord it over others;

Free to affirm but not to manipulate, pretend or
blame;

Free to hold a child's hand but not to imprison
his spirit;

Free to submit but not to be a doormat;
Free to define your own needs and dreams and
see them become reality but not at the expense
of those you care for;

Free to accept your femininity but not free to deny, degrade or imitate someone's masculinity;

Free to realize your equality but not to use it as an excuse for refusing to serve;

Free to talk but not at the expense of listening;

Free to believe but not without asking questions;

Free to ask questions but not free to expect all the answers;

Free to be positive but not free to be a pollyanna;

Free to laugh but never at the expense of another;

Free to be vulnerable but not free to force me to be;

Free to be creative but not to the exclusion of relationships;

Free to be hospitable but not for the purpose of showing off;

Free to pray but not free to procrastinate;

Free to be involved but not free to be consumed by busyness;

Free to face issues but not to lose sight of priorities;

Free to state your beliefs but not free to harbor anger and bitterness when others' beliefs are different from yours;

Free to face intimidation but not free to be intimidated;

Free to dream but not to forget that the dreams come from God;

Free to fail but not to abandon your dreams because you failed;

Free to be interdependent but not without first examining and rejecting the options of dependence and independence;

Free to see living as a privilege, not as a problem.

For the first time in many of your lives you are free to be yourself. You are free as an interdependent woman. Let's never choose self-imposed bondage again.

Remember always that *You* are God's way of being creative!

To God be the glory!

Notes

Chapter 1
1. From *A Woman's Worth* by Elaine Stedman, copyright © 1976; used by permission of Word Books, Publisher, Waco, Texas 76796.
2. From *There's a Lot More to Health Than Not Being Sick* by Bruce Larson, copyright © 1981; used by permission of Word Books, Publisher, Waco, Texas 76796.

Chapter 2
1. From *Why Am I Afraid to Tell You Who I Am?* by John Powell, S.J. © 1969 Argus Communications, a division of DLM, Inc., Allen, Texas 75002. Used by permission.
2. © Real People Press 1969. All rights reserved. Used by permission.

Chapter 3
1. Jim and Sally Conway, *Women in Mid-Life Crisis,* Copyright © 1983 by Jim and Sally Conway, Tyndale House Publishers, Inc. Used by permission.

2. Judy Haralson, "Freedom," *Faith at Work Magazine* (September, 1975). Used by permission.
3. From *There's a Lot More to Health Than Not Being Sick* by Bruce Larson, copyright © 1981; used by permission of Word Books, Publisher, Waco, Texas 76796.
4. Ibid.
5. Ibid.
6. William M. Kinnaird, *Joy Comes with the Morning,* Word Books, Waco, Texas 1979. Used by permission.

Chapter 4
1. Excerpt from START LOVING: THE MIRACLE OF FORGIVING by Colleen Townsend Evans. Copyright © 1976 by Colleen Townsend Evans and Laura Hobe. Reprinted by permission of Doubleday and Company, Inc.
2. *431 Quotes* by Henrietta C. Mears. © Copyright 1970, Regal Books, Ventura, California 93006. Used by permission.
3. From *There's a Lot More to Health Than Not Being Sick* by Bruce Larson, copyright © 1981; used by permission of Word Books, Publisher, Waco, Texas 76796.
4. Author unknown.

Chapter 5
1. "Because God Loves Me" by Dick Dickenson. Taken from *Improving Your Self Image* © 1983 Harvest House Publishers, Eugene, Oregon 97402. Used by permission.
2. If you'd like to learn more about this remarkable young lady and her great big God, I suggest *Michelle* by Carolyn E. Phillips, published by Regal Books, a Division of GL Publications, Ventura, California 93006.

Chapter 6
1. Walter Tubbs, "Beyond Perls." Journal of Humanistic Psychology, 12 (Fall 1972), p. 5.

Chapter 7
1. From SEEDS OF GREATNESS by Denis Waitley copyright © 1983 by Denis Waitley, Inc. Published by Fleming H. Revell Company. Used by permission.

Chapter 8
1. From the book, GET THE BEST FROM YOURSELF by Nido R. Qubein © 1983 by Nido R. Qubein. Published by Prentice-Hall, Inc., Englewood Cliffs, NJ 07632. Used by permission.

Chapter 9
1. From SEEDS OF GREATNESS by Denis Waitley copyright © 1983 by Denis Waitley, Inc. Published by Fleming H. Revell Company. Used by permission.
2. Anonymous
3. Leo Buscaglia, *Living, Loving and Learning* (NY: Fawcett, 1983), pp. 263-264. Used by permission.
4. Terry Hershey, *Beginning Again: Life After the Relationship Ends* (Laguna Hills, CA: Merit Books, 1984), p. 116.
5. From SEEDS OF GREATNESS by Denis Waitley copyright © 1983 by Denis Waitley, Inc. Published by Fleming H. Revell Company. Used by permission.
6. William M. Kinnaird, *Joy Comes with the Morning*, Word Books, Waco, Texas 1979. Used by permission.

Chapter 10
1. From *Improving Your Serve* by Charles R. Swindoll, copyright © 1982, used by permission of Word Books, Publisher, Waco, Texas 76796.
2. Reprinted from *To God with Love* by Dottie Versteeg. Copyright © 1980 Review and Herald Publishing Association. Used by permission.

Chapter 11
1. Taken from HEIRS TOGETHER, by Patricia Gundry. Copyright © 1980 by The Zondervan Corporation. Used by permission.
2. From *A Woman's Worth* by Elaine Stedman, copyright © 1976; used by permission of Word Books, Publisher, Waco, Texas 76796.
3. John Sterner, *How to Become Super-Spiritual or Kill Yourself Trying* (Nashville: Abingdon, 1982), p. 44. Used by permission.
4. Diagram reprinted by permission from the book, *When You Don't Agree* by James G. T. Fairfield, copyright by Herald Press, Scottdale, Pa. 15683.
5. Taken from HEIRS TOGETHER, by Patricia Gundry. Copyright © 1980 by The Zondervan Corporation. Used by permission.
6. From *Beyond Assertiveness* by John Paul and David Augsburger, copyright © 1980; used by permission of Word Books, Publisher, Waco, Texas 76796.
7. Reprinted by permission from HOW AM I SUPPOSED TO LOVE MYSELF? by Phoebe Cranor, published and copyright 1979, Bethany House Publishers, Minneapolis, MN 55438.
8. The word "liberation" refers to our freedom in Jesus Christ. We find true freedom only when bound to our Saviour and we *need* to be liberated into the awareness of what our freedom in Him means. I do not

agree with society's definition of liberation. Women who do agree with this definition are bound in hostility, bitterness and estranged relationships because they are reacting against dependency.

9. From IMAGES: WOMEN IN TRANSITION, compiled by Janice Grana, copyright © 1976 by The Upper Room. Used by permission of the publisher.
10. Mary Carolyn Davies, (public domain).

Chapter 12
1. Pearl S. Buck, *To My Daughters, with Love* (NY: John Day Company, 1967), pp. 184-186.
2. Terry Hershey, *Beginning Again: Life After the Relationship Ends* (Laguna Hills, CA: Merit Books, 1984), pp. 25-26.
3. From SEEDS OF GREATNESS by Denis Waitley copyright © 1983 by Denis Waitley, Inc. Published by Fleming H. Revell Company. Used by permission.
4. From *Self-Esteem: The New Reformation* by Robert H. Schuller, copyright © 1982; used by permission of Word Books, Publisher, Waco, Texas 76796.

PRAISE FOR RAFAEL ALVAREZ

This is a Baltimore that most of us have never seen. Behind the marble steps, the tightly shuttered windows of the silent row houses, the chugging tugboats and worn waterfront factories, was a magical old American city of immigrants and dreamers, drunks and gypsies, factory workers and watermen, saloon singers and bully-boys, all making it on nickels and dimes, conducting their lives in a silent symphonic march of gallantry, courage, and quiet dignity.

These are Americans we rarely hear about, told by a gifted native son, who can point to the place in the Chesapeake Bay where his father operated a tugboat and the factories where his grandparents left their sweat and blood. Alvarez's talents—poetic deftness, tight dialogue, burning descriptive passages laid out with seeming ease—show why he was one of the gifted writers that turned *The Wire* into the greatest show in television history. These are stories from the treasure chest of one of America's most talented scribes, and I am glad he shared them with us.

James McBride
Author, *The Good Lord Bird*
Winner of the National Book Award

More than anything else this is the story of a love affair; in this case, the beloved is a city.

Rafael Alvarez has no illusions about his city, he loves Baltimore despite its flaws, the violence, corruption, and the pain. He so deeply appreciates and articulates its unique if heartbreaking beauty amidst the ruins of a prosperous and glamorous past as well as its vitality, resilience, poignant sense of dignity and community.

Reading Alvarez's love story, I too began to see the city in a different light, wanting to know it better, even to live it.

Azar Nafisi
Author, *Reading Lolita in Tehran*
and *The Republic of Imagination*

BASILIO BOULLOSA STARS IN THE FOUNTAIN OF HIGHLANDTOWN

STORIES BY

RAFAEL ALVAREZ

COMMEMORATING THE 20TH ANNIVERSARY
OF THE PUBLICATION OF
THE FOUNTAIN OF HIGHLANDTOWN

CITYLIT
PRESS
BALTIMORE • MARYLAND

Library of Congress Control Number: 2017939758
ISBN 978-1-936328-22-2
Hardshell Edition
CityLit Project is a 501(c)(3) Nonprofit Organization
Federal Tax ID Number: 20-0639118

Front Jacket Photo: Amy Davis
Back Jacket Photo: Jennifer Bishop
Author Flap Photo: Sean Scheidt
Editor and Designer: Gregg Wilhelm

A note about the type:
The display font in the main titles is Kohinoor Bangla.
The rest of the type is set in PT Serif.

CITYLIT
PRESS

c/o CityLit Project
120 S. Curley Street
Baltimore, MD 21224
www.CityLitProject.org
info@citylitproject.org

Founded in 2004, CityLit Project is s nonprofit literary arts
orgnization based in Baltimore and serving the entire state of
Maryland. Its mission is to nurture a culture of literature by building
communities of readers and writers, and presenting programs that
bring people together to celebrate the literary arts. Launched in 2010,
the CityLit Press imprint publishes books of exceptional literary
merit and books of regional interest.

For Manny & Glo

CONTENTS

PUBLISHER'S NOTE

Believing Long Before Knowing

Twenty years ago, just five years into a publishing career, I had successfully pitched the idea of an independent press to the owners of Bibelot Books, a tremendous independent chain of bookstores in Baltimore. The imprint—Woodholme House Publishers, named for the flagship store's northwest Baltimore community—focused on regionalia and work by local writers. I was so surprised that the owners green-lighted the idea that I had neglected one important aspect: I had no one and nothing to publish.

I had long followed the bylines of writers for *The Sun*, Baltimore's remaining daily that I delivered as a kid, spread on tables for steamed crabs, and clipped bird cartoons by Jim Hartzell that depicted the previous night's Orioles' score. One of my favorite writers was Rafael Alvarez, a rewrite man who covered cops, obits, and City Hall cronies. Frequently, his name would be attached to stories about waterfront stevedores, bohemian ministers, button-festooned balloon sellers, subterranean kitchen klatches, bar bouncers, famous musicians—the authentic characters who contributed to Baltimore's hyperbolic quirk.

In the mid-1990s, Alvarez embedded himself into Baltimore's community of Orthodox Jews for a three-year series of stories about Passover and the transcendence of time, donning the black hat at bar mitzvah, the hulking station wagons at Sher Auto Sales, and evening prayers at Camden Yards. More than his mastery of prose, these stories revealed Alvarez's love of the worlds inhibited by souls who populated his hometown.

In those nascent Internet days, I crammed file folders and cabinet drawers with newspaper broadsheets, magazine clippings, and stapled photocopies of things I read that struck me about Baltimore that might find their way into the stew of a story idea of my own one day. I also learned from mentors at Johns Hopkins University Press that a solid article or column might be teased into a book project, which only fed my pack-rat habit. Under the pressure of finding something to publish, I dug into those files and found a copy of the Sunday *Sun Magazine* dated July 1994. The cover featured Rafael Alvarez, the reporter I admired, who had just won a prize awarded by organizers of Artscape, the city's sweltering summer outdoor arts extravaganza.

The prize was for a short story titled "The Fountain of Highlandtown." The first line—*I learned to live in the dark this year when I quit my job, sold everything I owned, and moved in with my grandfather*—hooked me like a rockfish reeled in from the bay.

The story economically told such a grand tale in three parts: an artist in one of life's liminal moments; a jaded girl to whom he reveals familiar turf as the Holy Land; his frugal grandfather in mourning but rich with memories. It was a story about a city and its people straddling old world and new, but so much more than that. It was about love dreams. It was a love dream.

I called the author and expressed my admiration. I asked if he had more stories. He lied and said "yes."

Six months later, Rafael Alvarez delivered the manuscript for *The Fountain of Highlandtown*. Artist Jonathon Scott Fuqua, an award-winning author in his own right, painted the perfect cover illustration of Patterson Park's iconic pagoda. Blurbs by Madison Smartt Bell and Stuart Dybek graced the back. A publishing house was born.

Since 1997, a lot of water has passed along Harris Creek, under Patterson Park, and out into the Patapsco "down at the end of Clinton Street."

Buyouts taken and scandals survived. Love found and loved ones lost. Kids grown, kids born. Little exiles in Hollywood and

Tampa. Too many Fleshtones shows to count. Unaware of what the day will bring besides the effort to write good sentences. A writer and his editor—two hometown boys—telling stories only we can set in a land only fiction can conjure.

This new collection, released to commemorate the original publication of *The Fountain of Highlandtown*, reintroduces an artist who paints memories so vivid that you will swear you saw them along The Avenue yourself. Publishing *The Fountain of Highlandtown* remains a highlight of my career and I am honored to team up with its author again. Books like this are exactly why I got into this tenuous business in the first place; twenty years later, we're both still pitching print in the age of streaming.

In my original copy of *The Fountain of Highlandtown*, dated August 18, 1997, Ralph scribbled "For Gregg, who believed long before I even knew he was paying attention." Let those words be solace to young writers, and an invitation to a new generation of readers.

Savor these stories the way you would old family recipes perfected over time by the pen and soul of Rafael Alvarez. Then anticipate what he is cooking up next.

"It's not too late, it's only..."

Gregg Wilhelm
Publisher, CityLit Press

FOREWORD

Exile on Macon Street

For forty years, Rafael Alvarez has been writing about home. But his great theme is exile, the heartbreak of leaving and being left behind. From the East Baltimore immigrants stirring the old country back to life in deep-bellied pots and cast iron skillets to the lovers stroking the relics of lost romance, Alvarez's characters yearn for the lost and struggle mightily to make memory as tangible as flesh.

The artist Basilio Boullosa, Alvarez's alter ego, lives in a house that he describes in "The Ganges of Baltimore" as "a reliquary."

In "The Fountain of Highlandtown," Basilio was a young man living with an old man, his grandfather, in the house on Macon Street. Even then, he was time-haunted, elegiac as the old man who refuses to turn on the lights. In the beautiful passage at the end of the story, Grandpop chants a litany of remembrance while Basilio paints his memories in a room without a roof, open to the stars that shine upon the living and the dead.

Past and present converge in an eternal now for both men, a now flavored with the ache of abandonment. Death is one kind of abandonment. Self-betrayal another. The yearning for home, a home left behind to enter this East Baltimore of struggle and sacrifice, a third.

Alvarez's characters are a particular kind of American—those restless souls who leave because they cannot stay but who refuse to surrender the sight, smell, taste and touch of that which has been lost. They live in a permanent state of exile but oh, how rich and deep is this liminal world of the present shot through with the past, how enchanting the ache.

In "Ganges," Basilio is older, with his own history of loss and abandonment fused with that of his city, his family, his house, his art. He corresponds with his old friend Hettleman who has left the city and professes not to miss Baltimore at all. Basilio is not buying it.

He knows that the past cannot be as casually discarded as a green plastic trash bag full of old clothes dropped off at Goodwill. His junk will never be someone else's treasure. In fact, he and Hettlemen turn junk, their own physical and emotional detritus, and that of other people, into art. "Any trace of the Baltimore that was gone pleased him."

But old junk can stab and shatter present pleasures as it does in this story when a crab shell ornament made by Basilio's great love Nieves interrupts a tender moment with a new lover. "The wound ran deep and Aubergine refused to go to the hospital."

The lady has her own old barely healed scars, after all, and is not unfamiliar with intimate pain. Yet even the mercurochrome Basilio applies to the wound is twenty years old. No antibiotic salve from Walgreens for him.

Hettleman has left it all behind, or so he thinks. He's sick of the past and of Baltimore in its decay and has lit out for pioneer country, the fragrant woods of Western Maryland. But the past isn't done with him. He's still scavenging and picking at his scabs. Even in the new world, still bleeding.

In exile, he makes a mask out of rain-soaked old cereal boxes and sends it to Basilio, along with a slew of letters raging against the machine.

Basilio puts on the mask and stirs a pot of cabbage soup. But Hettleman's mask—or perhaps the foolish dream of a fresh start for one so broken—angers the ghosts of the house, and the pot flies off the stove. "The mask fell into the mess on the floor, its edges fraying from the acid in the cabbage. He picked it up—stinking, dripping—set it on the table and cried, 'Come back...'"

Come back! Hettleman, Nieves, Grandpop and Francesca,

Leini and Orlo, all you lost.

"O, lost" as the quote by Thomas Wolfe painted on the transom of Alvarez's actual house on Macon Street whispers into the street. And the fragment of the quote not written on the door nonetheless echoes in the work: we seek the great forgotten language, the lost lane-end into heaven.

In this story, Hettleman learns the lesson Basilio knows in his blood. You can't go home again, but you can never really leave either.

Deborah Rudacille
2017 Guggenheim Fellow

INTRODUCTION

Spellbound in the Family Circle

> *"What are these picaresque tales of wandering sad sacks and love-fuddled stargazers if not road maps through the ineffable labyrinth, the heaped and swarming hive of our own sooty, shared Kingdom of the Patapsco?"*
> Tom Nugent
> Author of *The Strangeness*

Basilio Boullosa was born in darkness on the second floor of an East Baltimore rowhouse in 1989, a time of my life darker than the room where I scribbled the words that brought the young artist forth: "LIGHTS! LIGHTS! LIGHTS! LIGHTS! LIGHTS!"

A cry through the crepuscule...

I wasn't trying to write a story so much as leech some pain from the one I was living—stung by divorce, toking instead of typing, and thrown in with a shrewd old Spaniard who did not want me flipping on light switches much less living with him.

Yet without "Grandpop"—the one born in Galicia and his immortal double in the New World of fiction—there would be no Basilio nor a fountain by which his family is replenished to this day.

No hole cut in Grandpop's roof for moonlight to do what electricity cannot.

No Miss Bonnie's Elvis Bar where Basilio is struck sober on August 27, 1990, by a few true words.

And no clock on Eastern Avenue tolling: "It's not too late to imagine your way out of despair..."

•

"The Fountain of Highlandtown" won the 1994 Baltimore Artscape fiction award judged by James Alan McPherson [1943 to 2016]. That summer it was published in the old Sunday *Sun Magazine* and three years later became the title story of a collection of short fiction released by a publisher that no longer exists. I was 39 and it was my first book, something I had dreamed of since the third grade, the result of finally putting foolishness aside for a clear path to the typewriter.

[All of the stories in the first edition were sketched by hand and composed on manual typewriters—including a 1930s portable I bought for $20 at an East Baltimore Street sidewalk sale—serviced by Ken & Ray on North Avenue.]

Now, two decades and many books down the road, most of the stories in "The Fountain of Highlandtown" read to me like small talk about stick figures. All but that first one, my lucky charm.

Upon the foundation of Basilio and Grandpop, their narrow home on Macon Street, and the women who came to visit but not to stay, I have labored to build a house of many mansions.

A rowhouse pregnant with alcazars.

Within those palaces are long, linoleum-tiled hallways scrubbed by ghosts on their hands and knees. Did you know that when Francesca Bombacci's niece was a newlywed living with "Aunt Francie" and the elder Basilio ("Grandpop") the young couple washed their dishes in a claw-foot tub below a skylight shaped like a pyramid?

Through that same skylight passed enough moonbeams for me to scratch out my frustrations before passing out below it on the bed I slept on as a kid spending weekends with my grandparents.

Far below the kitchen basement where Francesca and her best friend Leini enjoyed sweet coffee and buttered toast are tunnels through which pigs fattened on chestnuts were driven to slaughter, their hocks destined for tureens of tomato broth served by Leini to customers at a Greek diner down at the end of Clinton Street.

And, rising high above the hole Basilio sawed out of the roof in order to paint the history of it all, a Moorish arch made of Baltimore brick through which Grandpop passed from his parlor death bed to ride wooden bicycles in *el mundo por venir.*

Thus, in this anniversary edition, I have scrapped all of the stories that don't feature Basilio and replaced them with new ones that do, adventures I could not have fathomed the night I scrawled the word "LIGHTS" on copy paper.

Beginning with a story about flying Beatle dolls in 1964—the year I figured out that my life was given to me and no one else— the narrative arcs toward Basilio's death eight decades later as he paints the circles below Anne Frank's eyes on the side of an abandoned building.

Along the way, the Cartographer of Baltimore introduces you to his daughter—the violinist India Jean Boullosa—but not the twins to which she will give birth, a boy and a girl destined to sit at the kitchen table on Macon Street after young Basilio has become Grandpop.

They will ask him the same innocent questions he once asked his grandfather, frustrating and delighting the aged artist four generations down the line from the rocky village of San Vincente.

"Grandpop, why did you fix the hole in the roof?"

"Grandpop, tell us about the time you and Mommy drove across the country for the whole summer."

"Grandpop, can we spend the night?"

Altogether a much bigger picture than the one that emerged from the carriage of my Remington portable between 1989 and 1997, an undulating Holy Land of dreamers and working people separated by two degrees or less.

Behold—

Basilio trying to remember if the young Greek mother who

walks her children to church was wearing a skirt of black or ivory or both for he has spent too many years behind the easel and his eyes play tricks on him.

"This is our Paris," he would say to her if given the chance, saying it to himself as he walks through alleys of rosebushes and trash cans, grape arbors and rats. "Our Jerusalem."

Nearing the gate to Grandpop's house, the spell is broken—these ruins are Baltimore, you fool—by Miss Helen, a proud Polack who shucked oysters on the waterfront during the Depression; tough old Helen Sadowski hanging over the wire fence separating her yard from Basilio's, calling out to him without so much as a how-ya-been.

"I miss my son," she says, turning away to take her wash off the line before Basilio can answer.

A canvas of bed clothes so much larger than ballpoint tears on yellowed scrap.

And far from complete.

Rafael Alvarez
Baltimore, May 24, 2017

I KNOW WHY I WAS BORN

Wigmann came to a few hours before dawn on Christmas Eve, face down on the sofa of a rowhouse saloon in the Holy Land. The old beer garden had been in his family since the turn of the century and passed down to him with the recent death of his father.

Wigmann rubbed the back of his neck.

"What am I going to do, Pop?"

The photograph stared back at him, mute alongside a bowl of ginger snaps soaking in sweet vinegar on the bar. The woman who'd promised to transform the cookies into sour rabbit and dumplings—a girl named Barbara he would introduce to the family tonight at dinner, the one who'd grown weary of apology—should have arrived hours ago.

A toy train emerged from a tunnel behind the wall with a shrill whistle and bubble lights percolated against the silvery sheen of a tin ceiling, reflecting in mirrors advertising "The Land of Pleasant Living," the destination Wigmann had sought while waiting for his sweetheart.

She'd many miles to cover and Wigmann had bided his time with one more beer.

Just one more.

Standing, he killed the train and walked to the front door, a draft frosting his toes as he turned the locks, the door bumping against something heavy.

Slipping outside, feet freezing against tiles that spelled out "645 Newkirk Street," Wigmann beheld a heart-breaking bounty.

A pile of presents, ribbons fluttering in the wind, were arranged around a roasting pan. Bending to lift the lid, Wigmann set his fingertips against the frozen skin of a cooked goose and began mourning the loss of his private Christmas: a German chapel crumbling inside an Italian cathedral.

Wigmann rifled through the gifts, but his beloved—who'd banged on the door with the heel of her shoe and let the phone ring a hundred times—had not left a note.

•

Tradition, Basilio's grandfather often said, is nothing more than hard work and planning.

The calendar is not a line, but a loop and you could not trust something as important as tradition—Christmas Eve the richest of all—to chance.

As Wigmann wept into his pillow, Basilio's grandfather stood at a basement workbench alongside a stone tub where eel would soon soak in milk. The Spaniard was hammering together a gift for his namesake grandson, an easel made from grape crates.

[The wine had turned out especially good that year, fruity and crude, the white better than the red and the words "Boullosa & Sons" written across clay jugs before gifts of it were made to friends and relatives who lived along the alley that separated Macon Street from Newkirk: an extra bottle delivered to Wigmann's Beer Garden to help ease the loss there.

As sad as it was, the dead man's son was supposed to bring a new face to the table and in this way—girded by hard work and new blood—tradition rolled with the calendar.]

Driving the last screw and oiling the hinges, Basilio's grandfather brought the easel from the back of the basement into the long kitchen where the feast would take place, where his Italian wife sat separating anchovies to be deep fried in dough.

"It's finished Mom," he said.

Weak-sighted, the woman wiped her hands on her apron and used her fingertips to make out the easel's form beneath a ring of florescent light on the ceiling.

"It's good."

"I think so," said Grandpop, putting away his tools.

Two floors above, Little Basilio slept with dreams coursing through his brain in the shape of his age: a pair of perfect circles, one set atop the other.

Inside the endless eight, the boy raced through the games he would play that night, felt the long wait ahead and realized why he was born.

[Born to paint the pictures in his head, to sketch the kitchen in the basement, to capture the clouds as the wind drove them past the bottle cap factory down by the railroad tracks, to capture the air that swirled across the tarred rooftops.]

The night before, Basilio had gone to bed knowing that he liked to draw.

Today, he would wake up with the knowledge that he was an artist the way his father was a tugboat man and his grandfather was a machinist at the shipyard.

A skylight above Basilio's head—hexagon panes embedded with diamonds of twisted wire—brought the breaking day into his room on a rolling bank of low, nickel-gray clouds, the kind that tease children with the promise of snow.

The boy opened his eyes and inside the skylight glass, he saw himself as a grown man living with his aged grandfather, painting the day-by-day story of their life together.

Basilio's father—at home with the rest of his family on a cul-de-sac where no one baked eel for Christmas—had slept below the same skylight thirty years before and told the boy over and over of the sacrifices made for a better life among the lawns outside the city.

Yet every weekend, summer vacation and Christmas Eve, Basilio's parents dropped him off on Macon Street.

To walk to the corner for wheels of fresh bread.

Wake up to the scent of smelts frying in olive oil.

And measure the universe by the width of a narrow rowhouse in the Holy Land.

Basilio heard his grandfather's feet coming up the stairs and knew it was time to go to the fish market.

Today was the day.

•

Wigmann took the gifts that had been left on his doorstep and packed them in his old man's car. He piled the packages on the back seat and set the roasting pan on the floor, thinking, as he walked back and forth between the house and the car, of the Christmas Eves of his childhood.

There was no place for goose at his family's feast. The tables pushed together in the basement of his aunt's house down the alley would be crowded with thirteen kinds of seafood in honor of the Savior of the World and the twelve who had followed Him.

Every year, Wigmann's father would lead all of the children from the crowded table to the beer garden to watch trains run through a sawdust village of 19th century Germany.

The big meal was a dozen hours away; his father dead and his sweetheart gone. Wigmann wasn't sure if he could stomach it this year.

The singing. The hugs. The love.

A basement filled with his mother's family: the bombastic Bombaccis.

Wigmann's mother Mary was the oldest of five first-generation sisters who lived up and down the alley.

Tonight's feast would take place in the middle of the block, at the home of Francesca Boullosa, the middle sister and grandmother of an eight-year-old boy who had just awoken with the knowledge that he was born to draw everything he saw.

•

Basilio gathered nickels and dimes and quarters from the top of the bedroom dresser, slipped them into his pockets with a few colored pencils and ran downstairs.

Next to the boy's place at the table—years later, the artist would stand in the basement and recite his family's seating arrangement for visitors—stood an easel Basilio would use long after the sidewalks had cracked on Macon Street.

"Sit," said his grandmother, touching the boy's head, buttered toast and hot Cream of Wheat on the table.

"When can I try it?" said Basilio.

"Eat," said Grandpop. "Then wash up."

In the car, as Basilio drew on the inside of the windows with his fingertips, Grandpop told the boy why the day was so special: "So you won't forget. The empanada, my mother made it with chopped nuts. Your grandmother uses raisins. Who knows what your mama will use? One day, if you marry the right girl, she will make it and I'll be gone."

"You're funny, Grandpop."

Together, they walked through the aisles of Broadway Market, and, as Basilio stared at pictures of his heroes hanging in a record store across the street, Grandpop pulled him toward the crushed ice of the fish stalls—do this in memory of me spiced with five pounds of shrimp—and told him again why this day was important.

But Basilio was thinking the thoughts of an eight-year-old who wakes up one day knowing why he was born: of listening to Beatles records with his cousin Donna and which new albums they might get as presents; of how long would it be before she walked through the front door of their grandparents' house with her red plastic record player.

"Today, we eat like kings," said Grandpop, preaching to a boy who had no idea what kings ate.

[Anyone who was blessed to eat their fill wore a crown. Enough potatoes. Plenty of fruit. And a sea of fish across three tables pushed together and covered with white cloth.]

The black eel—his wife's tradition, Bombacci and Boullosa mixed together in the restless boy like pigment on a palette—was a once a year treat: its sweet, firm length divided by the inch, breaded, baked, and piled on pastel china.

"You nail the head to a piece of wood and pull the skin back with pliers because she is too slippery to hold," said Grandpop as the fish man coiled three feet of eel into the bottom of a sack.

Basilio reached out and touched the creature just before it disappeared.

"Grandpop," he said, "can we stop at the record store on the way home?"

•

Wigmann sped east on Eastern Avenue with the roasted goose rocking gently near his feet.

Seeking absolution—the God of Second Chances was here Wigmann, right here in the Holy Land while you were passed out—he turned south onto Clinton Street and raised a cold cloud of dust, rumbling toward the water's edge, praying that a third chance would be the charm, a fat wad of inherited cash in his pocket.

Halfway down the gravel road, the mansion at the old Pound ship works began rising before Wigmann, higher than the tongue of flame above the Standard Oil refinery, an ornate, 19th century structure known as the Salvage House.

It looked worse for wear against the nickel gray skies over Fort McHenry as Wigmann pulled his old man's Volkswagen into the yard; the gutters sagging, paint peeling from the upper floors, and a quartet of gargoyle pigs sneering down from the four corners of the roof.

Wigmann growled at them as he got out of the VW with the roasting pan in his hands, drawing the attention of a gray-haired man slashing the thick skin of pig feet with an oyster knife before tossing the trotters into a black kettle over a backyard fire.

Orlo Pound was pickling enough Christmas pig feet to give to all of the people who had helped keep his secret and still have some left over to share with his lover, tending the pot in a small circle of peach trees at the edge of the Patapsco on a cold December morn; chuckling as he stirred it with a broom handle, a trio of Retrievers trying to stick their snouts in the bubbling vat, and an empty cask waiting to receive layers of pork upon layers of kosher salt, onions, and spices upon layers of pork.

Wigmann remembered coming down to the Salvage House when he was a kid with his father and how Orlo would give him gadgets from his great store of them; pocket watches without hands and port holes without glass that a kid could stick his head through and pretend to be Popeye the Sailor Man.

So many more thoughts of his old man in death than before; Christmas the time for remembering a wind-up toy the junkman called a "Dinky Doll," a monkey that hung from pipes on the ceiling while raising a tiny beer can to his lips; remembering how he'd lost Dinky before he could show it to anybody and how hard, being a big boy of eight or nine, he'd tried not to cry in front of his father.

"I don't want to cry," he had sobbed on the ride home from the Salvage House. "But my body does."

Back when Orlo had nothing but youth and conflict and yearning in his life—wanting Leini to be his and his alone, not caring to share her with her children much less her drunkard husband—the junkman had kept the mansion in perfect shape.

Now he was too content to get up on a ladder for minor repairs.

Laying churning stick aside as Wigmann approached, Orlo let out a belly laugh that smothered the sad world of pain he'd survived, recognizing in the disappointed face of the saloon keeper's son the little boy he used to know.

"Junior!" cried the junkman. "I thought that was you."

And in that moment—the boy gone but the dark hair, curved brow, and coal black eyes remaining in a man who looked nothing like his father—Orlo remembered that young Wigmann was the nephew of his lover's best friend.

Francesca Bombacci Boullosa and Eleini Leftafkis Papageorgiou

had been close as sisters since attending P.S. 228 together on Rap-
polla Street.

When the pretty girl from Greece enrolled in the fourth grade
without knowing five words of English, the feeble-sighted Francesca helped with her homework and invited her to big family
dinners along the alley separating Macon and Newkirk streets.

All these years later, Francesca remained the newly widowed
woman's best friend.

"Hi Mr. Orlo," said Wigmann, taking a seat in a metal folding
chair near the fire, freezing his ass off as the junkman par-boiled
a cauldron of trotters.

"What brings you down here after all these years? Doing some
last-minute Christmas shopping like your old man used to do?"

Once Wigmann hit puberty, he didn't want to hang out with
his father or tag along on the annual holiday visit to the Salvage
House for last minute gifts you couldn't get in stores.

One Christmas Eve, Wigmann told his father he didn't feel
like going to Mr. Orlo's, the same way—staring at a pile of gifts
on his freezing stoop that morning—he didn't want to sit around
and wait for Jesus to be born in Aunt Francie's basement.

The next year, the boy begged off again and after that Mr.
Wigmann didn't ask his son to go anywhere with him.

"Dad's gone," said Wigmann, taking the lid from the roasting
pan and ripping off a leg from the goose, the dogs jumping on his
lap.

"I know, I was at his funeral."

"How old are you now Mr. Orlo?"

"Sixty-seven last summer."

"Dad was only 52," said Wigmann, gnawing on the drum stick,
picking off pieces of the carcass and teasing the dogs with it. "It's
our first Christmas without him."

The bird was delicious and Wigmann wondered how it might
have been to share it with Barbara, warm from the oven, a white
tablecloth spread across the family bar. He threw a bone to the
dogs and started on a wing.

"Save me the wishbone?" said Orlo.

"What's your wish?"

"I'm building a star out of them."

Wigmann pointed to the kettle.

"What's that?"

"My holiday ritual," said Orlo. "Pickled pig feet with fig jam."

"For you and your friend? She used to give us Hershey bars wrapped in red and green cellophane when we were little. She still gives them to the little kids wrapped in five dollar bills."

"How can I help you, Junior?"

Wigmann lifted the goose from the pan like a football and tossed it into the middle of the yard. He watched the dogs rip the bird to shreds and then he startled himself.

"I need an engagement ring."

"Ah," said Orlo, covering the pot. "I got plenty of those."

•

Although Wigmann's vision was smaller now, Orlo's kitchen looked almost exactly the same as it did when he was little, when his father and the junkman would eat bowls of pig knuckles and spaetzle, washing it down with bottles of beer.

The junkman moved toward a stove near the hallway, bending over the oven and fiddling with the knobs as Wigmann inspected a china cabinet filled with records and buttons and school lunch boxes and pictures of three young men with long hair and guitars and one goofy looking guy with long hair and a drum set.

"What's this?" asked Wigmann.

Orlo turned the knob three-hundred-and-fifty degrees to the left, char-broil to the right, and two-hundred degrees to the left.

Wigmann heard a loud click and the oven door popped open.

"What's what?" said Orlo, pulling out a large tray of rings.

Wigmann tapped the cabinet glass.

"What are you doing with this kiddie stuff?"

"I've always collected fun things, Junior. You know that."

"But why this?"

"Because they're going to be huge and I like the way they cut-up," said Orlo. "This kid Frankie Lidinsky over near St. Wenceslaus gets everything the minute it hits the street and tells me what to look for."

"People are already throwing it away?"

"No," said Orlo. "There's just a ton of it out there."

"What's that hairy thing?"

"Hair."

"Who's?"

"John's."

"No."

"Yeah."

"I don't believe it."

"Don't."

"Where'd you get it?"

"From a friend whose old lady makes up beds at the Holiday Inn. She worked their rooms when they were here in March. Already been offered a grand for it."

"Gimme Sinatra and Dino," said Wigmann. "I can't stand that screaming."

"Some of it's nice," said Orlo, walking the rings to the kitchen table, the tray alive—a chest of pirate's jewels—in the sunshine streaming through the window above the sink.

Wigmann picked up the rings one at a time, slipping them on all of his fingers as far as they would go—"Okay, Ringo!" laughed Orlo—and began separating them into piles: diamonds, emeralds, rubies, ornate antique settings and sleek modern ones; sapphires, opals, and pearls.

"No prices on these," said Wigmann.

Orlo brought a cutting board to the table and began mashing cloves and grinding allspice across from Wigmann; a large bowl of kosher salt waiting, the room scented with the fragrance of nutmeg and cinnamon as a pot of figs boiled on the stove.

"Let me tell you about your father."

Wigmann stopped fiddling with the rings.

"Your old man was a character," said Orlo. "He'd come down here on afternoons when he couldn't stand being behind that bar a moment longer."

I know that feeling, thought Wigmann.

"And of course he loved everything German. He loved that Babe Ruth was German. That Mencken was German. These great Americans from Baltimore. I'd open up my German room, he'd put on lederhosen and we'd drink out of steins shaped like Bavarian castles."

"Can I see the room?"

"All doorknobs now," said Orlo. "Floor to ceiling doorknobs from around the world. After he had a few, he'd get very serious, almost grave, and start talking about how he envied me because I was a real American, free like other people aren't."

"He envied you?"

"He did and he didn't," said Orlo. "He envied how I could go anywhere at any time for any reason without having to explain. Still could if I didn't ache so much. He envied my freedom and I envied him his son."

"Me?

"Your father missed you coming down here with him. It upset him when you didn't want to come down here anymore."

"Ain't that I didn't want to."

"Only time I saw him cry."

"Is that true?"

"You'll hear it said that people love lies," said Orlo. "All I know about it is sitting on this table and out back in the pickling tub. Never been married."

"But I thought..."

"Nope."

"I've been messing up," Wigmann said. "I was expecting my girl last night and instead I got drunk and missed her. We were going to have an old-fashioned German Christmas, candles on the tree, just the two of us."

"Every year somebody burns their house down trying to have an old-fashioned Christmas," said Orlo.

"This is the big night, *the* night you wait all year for," said Wigmann. "And there's nothing I want to do less than sit around that table."

[I'd like to be there, thought Orlo, chuck this swine and enjoy a nice plate of fish. Wouldn't I love to hold her hand next to a cup of coffee and a plate of cookies.]

"Because your girl won't be there?"

"She might show up," said Wigmann, separating the rings into three piles: maybe, forget it, and gotta have it; his father's money tingling in his pocket as he played eenie-meenie-miney with an emerald and a ruby. "There's nothing I was looking forward to more than her knock on the door. It's Christmas and I feel bad about my father. Did he really say that about me?"

"Come on Junior. You come down here for the first time in a dozen years to ask questions there ain't no answers to and then you don't believe what I tell you."

"I wish he would have told me himself," said Wigmann. "I feel bad because I miss my girl more than I miss him."

"Of course you do," said Orlo.

"I want to chuck it all. Hop in Dad's car, find her and keep driving."

"I've ridden that train," laughed Orlo.

"You think it's funny?"

"I didn't then," said the junkman. "But I do now."

Jolly old Saint Orlo at the laughing stage after years of working himself to death to make Leini happy; the peace and wisdom of old age making him smile no matter how much his knees hurt, his back permanently wrenched after carting bathtubs from one end of the city to the other for his secret bride. In bad weather, his teeth hurt.

A year ago, in inexplicable sympathy with his adopted nation, Leini's husband had taken his life and Orlo hadn't stopped laughing since, not a whit of guilt.

"When was this?" asked Wigmann.

"Back in '55," said Orlo, chopping an onion. "Took the 2:12 Oriole Wing to New York City to see a Chinese witch doctor what was gonna cure what ailed us."

"I didn't say I was sick," said Wigmann.

Orlo remembered when he was Wigmann's age, it was the year Leini got married, a year into their affair. He'd sat brooding on the roof of the Salvage House as his lover's wedding guests danced in a circle behind Ralph's Diner.

Then, inexplicably, a softball game broke out, Leini at the plate in her wedding gown and then, less curious, Ralph's burned to the ground, Orlo watching from his roof across the way, harbor winds fanning the flames toward downtown.

As youth fades, the world beats acceptance into you or kicks the life out of you.

"All I want to know is where the train is going and when it's gonna get there," said Wigmann.

"That's all?"

"I wish you'd stop making fun of me," said Wigmann, who couldn't remember his father laughing much, even when something was funny. When his mother wasn't laughing or crying, she was yelling or preaching or asking her husband how in the goddamn world he could sit for hours without changing the look on his face.

"What makes you think I can answer these questions, Junior?"

"You're still making the pig feet aren't you?" said Wigmann, who'd only tried the trotters that sweetened his mother's spaghetti sauce.

"That I am," said Orlo. "You know what that goofy Chinaman wanted me to do?"

"What?"

"Drink the gallbladder of a bear crushed inside a milkshake."

"And?"

"That or go home empty-handed."

[I'm ain't going home empty-handed, thought Wigmann.]

"He said it would give us energy." said Orlo.

"We want children, too."

"Save your money on gallbladders," said Orlo. "It's cheaper just to love somebody."

"Didn't work?"

"There's a lot you could do with your time besides wait around for someone to see things your way," said Orlo.

"Did you know the city wants to put an expressway through this neighborhood?

"Already taking people's homes on Boston Street. Half the Polacks in Canton are dying of broken hearts. Crooks offered me $6,000, take it or leave it. They want to come right across the harbor with a double-decker highway to block out the sun.

"A mile the other way and they'd be coming for your father's bar. We could use somebody like you to help us fight the bastards."

Wigmann nudged the ruby to the side. Orlo turned down the flame under the figs on the stove and gathered up the salt and spices and onion to take outside.

"Did you hear what I said?" asked the junkman.

Wigmann held up an emerald in a half-century old basket setting.

"This one," he said.

"For that much you could have the Beatle hair," said Orlo. "It'll be worth ten times as much long after that ring is gone."

"How much?"

"Emeralds crack easy," said Orlo as Wigmann stood up to follow him outside. "Be careful with it."

Wigmann, took out his cash.

"Listen to me, Junior," said the junkman. "If they screw this part of town, Baltimore City is finished."

•

For all the stands of anticipation being braided in Little Basilio's imagination—his very pulse directed to the moment when guests would stream through the front door of his grandparents' house—that's how determined Wigmann was to avoid the evening.

Wigmann had been Basilio once. He'd walked through his Aunt Francie' door with his parents and a warm dish and expectations, stuffing himself with treats while waiting for the clock to move.

But Wigmann wasn't a little boy anymore and he knew it as he drove away from the Salvage House in a light snow, a backseat full of presents and an emerald ring in his pocket.

At the Broadway Market, Basilio and his grandfather carried a hundred dollars' worth of seafood out into the snow: scallops and a bushel of oysters. The snapper and two dozen clams. A fat rockfish. Shrimp, squid, and mussels.

It was cold enough for the fish to sit in the back of the car while Grandpop indulged Basilio in a visit to Kramer's, the candy store on Eastern Avenue where corn popped in the front window and a fan pushed the scent of hot caramel out onto the sidewalk. The scent was the only advertising Kramer's ever did; caramel and fresh popped corn mixed with the clean, brisk wind and the snow as Basilio walked inside with his grandfather.

The youngster would do all of his shopping here and go home with a dozen paper bags of sweets across which he would letter the names of the people he loved and draw pictures of birds and guitars and narrow houses along Macon Street.

Wigmann watched the boy and his grandfather from a pay phone across the street from Kramer's, rattling change in his hand, wondering what to do.

Above his head, the Great Bolewicki Depression Clock goaded him: "It's not too late to start a new tradition."

Sucking on a candy cane, Wigmann gave away three of the gifts left on his stoop to the first three people who walked by: a blind man drumming his fingernails against a metal pan rattling with change; a kid with a runny nose being dragged down the street by his mother; and a not-fat-enough man in a Santa suit ringing a bell in front of Epstein's department store.

"Thanks," said the old buzzard. "Nobody ever thinks to give a gift to Santa."

With one eye watching Basilio and his grandfather browse the candy store, Wigmann dropped a dime into the phone and called home.

"Hi Ma."

"How early did you leave this morning?"

"Did I get any calls?"

"No."

"You sure?"

"What's the matter, hon?"

Wigmann paused to search for his father's cool resolve but that was half-a-pause too long.

"I need a favor, Junior."

"What, Ma?"

"It's really your Aunt Francesca that needs the favor."

"What is it?"

"I don't know how my sister does it every year. All those people for a sit-down dinner. I hope you can be on time…"

"Ma, what do you WANT?"

"Watch yourself, young man."

"What, Ma?"

"Can you go down Pratt Street and pick up a Spanish man off a ship?"

"It never ends," muttered Wigmann.

"What's that?"

"Is the ship in yet, Ma?"

"I don't know. What's wrong, hon? I know you miss your father, we all do. But we've got to make the best of it and you know how good your Aunt Francie has been to us."

"What's the name of the ship?"

"Hold on, I got it right here."

Wigmann's mother put down the phone and he could hear her rummaging through her apartment upstairs from the saloon, picturing her in housecoat and slippers. By the time she was back on the phone, Wigmann was munching on a bag of Kramer's caramel corn.

"What are you eating?"

"Nothing."

"Junk? You're going to ruin your dinner."

"It is ruined," whispered Wigmann.

"What?"

"The name of the ship, Ma. What's the name of the ship?"

"The *Galicia.*"

"What pier?"

"I told you, Pratt Street."

"What's the man's name?"

"Mr. Steve. You remember Mr. Steve. He always brings goodies you can't get anywhere. Mr. Steve."

"I remember."

Wigmann hung up and leaned back in the booth to watch Basilio and his grandfather pull away from the candy store, munching a handful of caramel popcorn and wondering, in a swirl of flurries on Eastern Avenue, if he should go down to Pier Five or let Mr. Steve find his own way to Macon Street.

•

A letter from Spain was wedged between the storm door and the front door of 627 South Macon Street when Grandpop and Little Basilio returned from their errands. Grandpop shoved it into his back pocket and carried the food in from the car.

Basilio ran upstairs to arrange his bags of candy on the bureau beneath the skylight and draw a name on each one, but before he could smear the letters with glue and dust them with sparkles, he was called downstairs.

Taking the steps two at a time, he saw the easel alongside

the Christmas tree in the front window. Basilio's father and uncle had arrived while he was out, both were in aprons. Oil bubbled in a deep fryer and knives were sharpened against whetstones, the better to scale the fish and slice their bellies. Dough for empanada had been rolled out. It was time to work.

Little Basilio was assigned the tricky task of helping with the little stuff and staying out of the way. Up and down the steps they marched him for the right spoon, a certain bowl, and the colander. A thousand times, up and down, a thousand passes by the idle easel.

Walk, they said, don't run.

Amuse yourself.

Be a good boy.

The preparations took most of the morning and all of the afternoon. Christmas linen folded and waiting. A pyramid of fruit sat in the center of the table as the snapper baked in the oven. Basilio's father took off his apron, sent his son upstairs for a nap with a kiss on the head, and went home to clean up before returning with the rest of the family.

•

Like the screw of a great ship laboring against the current, Wigmann found himself on the parking lot of Connolly's—a green, ramshackle seafood house on Pratt Street—to sit and wait and do what he was told.

Wigmann brought a few presents in from the car, the pile now reduced to a single package on the back seat as he walked through a stiff wind into the fish house, sitting down at a wobbly wooden table. Tortoise shells and seaman's knots hung on pale green walls.

Wigmann set the gifts on the table and looked for a waitress. Aside from a few folks getting carry-out and a man shouldering a half-bushel of oysters to his car, the place was empty. A bus boy mopping the concrete floor began setting chairs on top of the tables.

"I'll start with a beer," Wigmann said to the waitress, unwrapping one of the presents when she left and finding a paperback of *The Diary of a Young Girl*.

The oddity of the gift—a kid's book about by a Jewish girl to celebrate Christmas—made Wigmann wonder what else Barbara had left that he'd given away. She inscribed it: "Anne just wasn't some kid who happened to keep a diary. She was a natural."

Flipping through the book as the waitress arrived with his beer, Wigmann found entries for late December and began reading.

"The Secret Annex has heard the joyful news that each person will receive an extra quarter of a pound of butter for Christmas. It says half a pound in the newspapers...but not for Jews who have gone into hiding."

"The oysters are good," said the waitress. "And the pan-fried rock."

Wigmann put the book aside to read the menu, his headache fading with each sip of beer.

"Something heavy," said Wigmann, "Liver and onions with mashed potatoes and gravy, a side order of baked beans, the coleslaw, and apple pie. And another beer."

The waitress left with the order and Wigmann turned to Anne's second Christmas in hiding as three red tugboats with white dots on their stacks pulled a freighter—"GALICIA" on her bow—into a slip one rotting pier away.

"I couldn't help feeling a great longing to laugh until my tummy ached," read Wigmann. "Especially at this time of the year with all the holidays...and we are stuck here like outcasts...when someone comes in from outside, with the wind in their clothes and the cold on their faces, then I could bury my head in the blankets to stop myself thinking: 'When will we be granted the privilege of smelling fresh air?'"

Outside, as the tugboats bumped and wedged the *Galicia* into her berth, the air was turning colder with the setting sun; a gray December cold that moved through the floor and into the soles of

Wigmann's shoes as his food arrived.

Wigmann ate fast, searched for comforting passages in the diary, ordered another beer, and stuffed himself until he was nearly sick, aware that a blessing over the meal on Macon Street would be said before the hawser lines were made fast between the *Galicia* and the cleats of pier 5.

How many sins could you commit in one day and still tell yourself that you were a good man?

Wigmann paid the bill, scribbled the waitress's name across another present he'd brought to the table, shoved the diary in his back pocket, and ambled out into the glorious fresh air of Pratt Street to watch the *Galicia* tie up and wait for Mr. Steve to come down the gangway.

On the way, the liver and potatoes sitting heavy in his gut, Wigmann passed a phone and dumped a pocketful of quarters into it.

"Thank you for the presents," he said, jingling the ring in his pocket.

"I'm glad you liked them."

"I'll leave right now," he said.

"No." said Barbara. "Don't."

Wigmann stood at the foot of the gangway making small talk with the man on watch while waiting for Mr. Steve. It was dark and the watchman looked up at the sky as he talked about a family he hadn't seen in half a year, at peace with a seaman's knowledge that he would see Christmas arrive from a folding chair on a foreign pier.

"Yep," said Wigmann, "I'm going to drop him off, drive straight to New York, and ask her to marry me."

"Good luck," said the watchman.

Wigmann took Anne's diary from his back pocket—the rising moon and a cross of white lights on the ship's stack glowing in the dark circles under the author's eyes—and handed it to the watchman as Mr. Steve appeared with a large duffel bag on his shoulder.

Wigmann drove Mr. Steve east on Lombard Street, past smoke hounds passing a jug around a fire in a barrel at the Fallsway; east toward the orange brick rowhouses of Highlandtown where Basilio was being told he must taste a bit of every dish on the table.

"How many children?" asked Steve.

"Where?"

"Tonight. How many children waiting?"

"At least three," said Wigmann. "But there could be a house full of them."

"Good," laughed Mr. Steve, his pockets jingling with silver coins. "Fill the house."

By the time Wigmann passed the Baker-Whiteley tugboats on Thames Street and made it around the harbor to the canning factories in Canton, the dishes from the first course had been cleared off and the three waiting children—Basilio, Donna, and Jose Pepper—had been excused from the table. They were joined at the record player upstairs by a neighborhood girl named Trudy.

Jose Pepper sat next to the portable stereo, more interested in how it worked than the music coming out of it; Basilio and Donna took turns putting on their favorite songs, the curtains parted in the front window, the tiny tree shining out onto the street as Wigmann pulled to the curb, deciding, that he at least had to help Mr. Steve in with his heavy bag and say hello to his mother.

Kneeling down outside of the basement window to glimpse the celebration on the other side of the glass, Wigmann watched the meal begin anew with each fresh face that came down the steps. He imagined his old man and Barbara at the table, himself between them, explaining the different foods to her as the plates passed by, his father approving.

Wigmann's seat was empty, his plate unsoiled, and his father's spot occupied by a heavy-set man from the Canary Islands peeling chestnuts with a penknife, his mother sitting close to her sisters and turning toward the steps every other moment to see if it was her son's footsteps coming down.

Wigmann belched—the invigorating cold not strong enough

to make him hungry again—stood up with Mr. Steve's bag under one arm and the last present from Barbara in the other, and went inside.

The house was warm with familiar smells, memories overwhelming a big baby who'd spent all day stuffing himself with distractions.

"Here," said Wigmann, handing the last package—obviously, a record—to Donna.

"The Beatles!" she cried, ripping the paper.

[Why them? Wigmann wondered. The Fab Four owned the world, Mr. Orlo was proof positive, but they hadn't played a part in his crumbling courtship any more than Anne's suffering.]

"Put it on!" said Basilio, hoping Santa would be as good to him before the night was out.

Donna spun the record—"Beatles '65"—and Wigmann took her by the hand for a quick dance, gliding the girl around the room on the top of his shoes. Trudy jumped up and down with Jose Pepper and Basilio watched, not understanding that the hotness in his chest was jealousy.

Downstairs, Mr. Steve took a ring of dried figs from a pocket of his suit and spread them out. A three-year-old circled the table, chased by a five-year-old. Glasses were refilled, dishes washed and dried and used again.

Catching the Mersey beat as it pulsed through the floorboards, Mr. Steve lit a long cigar and called for the children and his bag. The kids raced down the steps—strange guests to the house were always giving children something—and Wigmann followed with the seaman's bag.

"There you are!" cried Wigmann's mother. "Sit down. Eat."

Wigmann grabbed a beer out of the refrigerator, kissed his mother on the cheek, and stood near the children and Mr. Steve. After giving the youngest kids at the table silver coins from his pocket, the Spanish seaman dug deep in his bag and brought out a box of cigars, a bottle of Fundador cognac, a handful of unwrapped baubles, and then, one after another to squeals of delight, dolls of four young men with mop-top haircuts.

Made in Japan, no store or kid in America had the treasure being handed out on Macon Street.

"One for you," said Mr. Steve, handing the Paul doll to Donna. "And you," he said, giving Ringo to Jose Pepper, "and for you," as Trudy embraced George.

"And," he said extending John Lennon to Basilio, "for you."

"Dolls for a boy," scoffed Grandpop.

"They're kids," said Francesca.

"You should eat a little something and take the children over to see the trains," said Wigmann's mother.

Taking the doll from his son, Basilio's father ran his hands over John's head and disparaged it in Spanish. Wigmann caught the hurt on Basilio's face as the kid grabbed the doll back.

Lifelike down to McCartney's dimple, there was something odd about the dolls. Instead of arms holding guitars, the toys had wings—thin, holographic webbing of translucent plastic shaped like maple seedlings.

"They fly," said Mr. Steve, showing the kids how they worked.

"They fly!" cried Jose Pepper, jumping up and down.

"Like angels," said Mr. Steve.

Inside the boxes were launching pistols with zip cords. The feet fit into the pistols and when you pulled the cord, the doll twirled into the air. The harder you pulled, the higher they flew.

"A flying Beatle," marveled a guest as Ringo helicoptered from one end of the table to the other.

In a moment, nearly all of the adults were taking turns zipping the dolls around the basement.

Watching the dolls fly, Leini imagined the intimacy she would enjoy when the other women walked to Midnight Mass with their children and grandchildren. She picked at a fried tentacle of squid while savoring the prospect of sharing her secret delicacy in a few hours with Orlo.

But couldn't keep images of her husband, a suicide, dead almost a full year now, from jarring her thoughts, and worse, what would she and the junkman do if the Salvage House was razed for the expressway. No guilt, not a whit of regret as she reached out and caught George sailing by.

While others clamored to be the next to play—the kids jumping up and down for a turn, pulling at the hem of her black dress —Leini stared into the sweet face of the quiet one and felt an odd, wistful peace.

"Do you want to know a secret?" she hummed. "Do you promise not to tell?"

Leini gave the doll back to Trudy and asked Mr. Steve where she could get a set.

"Hell," said Basilio's other grandmother, a Lithuanian cannery worker. "By Easter they'll have shelves of 'em up Epstein's."

Mr. Steve leaned toward Leini with the self-assured smile that the Greek—still a beauty at 55—only saw in the faces of certain Europeans. He offered her a peeled chestnut.

"Not only did somebody figure out how to make them fly, but made sure they flew beautifully," said Trudy's father, a mechanic at Crown, Cork & Seal. "That's about as close to intangible as you can get."

Beautifully they flew until the Jewel Tea sugar bowl fell to the floor, a glass of wine tipped over, a baby who wanted a turn started to cry, and Grandpop slapped his palm against the table.

"What are we?" he demanded. "Americans?"

"Okay kids," said Basilio's mother, getting up to make coffee. "Take them upstairs."

Wigmann grabbed another beer from the refrigerator, told his mother he wasn't hungry, and followed the children up the steps. As the kids ran outside with the dolls, Wigmann picked up the receiver on the black wall phone in the kitchen to try Barbara again.

When no one answered, he trooped out into the cold with his beer to join the children.

Trudy and Donna and Jose Pepper were tentative pulling their strings; Paul, George, and Ringo barely rising higher than the wire fence before falling near their feet.

They turned to Basilio: "Your turn."

And for some reason—a vague feeling akin to the one he felt watching Donna dance with Wigmann, something close to the burn he felt when his father called the Beatles sissies—Basilio yanked the cord with all his might and John shot through the night sky as if fired from a gun.

Their heads tilted back, the children watched as the doll cleared the trees, and then the rooftops, soared beyond the chimneys and into the clouds and then—as though the stars reached down to receive him—John Lennon was assumed into the heavens over Highlandtown.

"Wow!" said Donna.

"Geezy," said Jose Pepper.

Wigmann whistled and Basilio began to cry.

"It's lost!"

"It's okay," said Wigmann, grateful for the most beautiful thing he'd seen all day. "We'll find it."

"I'm cold," said Trudy, picking up her doll and going inside.

"Me too," said Jose Pepper.

"Basilio," said Donna, rushing in the house and running back out. "Take your coat."

Basilio wiped his nose, put on his coat, and followed Wigmann into the alley.

"Don't worry," said Wigmann. "I knew a girl once just as talented as you, but her family was in such a bad way at Christmas that Santa brought just enough butter to make a few biscuits."

"I don't want biscuits," said Basilio.

["We *are* Americans," thought Wigmann.]

"I know," said Wigmann, scouring the backyards and trees for the doll. "I'm just telling you how it is sometimes."

At the end of the alley, Wigmann got an idea. He sat Basilio down on a set of cold marble steps across the street from the beer garden, told the boy to stay put, and slipped into the saloon. Inside, he ran to the top floor, opened a small hatch in the ceiling, and squeezed his way onto the roof.

Inconsolable, his teeth chattering in the cold, Basilio watched Wigmann's silhouette zig-zag across the rooftops as he checked inside the rain gutters and bumped up against chimneys. After searching from one end of the block to the other, Wigmann appeared before the shivering boy and said he was sorry.

Taking Basilio by the hand, Wigmann walked into the bar, hit the lights, poured the kid a Coca-Cola, and punched up "She Loves You" on the jukebox before tossing the soggy ginger snaps in the trash.

Pulling down an eight-foot-by-eight-foot wooden garden from the wall—five trains circling three platforms through secret passageways; farm houses; a town square with a water fountain and miniature Ferris Wheel—Wigmann turned the bar into a carnival.

"Maybe the Beatles are just for girls," said Basilio.

"The grown-ups are wrong on this one," said Wigmann. "Just like some people will tell you that nobody eats sauerkraut on Thanksgiving, but I do."

"You're a grown-up," said Basilio.

"Only because I'm older than you."

Leaving the boy alone with the trains, Wigmann walked behind the bar and into his bedroom. A moment later, he approached Basilio with open palms; a lock of brown hair in one hand and a swatch of bed sheet in the other.

"Merry Christmas!"

"What is it?"

"Stuff that's going to be worth a million dollars because of kids like you."

"Hair?"

"John's."

Basilio's heart jumped.

"No."

"Yes."

"Where'd you get it?"

"When they were here." said Wigmann. "I know somebody."

Wondering how you could know anyone that important, Basilio pointed to Wigmann's other hand.

"A piece of the sheets they slept on at the Holiday Inn, the one with the revolving restaurant on top, right there on Lombard Street. Suite 1013," said Wigmann. "Open your hands."

Wigmann set the hair and the linen in Basilio's palms and gently closed the boy's fingers around them. Over on Oldham Street, the bells of Holy Redeemer Chapel began ringing for Midnight Mass.

"Yours."

"All mine?"

"To keep."

"Can I tell?"

"They won't believe you."

Walking Basilio out to the alley, Wigmann handed the boy over to a parade of women and children making their way to church.

"Just showing him the trains," he said as Basilio skipped into line with Donna and Jose Pepper, hands tight in his pockets around the frankincense and myrrh.

"Say a few prayers for me, Ma," said Wigmann, giving his mother a hug before going inside to drink a beer and watch the trains run, twinkling lights glinting off a cracked emerald ring and a pair of scissors laying open on his bed.

CONKLING STREET CHRISTMAS

The last Christmas gift Basilio received from his mother was a Transfiguration High School jacket from Louis J. Smith Sporting Goods, 510 South Conkling Street at the twinkling crossroads of the Holy Land.

Corduroy: jet black with snow white stitching.

Two months pregnant with less than five months to live, Audrey Boullosa drove into the city from a cul-de-sac carved out of 19th century strawberry fields, her mission too important to trust to the suburbs.

Fretfully: What name to be sewn above her son's heart?

His given one—a thick cape of Iberia chosen by his father?

[The infant had been named for his grandfather, no discussion, no debate.]

Or the one his friends had called him—"Ringo"—the honor bestowed in the first grade when he was admonished by Sister Pamphelia (the nun who kept a parrot in the classroom) for drumming on his desk with No. 2 pencils.

Basilio was many Beatles' albums down the road from that now—"No one will be watching us," soon to be part of his catechism; a 14-year-old freshman at an Xaverian high school on the west side of town, ten miles from the corner of Conkling and Eastern and the one-eyed Santa in the tiny North Pole house of candy canes.

It was 1973 and, for a few more years—the briefest of calendars, ghosts walking the Avenue with a shopping bag in each hand—Highlandtown was still Highlandtown.

The greatest place in the world to feel—a sensation of the

blood confirming faith you weren't even sure you possessed—that Christmas was in you.

David Bowie had just released *Aladdin Sane* and Basilio had a date for the Christmas dance with a freckled bookworm from IND. He wore bangle bracelets when he knew his father wasn't around and did his best to avoid the barber.

At Transfiguration, instead of paying attention as Brother Declan told jokes the boys would not have thought funny even if they'd understood them, Basilio endlessly copied album covers—in exacting detail that would have put him on the honor roll—on pages of loose leaf.

These were his first commissions: Nils Lofgren and the Fat Man, twins glimmering under miles of moonlight, the Pontiff of Dirty Love of whom a statue would one day stand where the blind man sold pencils, and a guy from Jersey almost nobody had heard of; illustrations traded in the cafeteria for plates of French fries with gravy.

A year later—his mother in the breeze, father working as much overtime on the waterfront as he could get—Basilio would be good enough to trade his work for other things.

And no—no thank you, Brother Peter; I'm fine Father Fajardo, it's my allergies acting up—he did not want to illustrate the year book or draw cartoons for the school paper.

None of which had come to pass as his mother sat at the counter of the Little Tavern alongside the Grand Theater, eating sliders by the bag in the hunger of her first trimester, believing that the one thing to make her first-born happiest was a jacket that hadn't been popular since the Joe College boys were foolish enough to rumble with the Drapes in the alley behind G&A Coney Island Hot Dogs.

•

Audrey Paplauskas, a girl from Poppleton Street, was wearing a Transfiguration High letter jacket the night she met Basilio's father on a hayride in the distant farmlands of Harford County.

She came with a girlfriend and Henry had a jug of his father's homemade wine that stained her white blouse in the shape of a birthmark when the vino came her way. Henry's cousin Benny brought his accordion—you haven't heard the "The Tennessee Waltz" until you've heard it played on an Italian squeeze box—and the name over the left breast of Audrey's jacket said JOE in block letters.

Joe was Audrey's guy, a boy from her neighborhood on a baseball scholarship to Transfiguration. He was big and strong and he was a star—a lefty with more mustard on his fastball than Jimmy Farantos put on his G&A wieners. Scouts were coming around. The kid was going places.

But foolishly—even though Audrey had begged him—Joe did not go on the harvest hayride that first Saturday in October of 1950.

The Bombers were in the World Series against Philadelphia—the last all-white championship in the history of the game—and both teams had sent scouts to Baltimore that year to file reports on the Hollins Street Heater.

Believing (because he had reason to) that he might take the field in the majors the following spring and believing (because he had reason to) that Audrey would say "I do" on the day he signed, Joe spent the afternoon by the radio in his mother's kitchen, dipping cookies into milk as New York beat the Phillies 5-to-2 in the Bronx for the crown.

When Audrey stopped by just before heading east—"are you sure you don't want to go?"—Joe kissed his best girl and told her to have a good time.

Many hours later, after the long streetcar ride home without a lot to say to her girlfriend, Audrey put the jacket she'd worn every day for two years in a hall closet and that's where it stayed—from the Korean War beyond the sale of her parents' home after the King Riots—fraying into dust.

•

"Will it be ready by Christmas Eve?" asked Audrey, a bit of hamburger onion on her chin that the woman behind the counter gently wiped with a tissue.

"Oh, yes indeedy," said Miss Madeleine, whose father—Louis J. Smith—founded the store in 1927. "Spell the name again."

"B-A-S-I-L-I-O."

"That's what I thought."

"Do you need a deposit?"

"Haven't had a Transfiguration customer run out on a bill yet," laughed Madeleine. "Now Patterson, that's a different story."

Touching the cuff of Audrey's dark green coat, she said, "I'm just kidding, hon. It'll be ready in plenty of time for Sanny Claus."

Time enough to cross the street for caramel popcorn at Kramer's (a bag to eat now, one to hide for later), buy a chemistry set for Basilio's little brother at Epstein's (a curious child, Jose Pepper would blow up his goldfish on Christmas morning and, in a few short years, be expelled from Transfiguration for stealing balance beam scales from the science lab); enough time and loose change from the popcorn for the 50-cent ride through the Harbor Tunnel to make breaded pork chops and mashed potatoes for Henry and the boys.

•

As best as Basilio could remember (so much time had passed that he had decided to remember it this way) he'd only worn the jacket twice.

Out of respect for his mother: to Midnight Mass at Our Lady of Pompei after dinner on Christmas Eve, the IND girl on the other side of the church with her parents and a copy of *The Princess Bride*.

Out of respect for his mother: to her funeral at St. Peter the Apostle, around the corner from where he grew up and not far from his *alma mater.*

Long after that mild spring day, when Basilio met a profoundly bereaved warehouse laborer named Joe for the first and only time, the artist moved into the East Baltimore rowhouse where Christmas Eve endured in pots and pans, a 1948 Westinghouse refrigerator, and pale green Depression glass his grandmother used to serve deviled eggs.

Seeking succor and solace, he'd washed-up there after his divorce only to argue with his father's father about the cost of electricity, the rights of minorities, and, above all, how much longer he expected to live there.

Basilio never had a good answer and it wasn't long before Grandpop joined his wife and the other ghosts on the Avenue. When the house became Basilio's, he began putting a live tree in the front window even though the one from childhood was small and artificial, perched on an end table, the bottom of the stand swaddled in red felt.

Atop the tree, an angelus from Lithuania to honor the Hollins Market heritage of Audrey Paplauskas.

Next to it, hung in the window so the name could be easily read by people out on the sidewalk, a jacket that hadn't fit him for decades.

Jet black corduroy, snow white stitching.

TOO ROLLING TOOKIE

[January 15, 1976]

Five carving knives and a brown paper bag of plastic straws. Two ice picks, a wooden handled corkscrew, one large barbecue fork, and a 1950s Hamilton Beach Milk Shake mixer, a wedding gift to my parents.

I'm limping from tile-to-tile, yeah, man, me and Jimmy Page, we're "out on the tiles..."

No double-neck Gibson and a violin bow, just me and this broken leg, a clipboard and a retractable pen that says Tukulski Pet Food Supply. They're running stock cars on the dirt track in the woods across the road.

"Saturday! Saturday! Saturday! See the Fabulous Funny Cars at Diabolical Dorsey Drag Raceway!"

Even in the snow they gun those wrecks. And it's snowing pretty good now, good enough to cancel school. I'd give anything to be done with this stupid inventory and get out of the house.

Uncle Falooch pays me $20 a week to catalog every last spoon and No. 2 pencil in the house. They just passed the minimum wage, $2.30 an hour, so a twenty ain't bad, depending on how fast I go. Falooch has got plenty money, but he spends half of it on old radios and stuffs the rest under the mattress.

He lives here for free, he's Mom's mother's brother, so he makes up stupid chores for me to do and slips me a couple bucks so he don't feel like a freeloader. Mom says I waste the money on "worthless crap." She should know.

A pair of mounted butterflies; a large, porcelain wine decanter shaped like a poodle (poodle bites, baby, poodle chews it); more than a hundred "bingo daubers," in all colors of watery ink to mark bingo cards; a pair of burned pizza pans; and, above the stove, a saloon clock that reminds us at every meal that we are fortunate to be residing in "The Land of Pleasant Living."

Mom went bat shit when I told her what I was doing and ordered me not to "come near any of me and your father's personal stuff. Why the hell does he have to know what we got in the house. Ain't it enough he's in the goddamn house?"

In the foyer: a pair of antique barber chairs; a ceramic knick-knack of a rooster chasing a white girl paired with one of a black boy chasing a hen; a broken Montgomery Ward organ, more of a toy than an instrument, just another flat surface for my mother's knick-knack-paddy-whacked nightmare of frogs and lily pads and toadstools.

The closet: two tennis rackets, one wooden, one aluminum; nineteen assorted coats, including one with a moth-eaten fox head; and a canister vacuum cleaner: EUREKA!

I wish Basilio would come by and get me. That asshole never calls. He either shows up or he doesn't.

Above the kitchen sink, a gem Falooch has coveted since he got too old to live by himself, an Emerson my mother got when she made her Confirmation at St. Augustine's over in Elkridge. They call it a portable but it weighs a ton, like a car battery with a couple of knobs and a dial in see-through, salmon-colored Bakelite.

"Knock, knock..."

"Who's there?"

"Emerson."

"Emerson who?"

"Emerson big titties you got there, sister!"

HAH!

I got it tuned to WAYE-AM—Wishbone Ash as loud as it'll go. My parents are out trying to make all of the day's deliveries before the roads get too bad and Falooch is half deaf.

Man, it's really coming down. I can hardly see past the statue of the Blessed...

Well, whaddaya know! Here comes the Rock Star, banging up the drive in his mother's space station Pacer—Montrose, Space Station No. 5!—wearing state trooper mirror shades in a fucking blizzard!

Yee-haw!

I keep trying to talk him into running the Pacer over at the dirt track across the street.

"Right, Tookie," he says, dark brown Beatle hair down past the collar of his Quadrophenia army jacket. "Get in the fucking car."

What a car! "Mellow Yellow" paint job, brown vinyl bucket seats, fake wood paneling on the dash—Adjust-O-Tilt steering column!—and black vinyl roof. Factory-installed 8-track built into the console and a born-again bumper sticker on the ass.

"God Gave Rock & Roll to You."

My folks are gonna kill me when they find out I split, like they almost broke my other leg after I fell off the roof when I was up there drinking beer instead of cleaning out the gutters.

I'm supposed to defrost some chicken and start up the Crock Pot. Okay, done and done. What'd they expect me to do? Stay home?

Fucking Ringo!

Me and him are seniors at Transfiguration High, best friends. Rock and roll has never let us down and I ain't gonna let him down. If he's crazy enough to come get me in a blizzard, I'm smart enough to go.

Stove off, lights off, a quick shout up to Falooch—he's either dead or sleeping—door locked and I'm gone.

First thing when I open the Pacer door, a thick cloud of pot smoke billows out into the bite of January winter.

JOHNNY WINTER!

Basilio doesn't help me with the door, doesn't help me with my crutches, he just sits there swiveling his head as Captain Beefheart howls along with Zappa's guitar, Frank bending strings the way Einstein bent light.

[Beefheart's 35 today. Last week, Zappa told Dick Cavett (Basilio called the house late, "Turn on the TV! Turn on the TV!), Frank told Dick: "The disgusting stink of a too loud electric guitar. Now that's my idea of a good time."]

Basilio's got a paper cup of Dunkin Donuts coffee on the dash and a half-smoked joint in the ashtray. The new *Rolling Stone* is face-up on the passenger seat, Bob Dylan and Joan Baez on the cover all bundled up like they're on a fucking ski trip.

"What a pile of shit," I said, fishing the joint out of the ashtray as Basilio turns around in the driveway. "Keith Moon could eat Joan Baez for breakfast."

"Yeah, but Bob might give him a run for his money," said Basilio.

"Fuck Dylan," I say and he puts his nose close to the windshield to see the way down to the street, snow coming down harder than ever, Ringo heading for the place he was always headed: The City of Baltimore.

Rock and Roll.

[August 16, 1977]

Dear Tookie—

Hey, Crazy Motherfucker. Greetings from the poop deck!

The sun is going down over the Gulf and I'm hiding between containers topside, getting stoned with a couple beers I hid in the galley ice box.

The sunsets are stunning, breathtaking even before you catch the heavy-heavy, so you can imagine how sweet they are with a nice buzz. I started sketching the stern of the ship. I think I'm facing Haiti.

We're headed for New Orleans again, New Orleans every twelve days, coming in empty and going out with everything from frozen chickens to Kodak film. I'm too fried to draw so I thought

I'd drop a line. Been too long.

I think my work is getting better. I've been drawing the men who work in the steward department, their big faces poking into pots of boiling water. Most of them are Puerto Rican on this run, back and forth between San Juan and New Orleans, sometimes Beaumont, Texas.

When the rest of the crew headed for the whorehouse I looked up Johnny's parents in the white pages and there was his old man: John Dawson Winter, Jr. I grabbed a cab on the dock and rode by the house, but I didn't knock.

The chief cook sweats right on through the paper of his cigarette and every ten seconds wipes his face with a filthy rag and says, "It's a hot tamale today!"

He looks like Ernest Borgnine, only not as handsome!

I guess you know that Elvis died today. I was sitting in the galley waiting for chow and we were getting fuzzy reception out of Miami and there was Dave Marsh—I READ IT IN *ROLLING STONE*, IT MUST TRUE!—preaching on TV with news anchors like it was Dallas or something.

A black mess man looked up at the TV—it hangs on chains screwed into the ceiling—and laughed, hard and ugly.

He really put effort into it—HA! HA! HA!

I wanted to knock his teeth out. I used to catch a buzz with him in his focsle and listen to Parliament-Funkadelic and Sly. Didn't even know I gave a shit. I always thought the Beatles gave birth to themselves.

I was already cranky cuz I was coming down from tripping, couple hits of windowpane last night, didn't get a wink. You know how when the flashes are over and that Morse code runs up and down your spine for hours? Reefer buzz I got going now is taking some of the edge off and I'm hoping to sleep before the 4-to-8 rolls around again.

I dropped about an hour before sunset, washed it down with a beer, tied my ankles to the legs of the steel desk that's bolted to the deck in my room and hung myself upside down out the porthole.

They're big and rectangular now, not the round kind like on the *Titanic*. Secured my ass with a Baltimore knot. Know what a Baltimore knot is, Took? The bosun named it after me. It's a knot that's never tied the same way twice!

Tripping my nuts off, hanging out the porthole, my head just a foot above the waterline as the ship pushed through the ocean, spray soaking my head as I stared up at the stack and the stars, everything twirling like flying lamp shades. Black night, a million diamonds and I'm seeing the moon wash purple and pink and popsicle green.

When the guy from the 12-to-4 came to get me to relieve him, he had to haul me back in. The Baltimore knots held fast, though. Wouldn't be writing to you now if they didn't.

You know how I found out Elvis was important, Took? I mean really important? Scratch that mop, wrack that boiled noodle between your ears.

Howie Wyeth.

Remember the blizzard in our senior year when we went down the waterfront to see Mr. Orlo and bought that old Meerschaum? I almost pissed myself laughing when you called your parents after we got stuck down on Clinton Street. "Hi Pop, me and Basilio went to the library..."

Hey Took—YOU FORGOT ALL ABOUT THE LIBRARY LIKE YOU TOLD YOUR OLD MAN NOW!

We were making fun of *Rolling Stone* for putting Dylan and Joan Baez on the cover. That magazine got mixed in with all the shit I threw in my bag when I shipped out the day after we graduated. Finally got around to reading it.

Howie played piano on that Rolling Thunder tour—you taking $20 out of the register at the pet food store so we could see Foghat at the Civic Center while Dylan's putting on Ziggy makeup and rocking out with Mick Ronson and Roger McGuinn and a gorgeous fiddle player named Scarlet.

Holy Jumboly, she's hot! Like this crazy third mate on my

watch likes to say: "I'd marry her brother just to get in the family!"

Here's the line that stayed with me from that article. Somebody was talking about Elvis and then somebody pointed across the dressing room to Howie and said he played a piano that was "ancient, holy and American."

Man, I even like the way those words look on paper: ancient—holy—American.

I wanted to find him right away—in New Orleans you can find anything; maybe ask him about his grandfather, see if I could pick up a couple of tricks, but the closest I've gotten so far is a new album by a guy out of D.C. named Robert Gordon and Link "Rumble" Wray!

Rockabilly, Tookie: Elvis, holy American piano, amphetamines and the Killer!

I bought it on vinyl and one of the engineers (one of the guys who took the Elvis news hard, told the mess man to shut his goddamn mouth) has a turntable in his room and copied it onto a cassette for me before we shoved off.

Then I was looking through some other magazine, some newsprint rag they were giving away in a record store on Decatur, and some New York guitar player named Robert Ross said Howie used to play drums for him.

"If you ain't at your best," said Ross, "Howie's gonna bury you in a barrage of brilliance on a yard sale kit made out of trash can lids and spaghetti pots...very rare."

When I find him, Took, I'm going to ask him for both of us: What the fuck was Mick Ronson doing on tour with Bob Dylan?

Musicians are different from me and you. I'm not sure how, but they are.

You think Robin Trower wrote "Rock Me Baby"? Start reading the publishing credits and you'll find out who the real cats are. Everybody wrote that song, even some goof named Johnny Cymbal.

JOHNNY CYMBAL!

I'm learning so much stuff out here, Took, but not about being a seaman, I mostly fake my way through that. My old man was the real thing. He left Macon Street when he was 16 for his first run to Venezuela on a Beth Steel ore ship. I'm just playing.

But I like it and I don't think I'm coming back to go to college like my folks wanted me to do after we got out of Transfiguration.

Remember the day we got our diplomas? Me and you and Flannery racing up Charles Street in Mom's Pacer, passing a fat one and listening to Zappa doo-wop and then Trower kicking the shit out of "Too Rolling Stoned"?

Takers get the honey, Tookie Took. Givers sing the blues.

I told my father I needed a year to figure it out. Not sure how much I need now, but I know I need more. I got a cheap room near the SIU hall in New Orleans and between ships I stay in and paint. I don't even get high that much (not too much) when we're in port. Me and a hot plate, my brushes in vegetable cans.

I miss Trudy, but not enough to come home yet. She took a bus to visit once and I'm trying to get her to come again. Don't want to lose her. I'm gonna finish this beer and try to get some sleep. We hit New Orleans in a couple days and I'll drop this in the box.

Write to the return address: B.B.; Ordinary Seaman, c/o the S.S. Esmeralda, Navieras de Puerto Rico, 2700 Broening Highway, Baltimore, 21222.

Hey, Took, is it really running away from home if you're already gone but you just don't come back?

I remain, too fucking wild.

The extraordinary ordinary...

[January 7, 2006]

I buried Falooch today, just me and two or three people who knew him and weren't dead themselves yet. Fuck it was cold, the ground frozen and my bad leg acting up.

I kept turning around, thinking I'd see Basilio walking

through the tombstones with that "I'm smarter than you" smile on his face. Don't know why. Haven't seen him since the day we graduated. But that's what I was thinking, my mind wandering while the priest laid the mumbo jumbo on ole Falooch.

Last I heard, Basilio and Trudy got divorced and he was living in the house where his father grew up, painting pictures of crabs and rockfish on the sides of seafood trucks. I think he's got a grown daughter, that's what his father told my mom at the supermarket a while back.

When Mom passed, it was just me and Dad and Falooch and then it was just me and Falooch.

I bet that old goat has three hundred radios stuffed in here. I'll find out soon enough. I'm gonna inventory every stationary bike and Kewpie doll from attic to basement; even the nail the Sacred Heart is hanging on. And then I'm gonna sell all of it on eBay, air the whole joint out and sell it to the first asshole who shows up with cash.

What did Mom always say? The whole kit and caboodle.

I got the old A&P clipboard here on my lap, rolling a fat one—Basilio used to call them "Fidel Burgers"—4:30 in the afternoon and it's dark already, all by myself in this house, really alone, for the first time in my life.

This shit costs $100 for an eighth. You get about five skinny joints out of it. Me and Basilio used to buy a pound of tumbleweed Mexican for $140 in high school, sell three-quarters and keep the rest for our trouble.

Sometimes the only buzz you got was a vicious headache. A couple of tokes of this hydra-ponic shit—man, it's got colors I haven't seen since I played with crayons; half-a-doob of this and you're done for the day. I'll be cooked soon enough, laying on the twin bed Falooch slept in with the six-shooters carved into the headboard and ten million radios.

Falooch collected radios like other people bring home lost dogs. He'd find them in alleys and garbage cans, bring 'em home and patch 'em up. These shelves are just cinderblock and cut up plywood; rechargeable batteries and surge protectors and exten-sion cords all over the place.

Every night he'd tune all of them to a show on the same AM station: "George Noory's Coast-to-Coast," nothing but flying saucers, shadow people, and what Bowie asked back in '71: "Is there life on Mars?"

Before I started getting high and running out as soon as din-ner was over, I'd come in and listen with him. Falooch said he liked the show because it proved that man doesn't know any-thing.

[Man, this is good dope. Fifty times stronger than it used to be and I don't enjoy it half as much.]

Falooch always had his eye on my mother's Bakelite Emerson and when she died, the first thing he did was sneak it in here with all the others like I wouldn't know. I'd rescue it and he'd steal it back and I'd come and get it again until I got tired of playing and let him keep it. He's got it in a place of honor near the window, next to a 9-volt plastic Ferris Wheel from that dumb carnival show on HBO. We don't even have cable. Must have sent away for it.

Once, when it was just me and Falooch living here, fighting over who had to do the dishes, I saw a write-up in the *Sunpapers* saying Basilio's old friend Mr. Orlo had died and the new owner was going to sell all the junk for next-to-nothing.

I told Falooch about the radios Orlo had and talked him into getting out for a change. We got lost and came home, Falooch giving me a bunch of shit about why you shouldn't go any farther from home than your feel will take you.

People think it's a long way between the 'burb and the city because it looks so different, but if it ain't rush hour and you take the tunnel, you can be at Basilio's grandfather's house in fifteen minutes.

Twelve miles away and I never saw him again.

That snowy day when we drove to the junk house is one of my favorite memories of all time. Everything closed but hospitals and police stations but we went out anyway, riding around, getting high, driving up this lane of oyster shells covered with snow to a castle with SALVAGE HOUSE painted on the side in letters ten feet tall.

Basilio said Orlo used to give him a couple bucks and a six-pack to touch up the letters in the summer.

We looked through all of the junk, one room was nothing but door knobs and another was like a hippie museum. I found an original copy of *Look at Yourself* by Uriah Heep, the one that came with reflective foil on the front so you could, you know, look at yourself. Still got it, mint condition.

Basilio asked about some busted frames in a corner and Mr. Orlo made us hot chocolate. We walked out to the end of the pier with our mugs—the real deal, milk and Hershey's syrup, none of that Swiss Piss crap—and finished off the roach, watching the tugboats go back and forth past Fort McHenry in the snow.

Basilio kept saying that if he could just get that scene to yield. I always remembered that word he used, yield. If he could paint the tugboats riding past Fort McHenry in the snow the way he wanted, then he'd be a real artist.

I don't know what the fuck he was talking about. He could draw anything. Once this lady down the street from his parents' house gave him $100 and who knows what else to paint Dion DiMucci on one of her kitchen cabinets.

I was listening to "Coast to Coast" once and someone called in and told Noory that Dion was jogging down the street one day and saw God. Noory plays a lot of good music on his show when he's not talking to people who've had their appendix taken out by aliens.

Sometimes Basilio drew faces at the bottom of the letters he sent me from sea, the guys he worked with, his own mug, George and Ringo. I loved getting those letters, the stories he told. You know how people talk about something cool that they've seen but you haven't, like Niagara Falls or one of those skull mountains in Cambodia?

I never saw what Basilio saw. After high school, I started taking care of things around here. Never saw much outside of Dorsey, but I did see an eclipse once in the backyard.

Then the letters stopped. A couple of times I thought of calling, thought he'd come to my dad's funeral and then I thought he'd come to my mom's and today I thought I'd see him walking through the graveyard to ask if I wanted to get high.

Wish I knew what happened to his mother's car. I think Mr. Boullosa paid three grand for it at the AMC dealer in Glen Burnie in '75. It'd go for almost $6,000 today in good shape.

Me and Basilio thought 1976 was so un-cool. We said we were having fun—we did have fun, a lot of fun—but bitched a lot about how we'd missed the real stuff; daydreaming about things that happened when we were 9 and 10, the Greatest Rock and Roll Band in the World touring with Ike and Tina.

"Not bad," said Mick, peeping behind the stage curtain, "for a chick."

By 1976, Evelyn "Champagne" King had taken all the chicks away, the old Lion King Elton was on the throne and things just seemed to get worse every year, especially when Keith Moon died in '78.

There was the Ramones. God bless those glue-sniffing knuckleheads. They saved rock and roll for a couple of days but nobody was listening when they were alive. Joey dead, Johnny dead, Dee-Dee dead.

A couple years ago, they came out with Volume 5 of Dylan's Bootleg Series: *Live '75, the Rolling Thunder Revue.* I'm not sure I can hear Howie's "holy ancient American piano," but I like it, especially "The Lonesome Death of Hattie Carroll" cuz it's a Baltimore song.

They release everything today, all the stuff that used to be mysterious and legendary. It's all out there now; the vaults are empty and nothing's secret in the Information Age. Not even Brian's smile.

Humble Pie had this song we all listened to: "Thirty days in the hole..."

More like thirty years if you ask me. Whew, I'm buzzed. You can trip on this shit. Better stand up and put some music on, open the window on this witch's tit.

I'll tune 'em all to 105.7 FM, WKTK, Good Time Oldies: all Beatles, all Stones, a lot of Who, "Lola" by the Kinks at least once a day, Cream and Skynyrd, and, if you're really lucky, every now and then, some Nazareth, Mott the Hoople, and "Rebel, Rebel" by Bowie.

"Helter Skelter" as loud as it will go. I'm gonna dial 'em all up to the same station the way Falooch used to.

Me and Basilio thought we were cooler than everybody else because we could name all of Zappa's albums in order, from *Freak Out* right on through *Roxy & Elsewhere*.

We'd translate "knirps for moisture" to fuck with our Spanish teacher and thought Bob Dylan was square for playing cowboy music, not hip enough to know it was hillbilly music.

Who could figure out how Mick Ronson teleported from Bowie's Spiders to helping Dylan put on make-up for the Rolling Thunder Revue?

How do you get all those guitars out of your head so you can think straight?

Mick Ronson and Steve Marriott dead...

Howie Wyeth dead.

Elvis dead.

Zappa pink slipped with prostate cancer, just like my old man. How weird is that?

Beatle John and Beatle George.

First my parents and now Falooch, dead as a hammer in this bed just a couple days ago, all of his radios giving the morning's traffic report going at once.

The day we got our diplomas, the centennial class of the Transfiguration High School of Baltimore, was the last time I ever saw Basilio Boullosa.

For all I know, that crazy motherfucker's dead, too.

Good God, how we loved to ride around all day and all night, getting high and listening to Johnny Winter wail.

"*Every now and then I know it's kind of hard to tell...but I'm still alive and well.*"

WEDDING DAY

Sick to his stomach on the cool marble altar, Basilio Boullosa was dressed like a million bucks and dreaming of green bananas.

Bananas that rot before they ripen.

Green with envy.

Green with promise.

Green, straight to black.

From his spot on the altar of the Basilica of the Assumption of the Blessed Virgin Mary in Baltimore, the young painter could see everything.

The happy couple, the priest before them, and three hundred of their guests.

He saw his parents, his baby daughter, and a tear—for him—in his mother's eye.

Opposite Basilio, at the head of a row of bridesmaids, sweet icing on a bitter cake: Roxanne.

They'd been introduced just before the curtain went up on this cold, bright afternoon in late December, their conversation limited to which way to turn and when to do so; instructions for a parade route.

[The night before, since Roxanne hadn't yet arrived from out-of-town, Basilio had rehearsed with the bride's widowed mother.]

All he had pledged was to bear witness to love's great pageant, yet the young man who made his money painting signs was more spooked today than when it had been his turn, not so long ago.

You don't get a view like this when you are in the barrel, he thought, when it would be bad form to turn around to see what's behind you.

Joseph loves Mary.

And Mary loves Joe.

They do.

They do.

They do.

Basilio's best friend was marrying the girl of his dreams before God and family in the first Roman Catholic Cathedral in the United States.

And Basilio, who had not picked up a sincere brush in more than a year, who'd moved in with his parents after his marriage had died like an infant in its crib and had tried and tried and tried again to paint his daughter and attempted a portrait of Joe and Mary for their big day only to duck flying shards and crusty glue from his shattered sugar bowl; the same shit that rained down when he tried to capture Trudy the way he remembered her back when she wanted him: riding a bicycle through her parents' neighborhood; Basilio who every week sent Trudy a small support check by drawing crabs and fish on the sides of refrigerated trucks—this young man had agreed to testify to the power of love.

High Mass incense wafted over the 90-proof shot of courage in his stomach as Basilio managed to smile for the good things before his eyes; wondering why people say things they can only hope to be true.

Paint or die, the good news and hard truth.

The altar glowed in the warmth of three hundred faces bathing Joe and Mary in beams of joy, but it was a dim bulb next to the flood lights of devotion the betrothed poured into each other.

Basilio's wedding ring tumbled through nervous fingers in his tuxedo pocket and while he wasn't sure at age 26 that if your search is true you will happen upon another heart of contradictions that feels as you do, he still wanted it.

He'd rid himself of the ring today.

Leave it on the altar.

Or drop it in the poor box.

When Basilio was a boy and his family drove into the Holy Land for Sunday dinner at his grandparent's house on Macon Street, he'd lead the younger kids in make-believe Mass down by the bottle cap factory, consecrating sugar wafers into Hosts; all of the children kneeling together on the sidewalk to watch him scratch wedding cakes like flying saucers onto the sidewalk with rocks, the smart-alecks teasing him that he wanted to marry his cousin Donna and torturing him that he couldn't unless he wanted to go to jail.

In the Catholic church, matrimony is the only sacrament in which the priest is merely a witness; in truth, the man and woman marry themselves.

You make believe the way you make a painting.

The way Basilio had not for so long.

"Joseph and Mary, have you come here freely and without reservation? Will you love and honor one another until death? Will you accept children lovingly from God?"

Basilio tried to catch Roxanne's eye.

"All the days of my life," promised Mary.

"Each and every day," said Joseph.

The priest asked for the rings and Basilio had to think for a moment so he didn't pass his bad luck onto Joe.

He'd taken the dive before any of his friends.

"I love her, Dad," he told his father, arrogant in his youth. "That's why."

His parents were merciful when Basilio came back to the same kitchen table to tell of the collapse and ask for his old room back.

Taking the ring from Basilio and placing it on Mary's finger, Joe prayed that he would never take his wife for granted as his bride asked God to remind her to always give her husband encouragement.

As they exchanged rings, Basilio washed the cathedral with the busy brushes in his head, his real ones dry and brittle on a windowsill of the house he'd shared with Trudy, a red and gold umbrella behind him on the altar.

Red and gold: the colors of Spain.

Basilio's grandparents' marriage had been arranged in a basement kitchen in Highlandtown by people who knew better and it had lasted for fifty-seven years. He glimpsed his face in the golden chalice held aloft by the priest and he began whispering to his reflection: Take it easy. No big deal. You're just helping out a friend.

Not only had Joe done the same for him—best friends and best man—his old buddy from Transfiguration High spent a long evening trying to persuade Trudy to give it another try.

"What'd she say?" Basilio had pestered. "What'd she say?"

"She just said, 'Joe, I gotta go...'"

The bridal party was turned out in verdant shades of Eire with accents of orange in homage to Mary's dead, Protestant father; green and orange in tribute to the troubles her parents had overcome.

In Basilio's row: Emerald bowties and matching cummerbunds.

In Roxanne's: Kelly green and black velvet.

Satin sculpted and scalloped along white flesh and freckles and in each pretty head, fragrant blossoms of orchid: trellised, Dreamsicle petals of comparettia.

A wedding's worth of just-this-morning blooms had not come cheap, but Joe had paid the cost with the surety that it was money he'd never have to spend again. Mary hadn't need to grace her head with orange for it was a natural, coruscating copper, a crown trimmed in white lace.

The flowers took Basilio back to his childhood, back when Grandmom was living and Grandpop still slept upstairs in their bed; back to summer vacations painting flowers in their small backyard, adolescent easel built from grape crates and set beneath the clothesline, the alley behind Macon Street exploding with roses in May, tomatoes in July; sunflowers and figs as the summer wore on, the vegetable man idling through the alley in a pick-up with a scale hanging in the back.

If any of his juvenilia survived, Basilio didn't know where.

The Flowers of Highlandtown.

How to get back there?

Basilio traced Roxanne with desire dipped in paint; green satin and black velvet hugging plump curves; hair barely tamed around a pale, oval face from another country, another age; the kind of eyes that peered over golden fans at bullrings before her people were expelled from the land of Basilio's ancestors and a mouth like a baby's heart.

"I do..." said Joseph.

"I will," said Mary.

•

Two great Baltimore temples stand face-to-face on Cathedral Street: The Basilica of the Assumption of the Blessed Virgin Mary and the Enoch Pratt Free Library.

Joe and Mary strode from one to the other with the promise of Spring in their hearts, applause in their ears, and the bite of December at their backs. It was dusk, a few stars and a pale moon showing as a cop held back traffic for the bridal party to cross over to the reception.

Basilio wanted to say something to Roxanne—something new—but he couldn't think of anything and now the library was in front of them, its doors dividing a dozen display windows inspired by the department store palaces of the 1920s, windows dressed with the Story of Joe and Mary.

Baby pictures side-by-side, First Communion portraits, and posters of them at pastel proms.

The street lamps came on and flurries of snow danced in their margarine glow. Basilio breathed in the winter air, close enough now to dust Roxanne's every pore. Glancing down at his shoes and the thick white lines of the crosswalk, he said: "Just like Abbey Road."

In her best *scouse*, Roxanne thanked Basilio for taking her hand—"very much..."—as they stepped over the curb and he took it as a good sign.

The lobby of the library was crowded with long tables covered in white cloth, a ballroom walled with books, and Basilio and Roxanne stood together behind their chairs at the head table as Joe and Mary were introduced as man and wife for the first time.

Scanning the crowd for his parents and daughter, Basilio spotted a sign on a shelf above the bride and groom.

"Look," he said, touching Roxanne's elbow. "New Fiction."

What kind of good luck speech can a best man give when the thought of marriage is turning his stomach? The one he has rehearsed.

"GERONIMO!" shouted Basilio before tossing back a glass of champagne.

Taking his bride's hand, Joe took Mary out onto the floor for the first dance of their marriage, arms around each other, whispering and laughing, eyes locked.

Roxanne scanned the shelf at her elbow and pulled down a fat book of paintings by Chagall. Flipping through the pages, she happened upon a bride in a white gown wandering through a sapphire canvas of cocks and fiddlers.

"What do you think?" she asked Basilio.

"Nice colors," he said, moving an index finger across the lavender bridal canopy. "I'm going to find my family. Want to come?"

"I'll wait," said Roxanne, squinting past Basilio for a glimpse of his daughter; beginning to ache—not again, she thought, not here—the way Basilio had ached on the altar.

At his parents' table, Basilio kissed his mother, put his hand on his father's shoulder, and knelt down before India.

"Hey baby," he said. "Hey pretty girl."

"Da-da!"

"Baby doll," said Basilio, pressing his forehead against his daughter's stomach, making her laugh.

"Isn't her dress pretty, Daddy?" asked Basilio's mother, picking up the plate before her looking for her reflection in it. "Did I ever tell you about our wedding? The reception was downstairs on Macon Street. Those old Spaniards drank and sang for three days and the Polacks half-killed themselves trying to keep up."

She ran her finger around the gold leaf along the edge of the plate.

"We ate off of your grandmother's wedding china. It's still down there. Now that would make a nice picture."

"It's only a pretty dress on a pretty girl, Ma," said Basilio, kissing India on the top of her head and going back to his seat when the bridal party was invited to join Joe and Mary on the dance floor.

Basilio and Roxanne danced near the bride and groom; Joe winking at them over Mary's shoulder and Mary doing the same when they turned.

"Look at them," Roxanne said. "Complete happiness."

[Not that long ago, with no hope of any happiness, Roxanne had sent the father of her child-to-be away.]

"Complete?" laughed Basilio.

"Looks like it."

"Ever hear about Elvis' wedding?"

"No."

"They had a six-tiered cake five-feet tall," he said, holding his hand above the ground to show the magnificence of it. "Priscilla got pregnant on their wedding night."

"So why'd she leave him for her karate teacher?"

"Not right away she didn't," said Basilio. "Not at first."

Moving in time with the music, Basilio saw India bouncing in her chair and glimpsed a wisp of Trudy in his daughter's face.

"Have you ever painted her?" asked Roxanne.

"Priscilla?"

"Your daughter."

"Elvis took 'obey' out of the vows but only if Priscilla dyed her hair black and piled it up high in a beehive. Just like the old ladies up in Highlandtown."

"Highlandtown?"

"The Holy Land," said Basilio.

Late in the party, Mary asked the band for "Daddy's Little Girl" and walked out onto the floor to greet the melody alone. Her mother joined her after the first verse, their arms around each other's neck as Joe stood on the side and watched his bride grieve on her wedding day.

Roxanne's gaze was drawn to a far corner where Basilio danced with India in his arms.

"What are we gonna do, baby?" he whispered, running his lips over the curve of the girl's ear. "What we gonna do?"

The song faded and it was time to go. Basilio handed India to his mother—"Be good for Grandmom..."—and Joe grabbed his shoulder.

"Thanks a million," he said, a little drunk.

"It was all you, man," said Basilio.

"Take a walk?" said Joe.

"Where's Roxanne?"

"She's still here," said Joe, pulling Basilio into a back hall, past rooms dedicated to Mencken and Poe and Maulsby, the two friends side-by-side and quiet; Basilio guessing that Joe wanted to catch a little buzz the way they used to in high school, Joe about to roll one up when they heard laughter rolling down the hall.

"Manners," said Joe.

"Manners," agreed Basilio and they crept down the hall to a reading room where Seth Manners, another mug from Transfiguration High, was pitching woo on a red leather couch with one of Mary's married cousins.

Joe and Basilio held their breath on each side of the door.

Manners had a hand up the woman's dress. She'd come to the wedding alone because her husband was working overtime to pay the mortgage on their dream house, the one they'd promised themselves, the one they deserved.

Manners was single for the same reason Mary's cousin would be one day and as he worked his way into the woman's panties,

Joe inexplicably whispered: "How's Trudy?"

Basilio turned his back and headed for the reception.

"Sorry," said Joe, catching up. "Everybody misses Trudy."

"There he is!" cried Mrs. Boullosa, standing with Roxanne and India as Basilio walked into the nearly deserted lobby. "Where've you been?"

Basilio fastened the top button of his daughter's coat and hugged her until she cried. Roxanne took the orchids from her hair and set them on the baby's head.

"I'm ready," she said.

•

Basilio drove east with Roxanne for a rendezvous in the Shadow of the King; east into the Holy Land toward Miss Bonnie's Elvis Grotto. It was almost 11:00 p.m. when they pulled up to the corner of Fleet and Port.

"Where are we?" asked Roxanne, scooting up to a plate-glass window where a bust of the King stood in a carpet of poinsettia leaves, lights twinkling around his neck.

"We're here," said Basilio, holding the door open.

Roxanne stepped inside, her pupils opening wide in a poorly lit sanctuary for people who have nowhere to go on days when everyone is supposed to have a place to go.

Three solitary regulars looked up from their drinks to give Basilio and Roxanne the once over: a wrinkled dwarf in white face; a woman who couldn't hold her head up; and an old foreigner who needed a shave falling forward on an aluminum walker.

A cold cut buffet was set up against the wall; behind the bar, goldfish floated in and out of a white mansion sunk in a long aquarium; 45 rpm records spray painted silver and gold hung from the ceiling and Elvis crooned: "The hopes and fears of all the years are met in thee tonight..."

No one spoke until Miss Bonnie—deep in an easy chair at the back of the bar, savoring a voice that came to visit but not to stay

—noticed her visitors.

"Why darlin'," she said, putting down a movie magazine. "I was wondering if my boyfriend was gonna remember me on Christmas."

Basilio blushed and stepped over the threshold with Roxanne.

"Miss Bonnie," he said. "This is Roxanne. Roxanne, my sweetheart Miss Bonnie."

"Why hello honey," said Bonnie, giving Roxanne a hug. "Don't you two look gorgeous."

Roxanne gazed over Miss Bonnie's shoulder to a life-sized crèche in the back, a manger of limbs from trees that grew along the waterfront before the piers were poured from cement trucks; tall plaster figures of beasts and blessed.

She had never been this close to one before, never one this big—not figurines behind glass, but life-size statues out in the open and she slipped Miss Bonnie's embrace to get a closer look.

She crouched for a lamb's eye view, her satin gown stretched tight across full thighs and wide hips, knees up against her chest as she peered through wooden slats to see the infant.

"She's a keeper," whispered Bonnie.

Closing her eyes, Roxanne asked the Universe for forgiveness, a clenched fist between her breasts.

Stand up, she said to herself.

You better find a way to get up.

Reaching through the slats, she plucked a stalk of hay from the manger and with swift élan, used it to gather up her great mane before returning to Basilio and saying: "You like?"

Too much. The last straw.

Basilio took Roxanne's shaking hand, stood in front of Miss Bonnie, and said: "I can't keep it in anymore."

"What?" asked Roxanne.

"What, Hon?" said Bonnie.

"We just came from the priest!" he shouted. "We're married!"

Roxanne flinched.

"It's true," said Basilio, pulling her hand to his lips. "By God, it's true!"

"Hallelujah!" cried Bonnie, coming in for hugs.

Roxanne smiled at Basilio over Bonnie's shoulder, mischief replacing guilt as she waved a naked ring finger before him with a look that said: "You didn't think of everything, Mr. Smarty Pants."

"Lock the front door," said Bonnie. "We got us a wedding here."

Fussing over every little thing, she smacked Basilio's fanny and said: "Honey, you shoulda gimme some notice."

"Wasn't any notice," said Roxanne.

"Oh Christ, one of them," said Bonnie. "Two of mine were like that."

And then she turned a cynical eye on Basilio.

"Catholic?"

"Of course."

"How the hell did you get a priest to say the magic words without jumpin' through all them goddamn hoops?"

Basilio rubbed his thumb and forefinger together.

"The usual way," he said.

"Well, well," laughed Bonnie. "It's good to know they didn't change everything in the Church."

"Didn't all go so smooth," said Basilio.

He held Roxanne's hand in the air and said, "No time for a ring."

"Stores closed," said Roxanne.

"Wedding rings?" said Bonnie as though they'd asked her for a bag of chips.

"That's it," said Basilio.

"That's all," said Roxanne.

"Hell," said Bonnie. "Come here girl."

Roxanne walked behind the bar to the one-hundred-gallon home of a submerged Graceland and three generations of Holy Rosary Spring Carnival goldfish floating in and out of the mansion's empty rooms, the path to the King's front door paved with bands of gold.

"Ever been fishin' honey?" said Bonnie, reaching behind the cash register for a toy rod with a paperclip hook.

Basilio hopped up on the bar, his head over Roxanne's shoulder, and the regulars followed: Ted the Clown, still in make-up from a nursing home gig; the drunken Carmen; and Mr. Voliotikes, leaning hard on his walker.

"Fish?" said Roxanne, taking the rod.

"Don't wanna stick your hand in the muck," said Bonnie, pointing to five rings nestled in slime.

"Go fish," said Basilio.

Ted scurried around the bar to stand alongside Roxanne and Carmen twirled on a barstool like a kid.

"Don't hurt the fish," said Carmen, twice divorced.

"You can't hurt them fish," said the clown.

"Don't crowd her," yelled Bonnie.

"Which one?" asked Roxanne, dropping the line into the tank.

"Any one," said Bonnie as the hook dragged gravel.

"Got one!" squealed Roxanne.

"So quick," said Carmen.

"Lickety-split!" yodeled the clown.

"Told you," Bonnie said.

Roxanne turned to Basilio with the dripping ring, but when he reached out for it, Bonnie snatched it away and wiped it clean.

"Not yet," she said, passing the rod to Basilio. "Your turn."

Oh boy, he thought, hopping down from the bar with the ring Trudy had once slipped on his finger deep in his pocket. Holding the rod over the bubbling water, Basilio asked Bonnie which ring came from which husband; if, he wondered, one was any luckier than the others.

"You see where they wound up," she said.

Basilio let the hook sway above the tank until the crowd was hypnotized, lowered the line and slipped a hand into his pocket.

"Bingo!" he said.

Turning to Roxanne, Basilio stood with a dry ring on the end of his hook, unsmiling, four others still in the drink.

Such dexterity, at turns charming and nauseating, had ultimately convinced Trudy to leave, a truth that Basilio would try to stuff into poor boxes and sewer holes for years to come.

Bonnie led the couple out from behind the bar, handed Basilio the ring Roxanne had plucked from the aquarium, gave Roxanne the ring Basilio had reeled in and ordered them to trade.

Roxanne's ring was too small, stopping at her knuckle and she slipped it on her pinky. Basilio's moved along his finger without a hitch.

"Now kiss her," said Bonnie.

"Yeah!" said Carmen.

"Right in the kisser!" said the clown.

"Show some respect," said Mr. Voliotikes.

Their lips touched and a current passed between them to light every bulb in the bar and run the ice machine.

"Love...," marveled Bonnie before turning for the stairs that led to her apartment above the bar. "You kids enjoy yourselves. I'll be right back."

In Bonnie's absence, Ted the Clown took over, guiding Basilio and Roxanne to a table against the wall as they stared at their rings.

"We're married," said Basilio.

"What now?" asked Roxanne.

Ted slipped behind the bar to tipple a little of this and some of that before bringing Basilio a beer and a glass of white wine.

With the goo-goo eyes of the regulars bearing down upon them, the newlyweds could not enjoy themselves or leave without saying goodbye to Bonnie, whose absence had changed the room.

"This was just another neighborhood gin mill selling boiled eggs and pickled onions until Bonnie's last husband died," said Basilio. "When he dropped dead Bonnie started putting up pictures of Elvis to make herself feel better."

Roxanne shifted to take in the massive collage that was Miss Bonnie's Elvis Grotto and was particularly taken by a Graceland postcard of the tux and gown that Elvis and Priscilla had worn on their wedding day, an exhibit of empty clothes.

"And then Presley died," said Basilio. "And everybody began loading the joint up with the King, but none of it made Bonnie feel any better."

Feeling ignored, Ted leaned across the table so far that his rubber nose nearly poked Roxanne in the face, his head bobbing on a pencil neck.

"You don't think people marry clowns?" he said, smacking himself on the back of his head until the red ball popped off of his nose. "Happens every goddamn day."

Ted stuck the rubber nose on Basilio and lamented: "But all them gutter balls. Maybe that's the way it oughta be. That's the way it is."

"Dog shit!" shouted Carmen, drunk on gloom and schnapps, edging her way to the table with Baby Jesus in her arms, tripping toward Roxanne when the clown grabbed her ass.

Carmen dropped the infant and it shattered on the floor. Roxanne screamed.

"Oh my God," said Basilio, picking up the pieces. "Ted, you mental patient."

"I didn't do it," shouted the clown. "I had nothin' to do with it."

Carmen stood over Roxanne like a runaway, tangled hair in her eyes as the lights blinked on and off across the stucco paste of her face.

"Goochie-goochie goo," she warbled. "Goochie-goochie goo..."

"Oh Christ," said Basilio, on his knees. He hurled the rubber nose at Ted and held Roxanne's ankle as she cried. Ted polished off everyone's drink and slipped out the side door as Mr. Voliotikes lumbered toward the head of the table.

"Out of my way," he roared, kicking Carmen with his good foot.

"Why?" he asked, taking Roxanne's hand. "Why you do this without your mother and father?"

Roxanne wiped her eyes on the cuff of her gown and blew her nose in a napkin.

"It's my life," she said, pulling her hand away as Bonnie came down the stairs with a sheet cake in her hands. Stopping halfway down, she saw Basilio piling pieces of Jesus on the table, Roxanne in tears, Carmen passed out on the floor, the old Greek preaching, and no sign of the clown.

"What the hell's goin' on here? I can't leave for five goddamn minutes without you smoke hounds turning a wedding into a wake? For Christ's sake, this is the best thing that's happened here in years and you rumpots ain't gonna poison it with your goddamn war stories."

"Carmen? CARMEN! Get the hell off the floor. What's wrong with you? Somebody help her up. Mr. V, wipe your eyes and sit down. That girl don't need no Daddy. She's got a husband now."

Walking the cake over to the table, Bonnie rubbed Roxanne's shoulder and told her not to mind the others: "They ain't right."

Putting her arms around the guests of honor, she assured them, "We're making our own happiness here," and brought over a fresh pot of coffee to go with the cake.

"Okay," she said. "Mr. V, say a nice grace for us. Something for a Christmas wedding. In English."

The old man closed his eyes, bowed his head, and was just starting to get warmed up—"Forgive us, Father, for the vows we could not keep"—when Bonnie shouted "Amen" and began cutting the cake.

The caffeine and sugar gave Roxanne and Basilio new strength, and when Bonnie started clinking a spoon against her coffee cup for them to kiss, he put his lips next to Roxanne's ear and said: "Let's get out of here."

"Miss Bonnie..."

"I know, you gotta go," she said. "Let me give you something first."

From a shelf behind the bar, she took down a bust of Elvis made into a lamp and handed it to Basilio at the front door.

"Works on batteries," she said, flicking the switch on and off.

He thanked her with a kiss on the cheek and said: "You made this a special night for us."

"I didn't make it special, hon. It is special."

And the heart-shaped clock on the wall said it was time.

"Now out with you," said Bonnie. "Out you go."

•

The cold slapped color into Roxanne's cheeks and bit through Basilio's pants as they hurried to the car. Basilio put Elvis between them on the front seat and waited for the engine to warm up.

Stuffed with their rich lie and too full to speak, a young man and a young woman who'd never met before that day drove through the Holy Land with rings on their fingers and wedding cake in their pockets; the city as silent as the bride and groom as Roxanne stared through the darkness at rows of narrow brick houses and Basilio drove south to the water's edge at the end of Clinton Street.

The road was unpaved and the moon made silhouettes of coal piers and cranes, fuel barges and corrugated fertilizer warehouses. They drove past the hulk of the S.S. *John Brown* Liberty Ship and Schuefel's, the saloon where a monkey named Dinky drank beer from a can.

Gravel crunched under the tires until the road stopped at a wooden pier jutting out from the front yard of a house with "SALVAGE" painted across its side.

Basilio parked in front of a twisted guard rail as a red tugboat with a white dot on its stack pulled a barge across the harbor, the flag over Fort McHenry starched in a stiff breeze.

Engine running, heater on, he pushed the seat back and closed his eyes, fresh out of script until Roxanne opened her door and a blast of winter air accompanied her command to get out and bring the lamp.

Basilio sat up to see her walk down a warped pier beneath a feta moon, high heels steady on the splintered boards, black hair flying in a nocturne of ebony and cream. Hurrying to catch up with Elvis in his arms, he found Roxanne sitting on the edge of the pier with her legs over the side. Basilio set the lamp down and sat beside her. It was freezing.

Roxanne turned the switch on the lamp and a pink halo floated up from the pier into the night.

"Have your fun?"

"Didn't you?" said Basilio, numb fingers struggling with the ring on his hand when Roxanne kissed him with an open mouth, her saliva freezing on his chin.

"We'll die out here," said Basilio, sliding his palm across the front of Roxanne's gown to her left hand, tugging the ring free from her pinky and shaking it with his own like dice before tossing them into the harbor.

Opening her coat, Roxanne pulled the velvet gown from her chest, her breasts snug in a strapless bra.

"What are you doing?" said Basilio, laying his head against her chest, no room of his own to set up an easel, much less rattle a headboard.

Defiant against the cold, Roxanne freed her breasts one at a time, looked down at Basilio and said: "Paint my portrait."

"Nude?"

"With India on my lap."

"Just you."

"Let's go," she said, and as Basilio began buttoning Roxanne's coat, he remembered the good morning light that came through the window near the sink in his grandfather's kitchen and work not yet begun that had vexed him since he was a boy.

THE FOUNTAIN OF HIGHLANDTOWN

BASILIO

I learned to live in the dark this year when I quit my job, sold everything I owned, and moved in with my grandfather.

This new life makes the simplest things complicated, even for a guy who decides one day to quit his job, sell everything he owns and go live in the dark.

But that's my problem.

Grandpop would tell you that.

It's a fine summer night in Baltimore and I am walking from Grandpop's house to meet Katherine, who is young and beautiful and smart and almost completely unknown to me.

I haven't told her much about myself, hardly anything except that my grandmother died in the hospital where she works, that my grandfather stopped sleeping in their bed the day she passed away and that it would be better if I met her where she lives than the other way around.

I said all this last week when I found her standing in line at the Broadway market. I was buying fresh fruit for Grandpop and she was picking up scallops and shrimp and pints of shucked oysters for a dinner party at her apartment.

Okay, she said, maybe we can do something, and borrowed a pencil to scratch her number across my bag of peaches.

And so, I am walking from the little Highlandtown rowhouse where my father was born and raised, passing bakeries and record stores and coffee shops, on my way to Katherine's apartment a few miles away, up around Johns Hopkins Hospital.

It's early (I had to get out of the house) and there's still a pink wash of early evening light across the sky as I walk down Macon Street to Eastern Avenue.

The street jumps with kids on skates, Saturday shoppers coming home with carts and bundles, and heavy women squirting down the gutters.

On the Avenue, middle-aged sports with slick hair and brown shoes with white socks wait on the word; Greek men who haven't shaved for two days stand on the corners, telling lies; packs of heavy-metal kids graze for drugs and kicks and young girls walk by, dressed up for each other.

My eye swims through the center of the composition but the margins are crowded with thoughts of Katherine.

What will she wear?

What does she smell like?

What hangs on her walls?

I think: How will our time pass?

And, if things go well, will we find our way back to Macon Street?

Fat chance.

My world is ruled by Grandpop and he is driving me crazy.

Right up the wall.

I am afraid that it won't last long enough for me to get everything done.

Every morning at breakfast he says the same thing: "Why are you here?"

Like he forgets that I am living with him between the time we go to bed and the time we wake up.

All night, Grandpop tosses and turns on the sofa bed downstairs, like he's being chased, until the break of day when he asks: "Why are you here?"

And then: "It's morning, turn off that light. You think I'm a millionaire? How were you raised?"

Grandpop was so poor growing up in Spain that one summer he carved an entire bicycle out of wood, wheels and all, so he

THE FOUNTAIN OF HIGHLANDTOWN • 79

would have something to ride besides an ox-drawn plow.

It doesn't matter that he's had it good in this country for sixty years, that, in his own words, he "eats like a king" and can lock the front door to a warm home he has owned for twice as long as I've been alive.

It does not matter that he's got a good pension from the shipyard and Social Security and more money in forgotten bank accounts than I have made in twenty-eight years on Earth.

None of that means shit if you are foolish enough to leave a light on in a room you have left or care to read or draw or scratch your ass by electric lamp before the sky outside has turned to pitch.

And there is no reason to use lights at night because at night you sleep.

Electricity, says Grandpop, is money. And a poor man cannot afford to waste either of them.

Bent over and angry, pointing to an offending fifteen-watt bulb, he says: "You think I'm a millionaire?"

When I try to tell him not to worry, that I'll help pay for it and its only pennies anyway—when I smile and say, "Hey Grandpop, we got it pretty good in this country"—he says I can go live with somebody else if I want to waste money.

He asks: "Why are you here?"

But he doesn't charge me a dime to sleep in his bed and eat his food and he doesn't say a word when I do what I need to do to get my work done.

Just as long as I don't turn on any lights.

God Bless America.

God Bless Grandpop.

I cross Eastern Avenue and dart between traffic into Patterson Park, where Grandpop used to play soccer way back when with other expatriates from around the world.

It's hard for me to imagine his legs strong enough to kick a ball the length of the park; he's barely able to climb the steps in the middle of the night to make sure I'm not reading under the covers with a flashlight. But up on dusty shelves near the sofa where he lays at night and talks in his sleep like he's trying to make someone understand, there are trophies to prove it.

"Grandpop," I say. "Tell me about playing soccer in the land of baseball."

The Pagoda sits on the highest hill in the park, a surreal stack of Oriental octagons in the middle of a wide, rolling lawn; a weird obelisk of Confucius bordered all around by narrow brick row-houses, the first in Baltimore with indoor bathrooms.

When you stand atop the Pagoda you can see all of the Holy Land, all the way past Fort McHenry to freighters in the harbor and the Francis Scott Key Bridge in the mist.

I would like to take Katherine up there and present her with the view, but it's only open on Sunday mornings when the Friends of the Park are around to let you in and keep an eye on things.

Grandmom and Grandpop used to walk me up here when I was a kid and you could go up to the top and see the whole city. They would stay down on the ground and wave up to me and I can see them now like it was yesterday, smiling through their broken English: "Doan breaka you neck."

After a while Grandmom couldn't make the walk anymore and as I got older other things became important and I didn't care to visit Macon Street so much.

The city let the Pagoda rot while punks and drunks and whores and glue-heads got up inside of it, doing things that made the paint peel. The city tried to tear it down a few years ago, when some goof on dope fell off and killed himself but the good citizens saved it and now you can only go up on Sunday mornings.

I tried to paint the Pagoda for three years before I moved in with Grandpop and I never got it right.

I stare up at it and fix its scale in my head.

I wonder: Does Katherine know any of this stuff? Does she care? Will she want to know once she knows how much I care?

What I know about Katherine you could pour into a thimble with room to spare. She is young and beautiful and smart and puts on dinner parties with scallop and shrimp.

I don't even know if she's from Baltimore.

I leave the Pagoda and walk out of the park onto Pratt Street, passing families of Lumbees and Salvadorans and black folks as the neighborhoods change the closer I get to downtown.

I hit Broadway and turn north on a wide stretch of asphalt that rises up beyond the statue of Latrobe and the derelict housing projects named in his honor; up from the harbor a good mile or two where Broadway meets Hopkins, where my grandmother died twenty years ago, leaving Grandpop all that time and how much more to lie in the dark, conserving kilowatts to save pennies he doesn't count anymore.

Katherine's apartment is in the shadow of the hospital's great dome.

The neighborhood used to be called Swampoodle before Hopkins started gobbling it up, back when Bohemians lived there, in the days when Grandpop played soccer in Patterson Park and Grandmom sat on a bench with her girlfriends and watched.

I tried to paint the Hopkins dome too, in the last days before I moved in with Grandpop, but all I could think about was what we lost there.

I smeared the canvas with vinegar and vowed that I would not paint pictures of buildings anymore.

KATHERINE

I didn't know what to expect with this guy.

I haven't dated much lately because they've all been the same, but I said yes to this guy right in the market. I knew it would be different, but I didn't know how.

I certainly didn't expect to be picked up for our first date on foot.

He knocks on the door, comes in with a polite hello, and looks around.

Next thing out of his mouth: "I walked over because I sold my car when I moved in with my grandfather."

But he doesn't say what one has to do with the other.

He tells me that my dress reminds him of the sunflowers his grandmother used to grow in her backyard until the summer she passed away "right there," and he points through the window to the hospital.

"That exact same color," he says, staring just a little too long before telling me "it's gorgeous outside," and would I like to take a walk?

He's cute, in a funny way, like a kid; younger than me and a nice change from the clever men with tasseled loafers and Jaguars, so suave and witty until they find out I'm a doctor and then they really start acting like kids.

I don't mind walking and out we go, strolling south on Broadway toward the water.

I'd bet you a lobster that we're headed for the bars in Fells Point, where every man I've dated in this town goes sooner or later, like it's the only place in Baltimore that sells beer.

But he doesn't mention Fells Point or any special restaurant or destination; he just keeps up a pleasant chatter about things you can't imagine—bicycles and chestnut trees and the Rock of Gibraltar (I've seen it, he hasn't)—and now we're cutting across the side streets and through the alleys, moving east to the neighborhoods where my patients live and die.

He doesn't say what he does for a living and I wonder if it's anything at all, if maybe the good doctor is out for an evening with the unemployed. He must do something because his shoes and pants are speckled with little smudges of paint.

Maybe he's the Cartographer of Baltimore, so well he knows these cobbled paths crowded with dogs and kids and garbage cans.

"You know what I love?" he says. "I love to walk through the alleys and look in peoples' houses. Especially at night when the lights are on and the shades are up. You can look right in and see people eating and watching TV, talking to each other, you know, just living."

He doesn't ask me what I do and it's a relief not to have to answer all the questions, a blessing not to feel the evening turn when it finally comes out.

It seems enough for him just to know that I work in a hospital.

Our walk is slow and evening falls with a warm, clean breeze from the harbor.

How odd, I think, looking into the tiny concrete yards where kids splash in wading pools, Moms watching from lawn chairs with their feet in the water, old men in their undershirts, listening to the ballgame and drinking beer; how pleasantly odd not to talk about what you do for a living.

I will extend him the same courtesy for as long as it lasts.

At the end of an alley we stop in front of a corner bar called Miss Bonnie's and he points out the red and blue and green neon floating out from behind block glass in the windows.

He talks about colors as if they are alive and in between all the loose words he talks about his grandfather.

"Grandpop won't let me turn on any lights. He sits at the kitchen table all day circling crime stories in the paper with a red pencil. Nothing bad has ever happened to him here, but he says America is going to the dogs."

A native girl on a tricycle zips between us and he talks about the shades of red and brown in her cheeks, "like autumn leaves."

He says that American Indians are the only minority his grandfather has any sympathy for because there was no New World left for them when things went bad at home.

Now we're in the park, walking quietly until we reach the Pagoda, the sun going down behind it like a tangerine, that's what he says, "a big, fat tangerine."

He shakes the gate on the iron fence around the Pagoda but you don't have to shake it to see that it's locked.

"Grandpop forgets that I'm living with him between the time we go to bed and the time I come down for breakfast. Every day we start from scratch."

"So why do you stay?"

He turns from the Pagoda and we walk east across the park toward Eastern Avenue and the Greeks.

Just beyond the railroad bridge marking the incline that gives Highlandtown its name, he spies a wooden stand on the sidewalk and says: "Wanna a snowball?"

I get chocolate with marshmallow and he asks for grape, fishing out a couple of dollars from the pockets of his white jeans.

We pause at a bus stop and I wonder if maybe we're going to catch one to take us to God knows where.

Holding out his palm, he invites me to sit down and I think: This bench is the sidewalk cafe in Paris that the plastic surgeon wanted to take me to last month until he found out that a ticket to France would get me across the ocean and wouldn't get him anywhere.

We sit, the distance of five hands between us, and I look up to see that above our heads hangs one of the most bizarre landmarks in a city filled with them.

Up against the sky: The Great Bolewicki Depression Clock.

Bolted to the front of an appliance store called Bolewicki's, it has a human face and crystal hands filled with bubbling water— the little hand bubbling lavender and the big hand bubbling pink —and around it glows lights shaped into words that say: "It's not too late, it's only..."

And then you read the time.

Like right now, eating snowballs at a bus stop on a Saturday night in Baltimore, it's not too late for anything: It's only ten past seven.

"I've been to Germany and Switzerland a half-dozen times," I say, "and I've never seen a clock like this."

"It's something," he says. "I tried painting this clock for three months."

"How many coats did it take?"

That does it!

He starts laughing and can't stop; a wild, crazy laugh from

way back in his throat and I start to laugh too because he's got such a funny, genuine laugh, like some strange bird.

Tears come to his eyes and he's spewing crystals of purple ice, trying to catch his breath.

And somewhere inside of this laugh I decide that I like this man and surrender to whatever the night may bring as the No. 10 stops to let people off beneath the Great Bolewicki Depression Clock in the middle of Eastern Avenue and my date with a guy named Basilio whose tongue is the color of a ripe plum.

He gets a hold of himself and says: "I wish old man Bolewicki would let me paint his clock. It would be the first money I've made with a brush in a long time."

He looks me in the eye.

"I tried to paint a picture of it."

"You're an artist?"

"I guess," he says, looking up. "This thing was so hard, Katherine. You see the water bubbling in those hands, like bubble lights at Christmas...did your tree have bubble lights when you were a kid? I loved those things, you don't see 'em anymore. But I couldn't get the water right, I couldn't make it look like it was really bubbling."

I watch as he loses himself in the clock, the big hand bubbling pink and the smaller one pumping lavender—"It's not too late, it's only..."—and he catches me looking.

"Let's go."

We walk deeper into the neighborhood and he points out things I know and things I don't.

"That's a great little place," he says as we pass Garayoa's Cafe Espanol, where, he tells me, they serve squid stuffed with their own tentacles and cooked in a sauce made with the ink.

I don't tell him that I have broken bread there with an investment banker, a screen writer and a child psychiatrist.

"The ink bubbles up in a thick dark sauce that shimmers deep green just above the surface," he says. "I tried painting with it once. Thought it would be perfect for a sad night sky. But it dried ugly brown."

At the next corner, Basilio passes our empty snowball cups to a short man selling produce from the trunk of a gigantic Pontiac and in return the man hands each of us a small, brown pear.

"Lefty," says Basilio, shaking the guy's hand.

"Senor," says the man with a Greek accent, looking me over and winking at Basilio. "How's your old abuelo my friend?"

"He's good Lefty, real good," says Basilio. "I'll tell him you said hello."

"You do that, senor," he says. "Enjoy your evening."

We move away in silence, biting the fruit as the sky turns dark and pear juice runs along my mouth. Basilio pulls a spotless white handkerchief from his back pocket and wipes my chin, cleaning his own with the back of his hand and it is all so very simple and nice...

Until we come upon a narrow lane paved with brick and identified by stained-glass transoms as the 600 block of South Macon Street.

Basilio points down the long row of identical rowhouses, orange brick with white marble steps before each of them.

"I live down there with Grandpop," he says, pausing like someone trying to decide if they should show up unannounced at your door, making me feel like he's talking to himself and I am no longer here.

Over the next curve of the Avenue, beyond a cluster of blue and white Greek restaurants, I see the Ruth Tower rising up from the University of East Baltimore and since there seems to be no agenda and Basilio's verve faded at Macon Street, I point up to the tower where I had a blast as an undergraduate, a stone room —cool and round—with a bar and a view you can't get from two Pagodas set on top of one another.

My turn: "Up there. Let's go."

It is night now and we move through the dark campus toward a granite spiral tiled with all the great moments of the Babe's career.

It is the Bambino's only gift to the city of his birth.

Bolted to the base of the tower is a plaque quoting the slugger at the dedication: "Let the poor kids in free and name it after me."

We walk inside and start climbing, round and round, up to the sky.

I tell Basilio that when I first came to Baltimore—Good Lord, it seems like nine thousand dead teenagers ago—the top of the Ruth Tower was *the* spot: strong Greek coffee, Delta blues, oval plates of feta and black olives, crusty bread, cheap beer, and young people from around the world shouting at each other about what it's all about.

He says: "I was in the suburbs back then."

"Did you ever try to paint this?"

"Sure. Grandpop brought my old man here to see the Babe when Dad was a kid and Ruth was half-dead with termites."

We walk in and I head for the bar, reaching into the pockets of my dress for money, feeling Basilio behind me, looking around.

"So this is college," he says.

I hand him a draft beer and steer to a table with a window facing west, back toward downtown where Baltimore's money finds Baltimore's art in chic storefronts along Charles Street.

The docs I work with write big checks for paintings that probably aren't any better than the ones Basilio destroys, but I really don't know if he can paint or not. All I know is what didn't turn out: half the real estate in East Baltimore.

I sip my beer and think that maybe I can help this guy.

"Tell me about the paintings you're happy with."

He gulps beer and ignores the question, shifting east to play tour guide again: Over there is the National Brewery, home of the One-Eyed Little Man; and the Esskay slaughterhouse is there, they've got some great stainless steel letters out front; and way over there, he says, beyond the rooftops, is a graveyard where four Chinese sailors who capsized in a 1917 hailstorm are buried.

I think for a moment that he's a fraud and I will be sick.

Turning his head with an angry finger, I direct his gaze toward the Hopkins dome.

"And over there is where I fish bullets out of 14-year-old boys on Saturday nights just like this before I have to tell their 27-year-old mothers they didn't make it. Take me to see your work or take me home."

And still this hard-head gives me words instead of pictures.

Grandpop skinning squirrels for dinner at the stationary tubs in the basement; Grandpop lecturing a little boy at those same tubs that a man really hasn't washed up if he hasn't washed his neck; and Grandpop making love to his bride on Macon Street, conceiving the man who would seed the artist.

"Those," he says. "are pretty good."

As we take the steps two at a time, he takes my hand.

At the front door to 627 South Macon Street, just before turning the key, Basilio tells me to take off my shoes and leads me in, dim light from a streetlamp falling across a small figure sleeping in the middle room.

"Grandpop," he whispers as we creep toward a staircase along the wall.

No one answers and as I move up the stairs, the old man stirs in his bed and my dress flutters around my knees.

Basilio keeps moving and I am right behind him, shoes in my left hand and my right against the small of his back as we climb together.

When we reach the top, he whispers in my ear, his "hallelujah!" warm and sweet.

He says: "I've never done this before."

Neither have I.

A door creaks open before us as Basilio turns the knob and I slip in behind him.

We stand still in the darkness, just inside the door, and my nose stings from the turpentine. As my eyes adjust I sense that this is the biggest room in the house, that there is only one room on this floor—as long and as wide as the house itself—and I am in it.

Basilio escorts me to a saloon table against the long side wall and sits me down on a stool before crossing to the other side of the room.

"Ready?" he asks, holding a cord.

I answer "ready" and he pulls it.

A tarp whooshes to the floor, night fills the space where the roof ought to be, the light of a nearly full moon and a sky of stars floods the room, and in one clear instant I see the world this man lives in.

"There's no roof!"

My head spins as I try to take in the sky, the paintings, the smile on Basilio's face, and the colors everywhere.

"I told you, Grandpop won't let me turn on any lights. I cut the roof out a little bit at a time and paint with what it gives me. I never would have thought of it if I didn't have to."

I stand, dumbfounded.

"You can't turn on the lights, but you can saw the roof out of his house?"

"He's never mentioned it. As long as I don't use electricity or bring women home, he pretty much leaves me alone."

I move close to his work, the silver light from above giving each painting a glow I've never seen in any gallery in the world and on one canvas after another I read the narrative of his grandfather's life.

Grandpop as a boy, sitting on a rocky hill, carving a pair of handlebars from the limb of a chestnut tree; Grandpop shoveling coal on the deck of a rusty freighter, Gibraltar bearing down in the background; Grandpop kicking a soccer ball, his right leg stretched out in front of him as the ball sails across Patterson Park, the Pagoda perfect in the background; Grandpop strolling down Eastern Avenue, all dressed up with his wife on a Sunday afternoon, the Great Bolewicki Depression Clock bubbling pink and lavender to beat the band.

And then, running the length of a single wall, a huge canvas of a bedroom cast in moonlight and shadows.

In the bed is a young man who looks a lot like Basilio, a white sheet draped across his back, arms strong and taut as he hovers over a dark-haired beauty with stars in her eyes.

I am transfixed and wonder if there is a cot in the room.

"What do you call this one?"

"The Fountain of Highlandtown."

GRANDPOP

Suenos. Siempre suenos. Dulces suenos y malos suenos. Suenos de amor.

I can feel it.

Basilio must be making a pintura of a woman upstairs.

I can feel it in my sleep, like she is in the house.

He must be getting good.

"Grandpop," he says at my kitchen table every morning, up before me, coffee ready for his *abuelo*, this boy is a man, doesn't he have a home?

"Grandpop," he says while I'm still trying to figure out what day it is and why he is living with me.

"Grandpop, do you remember what Grandmom looked like the first time you saw her?

"What did her skin look like?"

I say: "Basilio," (he was named after me, two Basilios in one house is one Basilio too many); I say: "What are you doing, writing a book?"

"Something like that," he says.

Last week it was questions about the shipyard, before that it was Patterson Park, now it's about Mama and I don't have the patience for it.

Questions and questions and questions as he makes little pencil marks on a napkin.

"Grandpop, tell me about Galicia and the corn cribs on stilts and the baskets your father made."

"Grandpop, tell me about the ox and the cart and the *cocido* your mother stewed over the fire in the black pot."

"Grandpop, tell me about the first time you saw Gibraltar."

Why does he want to live with an old man who is so mean to him? He is good company, this boy with the questions, even if he has to turn on a light to clean the kitchen in the middle of the afternoon.

"Grandpop," he says to me on his way out of the house to-night (where he was going in the shoes with the paint on them, I don't know, he should get dressed and go out with a woman before he gets old); "Grandpop," he says: "What did Grandmom's hair look like on your wedding night?"

I told him: "Turn off the light and lock the door when you go out."

This is what I didn't tell him: It was black, Basilio, black like the coal I shoveled out of ships at *la Roca*; black like a night at sea without stars and it fell down around my shoulders when she leaned over me; *que linda Francesca, que bella Francesca, que guapa Francesca para me y solamente para mi.*

He asks in the morning while we eat our bacon and eggs; eggs he makes like I made for him when he stayed with Mama and me when he was a little boy (even then he wouldn't listen); bacon fried crisp and the eggs on top, grease spooned slow over the yolk.

I say: "Basilio, what are you doing here?"

And he answers: "What did Grandmom's eyes look like when she told you she loved you?"

And after all these years, the thought of her kiss (I can feel it at night, on nights like this, Basilio you must be painting upstairs), the thought of her still makes me excited, *un caballo fuerte*, and it makes me ready, so sad and ready, and I get mad to answer this boy with skinny brushes and silly paints and goddammit, why doesn't he go and live with his father in their big house in the suburbs?

My house is small and life here is finished.

I get mad and tell him he's too much trouble, that he's wasting my money leaving the lights on.

You don't turn on lights in the daytime and a boy doesn't ask an old man so many questions.

But he doesn't get mad back at me, he just touches my arm and gets up to wash the dishes saying: "I know, Grandpop, I know."

What does he know?

By the time I was his age I spoke good English, had three kids, a new Chevrolet and seniority down the shipyard.

What does he have?

My electricity and *no trabajo*; pennies he saves for paint (where his pennies come from I don't know, maybe he finds them in the street, he takes so many walks); and a loaf of bread he puts on the table every day before supper; one loaf of bread fresh from the Avenue in the center of my table four o'clock every day without a word.

I should go easy on him.

He's the only one who really talks with me.

The only one who comes to see his old *abuelo*.

But when did he move in?

How did that happen?

That's the question you never asked, Basilio: "Grandpop, can I live with you?"

Suenos. Dulces Suenos.

He must be painting upstairs.

I can feel it.

I remember when his father was just a baby and I called her Mama for the first time and she became Mama for all of us; Mama de la casa and his father would wake up in the middle of the night and scream in his crib and nothing would make him stop, nada, and Mama would get so exhausted she would turn her back to me and cry in her pillow.

I would smooth her hair—it was black, Basilio, as black as an olive—and I would turn on the radio (electricity, Basilio, in the middle of the night), to maybe calm the baby and listen to something besides the screaming.

Mama liked the radio, Basilio, and we listened while your father cried—*cantante negra, cantante de almas azules*—and it made us feel a little better, helped us make it through.

I had to get up early to catch the street car to the shipyard, but when the crying finally stopped sometimes the sun would be ready to pop and Mama's breathing would slow down and her shoulders would move like gentle waves, sleeping but still listening, like I can hear her now on this no good bed, and Basilio—*Mira, hombre*, I will not tell you this again—if I moved very close and kissed her shoulders, she would turn to face me and we would have to be quiet Basilio, under the music, very, very quiet...

So, this I want to know Basilio.

This, if you want to live on Macon Street for another minute.

Can you paint an apple baked soft in the oven, an apple filled with cinnamon and raisins?

Can you paint such a woman?

Are you good enough yet with those brushes that she will step out of your pictures to turn on the radio in the middle of the night?

Will she visit an old man on his death bed?

If you cannot do that, Basilio, there is no need for you to live here anymore.

BASILIO AND GRANDPOP
AND NIEVES

"The cuckoo, she's a pretty bird, Lord she warbles as she flies..."
—a plastic radio on the kitchen sink

Basilio had been calling himself "the Cartographer of Baltimore," since he was 17 and the subject of his paintings—the circles beneath Anne Franks' eyes on an abandoned confectionary, old men crabbing with chicken necks downwind from the soap factory—rarely strayed more than a mile beyond the glittering shithole he called the Holy Land.

He never drew a barn much less a cow. Tears shed over rivers of spilled milk he applied to the canvas with a butter knife thick with bee's wax.

A dozen years and a hundred sketchbooks down the line from the Carter Administration (voting for the first time, Jimmy pardoning the Vietnam draft dodgers), Basilio began using his work as currency.

You wouldn't believe how many egg sandwiches you can get with a wheat penny upon which the visage of Elvis Presley is painstakingly painted over Lincoln.

"You're gonna get me in trouble," said one aproned Betty when Basilio played the game for the third time in a week.

"I just bought a flying saucer off of Vernon," winked Basilio. "If the Greek fires you we'll go for a ride."

There was plenty of trouble for Basilio across the summer of 1989, the season opening on Memorial Day with the arrival of Nieves—both kin and stranger, all of nineteen years old—at the small house Basilio shared with Grandpop near the Patapsco.

A distant cousin, she landed on short notice and ushered in a delightful, more difficult, and eventually dangerous trudge through the humidity and thunderstorms of Baltimore in July and August. From her first glass of wine in the backyard with the old Spaniard (barefoot, the hem of her only pair of pants wet from the garden hose), Nieves turned Macon Street upside down.

Basilio moved in with Grandpop without asking nearly a year ago. Almost all of the artist's battles with the old man evaporated when he brought a woman to the kitchen table for cake and coffee. Which was fine with the *antiguo caballo fuerte* until the knives came out.

Many were prettier, few were smarter, and none half as seductive as Nieves, more alluring with each stone she skipped across the shrinking pool of Grandpop's life, charming a house cat that smiled like a young Tom.

"*No hay trabajo en España, Tío,*" she said, licking icing from the back of a fork. "I saved money to visit you washing dishes for my father."

All the while Basilio filled notebooks with every move she made, ear lobes to ankle bones.

•

About six weeks after moving in with Grandpop and Basilio, Nieves began stealing clothes from unlocked cars, wearing the stuff that moved her and selling the rest at vintage stores and junk shops.

Her earrings—bolls of Spanish gold which she had managed to hold onto from Vigo to Madrid to Marrakesh—soon followed and she began spending time with the young mother across the alley, a child whose husband said they didn't have the money to plant a garden but bought himself a set of golf clubs to get ahead in the world. Nieves befriended Elisabeth with a tomato seedling in a milk carton.

Basilio knew his cousin and the girl across the alley were

together somehow; Nieves and Elisabeth together in a way that Basilio had not been since he began dating the girl who would become his wife when Jimmy left Plains for Washington. He knew it like he knew every color possesses a numerology unto itself, the way he did not know that the spiritual world has its own system of justice. [Though he would one day soon.]

Standing before an upstairs window in the back of the house late one night, he watched as Nieves was transfigured beneath the street light in the alley before slipping inside E's basement door. Downstairs on the daybed, Grandpop was invigorated by the *torrijas* Nieves had cooked that morning, wine and sugar and bread and energy to shine a pair of shoes he hadn't worn in a decade before curling toward the wall to sleep.

What did Nieves give Basilio besides a stomach ache and ill-advised dreams?

A sense of being in Spain though he'd never been, a transcendence of time and place he tried to understand but never felt from the stories he'd heard from Grandpop all his life, the stories he'd begun to paint after moving in. It was a just-beyond-the-fingertips quality halved in Basilio's father out in the suburbs and watered down to two-bits in Basilio, a Beatles-on-Sullivan cul-de-sac kid with an Old World name so ornate that his friends had been calling him Ringo since the first grade.

But when Nieves so much as laid an anchovy on a cracker, the narrow rowhouse was perched on a Galician hillside far above the fishing boats of Vigo, the city which Grandpop had left by stage coach more than sixty years earlier.

Basilio was convinced it had something to do with smell, the way Grandpop's vestibule always carried the scent of old keys and coffee grounds boiled in a sauce pan. If a butter knife oily with fish could do that, how much more might...

He opened the window to smell the hot night air—the dank harbor mixed with black pepper, the blouse Nieves arrived in at his nose—staring at the door across the alley as it closed behind her, wondering...

"What do they know that I don't?"

•

From the time of crayons, Basilio's art existed at the exclusion of everything but girls who enjoyed looking at what he drew.

After his mother died, he never made a bed again and when he was exhausted (constantly during the Summer of Nieves), the cot in his studio down the hall from the window where he spied on Elisabeth was his pallet.

One Basilio dying downstairs, the other Basilio a floor above with the knowledge that most things cannot kill you without your cooperation. Two hardheads.

Tired, frayed, broke, and in deep on both sides of the alley, Basilio should have spent less time dreaming in his sketch book and more painting signs, the work that allowed him to put groceries in Grandpop's 1948 Westinghouse refrigerator, a tank with more steel in it that the piece-of-shit Chevette Elisabeth drove in carpool.

The best advice his mother ever gave him, back in the third grade when he began making noise about becoming an artist: "Learn your letters..."

It took a while but he'd done it; became a one-man typography shop, a bread and butter skill too often set aside in his desire for cake.

Forget painting crabs on the sides of seafood trucks, once Nieves arrived Basilio's work took a dive for the absurd, away from the native narratives of Caitlin and headlong into the carnivals of Miro.

His first leap—from Crayola to Faber-Castell—took place on the curb in front of Grandpop's house in 1967, the first of many Summers of Love on Macon Street, a little kid teaching himself depth and shading by trying and failing and trying again to sketch the identical houses and their steps of marble across the street.

From there he moved to watercolor, concentrating on the

Crown, Cork & Seal building a block away from Grandpop's house when Grandmom was still alive, sitting cross-legged at Foster and Lehigh in the rattling behemoth's last year of production.

How to make the freight cars grinding past the bottle cap factory look like they were moving?

More failure, more hours, comforting himself when it got too hard by using felt tipped pens to render a stray soda cap—ALMOND SMASH—with the precision of a laser.

Now, agitated in the extreme—lush oils of the alleys of Crabtown oxidizing as Nieves made friends where those alleys ended in sewer grates—Basilio's work took a turn for the Big Top.

"No," said Nieves when Grandpop asked if there was work for young people in Villamayor de Boullosa, the village where his parents met.

"Never," said Basilio, fingering the brim of his Orioles' cap when Nieves asked if he'd ever thought of moving to Europe to paint.

"Soon," said Elisabeth when Nieves asked when she would accept her invitation to disappear.

The circus was in town, Basilio's new work the absurd response to the absurdities that followed Nieves to Macon Street and the vigor her presence awakened in Grandpop.

He never knew that his grandfather butchered a live turkey in the basement every Thanksgiving—a holiday the Spaniard did not fully understand—did not know that his grandmother once lost her grip on a guillotined bird and it ran around splattering blood on the whitewashed walls.

But he knew seduction when it squeezed and was stunned by how easily Nieves made herself at home in the house Grandpop had bought on a laborer's wage at the shipyard when Basilio's father was an infant, before World War II opened up the skilled trades at Bethlehem Steel.

Stunned and too self-absorbed to remember that he'd never asked Grandpop *if* he could move in.

Basilio opened the jalousie storm door (a sticker on a glass

slat reading LIVE BETTER/WORK UNION) to let Nieves in and
paid the cab that brought her from the bus station: Casablanca
to London to New York to Baltimore with a dollar in her pocket.

Carrying her cracked leather suitcase upstairs by its broken
strap, he was so viscerally unnerved by this stranger (hung over,
not quite four hours sleep) that he dropped her bag at the top of
the stairs and threw up in the bathroom sink, the indecipherable
Spanish of his Prado heroes floating up from the kitchen.

"*Todo el mundo envía su amor, Tío Basilio...*"

Spanish spoken once more on Macon Street!

As it only did when Grandpop had the rare visitor; his long-
dead wife from a part of Italy called western Pennsylvania, his
children solidly American and his namesake grandson claiming
the neighborhood as a nation unto itself.

Rattled to the point of nausea as this distant cousin brought
Grandpop back to life, the two of them getting right down to it—
Mi padre es un hombre enojado—Basilio hacked up the phlegm of
that morning's coffee-on-an-empty stomach in a porcelain sink
brown with Rothko rust.

In one of the few reviews written about his work, a critic from
D.C. wrote: "...Boullosa finds deep pain in the good humor of his
provincial subjects and absurdity in the grief of neighborhoods
he calls 'The Holy Land.' Taken together, his work is a mural of
anguish..."

As Grandpop liked to say when the truth was as plain as his
pointy nose: "You ain't just-a kidding."

Basilio stifled an urge to rifle her satchel.

Where will she sleep?

Upon moving in with his namesake (barging in by degrees,
one day a tube of cadmium yellow, the next a tube of toothpaste),
Basilio set out to stanch his wounds by working like he believed
he could not while married, struggling to paint the peripheral
histories of Baltimore through the wide lens of family.

But it was not his work that blew up life with the woman he'd
met when they were teenagers, with whom he had a daughter and

hoped—in moments of delusion well beyond what was about to take place at Grandpop's, Nieves a time-bomb in the guise of a salve—to one day have a son.

HAH!

Basilio sketched his way through every misfortune that crossed his path but he'd never painted the way he'd always hoped he would, believed (still) that he could. At his mother's funeral, a high school freshman, he'd fidgeted in the pew, sketching the design of the altar linens on the back of her Mass card. But nothing had yet come ashore like the girl downstairs explaining to Grandpop not only that Spain had changed with "*la movida*," but from Valencia to Valenzuela, "*Es un mundo nuevo tío Basilio.*"

His sketchbooks were filling up quickly now along with note-books busy with descriptions of Elisabeth, over whose roof his "Flying Beatle" John Lennon doll had disappeared before she was born—drawings of her husband (always from behind), her chil-dren (blonde-haired ragamuffins), the shovel they played with, and the rosebush she couldn't keep alive.

Elisabeth, not far from a ragamuffin herself, beautiful like an advertisement for Ivory soap; Nieves a walking narcotic, funny looking in a pinched, *gallego* way; Basilio unable to find his ass with both hands and a map.

Within moments of Nieves' appearance on Macon Street, life began to spin too fast for the whir of a Super-8 camera much less Basilio's skinny brushes. Before she fell from the same sky into which John had vanished, Grandpop's life in the New World was a still life becoming stiller by the day, a cart of apples going soft in the sun.

["Can you paint such a woman, Basilio? A *manzana* cored and filled with raisins and cinnamon and baked in the oven?"]

The elder Basilio had fled a medieval village in the province of Pontevedra in 1921 just to be able to eat every day. Where he came from, you worked all day, went to bed hungry, and the only fat guy in town was the village priest.

To hear Nieves tell it not much had changed. Basilio didn't

know. He'd never been, had no means to go.

But in the United States, said Grandpop, if you worked you were guaranteed a heaping plate when the whistle blew: liver and onions with mashed potatoes and gravy, apple pie for dessert, hot coffee and beer. He chased that promise at 17 with a shovel, muscling coal into the boiler of a tramp steamer that stopped in Baltimore every four months and one night left the Pratt Street piers without him.

[A month before Nieves arrived, Basilio painted Elisabeth's backyard onto a piece of plywood he found in the alley, imagining the shovel her children played with was the one Grandpop had used to shovel coal, his un-calloused hands not knowing the difference between a flat head coal shovel and an oval garden shovel.

The fresh carrot laid before Basilio the younger did not pivot on the blue plate special: If you study hard and don't fuck up you can be anything you want.

At 17, Basilio was skipping past those same Pratt Street piers (once brisk with men and cargo, then ruined and rotted, now a shopping mall) waiting for a postage stamp of LSD to melt on his tongue.

Basilio knew that his Italian grandmother was dying at Johns Hopkins but he didn't believe that particular day would be the day; the kid for whom she'd made buttered toast every Sunday morning while Grandpop shaved at the same concrete stationary tubs where he once slaughtered turkeys was blind in the glare of synthetic epiphanies...

About to make his own decisions without aid of counsel yet ignorant that every one of the greats paid for their pictures with their lives, Basilio saw that all the material he'd ever need danced before him from one side of the Patapsco to the other.

A teenage Hopper all hopped-up, he walked clockwise and counter-clockwise around the harbor rim until the cheap drug wore off enough for him to take his place with the family at Grandmom's bedside.

"Don't get lost," his father had been telling him for a week. "It's going to be soon."

But didn't say that it was that morning that the person he loved most in the world would succumb to non-alcoholic cirrhosis while he chewed the inside of his cheek raw and stared at bronze dapples of sunshine across brown water.

Was that her spirit gliding by on its way to the other side?

He reached out for it and a cop asked if he was all right.

"Yes."

"You need help?"

"No."

"Then get the hell away from the edge and stop talking to yourself."

Nieves also worked for her daily bread—either the hustle of finding what she needed or the torture that she wasn't going to get it in the moment, the latter always the more difficult. She'd left her father's house more than a year ago, swept up in *La Movida* that took her to Madrid where she learned the hard way that if you let the Devil ride, that horny prick is going to drive.

While sweating it out in Morocco—somebody said they knew where Paul Bowles lived, somebody else robbed the wrong person of the wrong shit—Nieves became besotted with the idea of visiting relatives in the United States with whom she was barely acquainted and had never met, an addict in withdrawal somehow convinced there might be less heroin in Baltimore than North Africa.

In this fancy, she vowed to become an artist and knew from long-ago Christmas cards that a cousin in Baltimore a generation older than her was one as well. Nodding in the Moroccan sunshine, she decided to paint a swarm of Barbary flies looking for a place to land.

Does the world really need another Spanish painter?

Just a visit, said the letter that arrived from Ceuta less than twenty-four hours before she did, "*solamente hola y adios.*"

And she wasn't far from wrong.

Grandpop had chosen Baltimore with even less care than Nieves did, getting drunk and passing out in a Spanish seamen's club near the docks, missing his ship and finding new work with a shovel made of U.S. steel.

The elder Basilio was the youngest brother of Nieves's great-grandfather, long dead. Basilio wasn't sure what kin that made this young woman to him and he didn't want to know, a familiar cloven hoof hard on the pedal from the moment he met her at the storm door embossed with an aluminum "B."

Throwing water on his face upstairs, looking in the mirror and unsure what was looking back at him, Basilio heard Grandpop opening the metal cabinet in the kitchen to set a plate of stale cookies alongside of juice glasses for wine.

The old man finally had company, real company.

•

The pageant that Basilio spattered across the wallpaper of Grandmom and Grandpop's old bedroom on the second floor—Miro mixed with chestnut leaves and Mad Dogs and Englishmen (a song for you, E; a song for *YOU*, Nieves)—glittered like harlequins leaping through starlight.

Nieves did not know Leon Russell from Leonard Cohen but she'd seen plenty of Caballero Joan in her wanderings.

"At his house, I was," said Nieves her first time in the studio. "*Su museo está en una colina llamada Montjuïc.*"

Basilio nodded, wondering if a long walk around the harbor to the American Visionary Art Museum on Key Highway—this is where Grandpop dropped anchor before your Civil War, he'd tell her, this is where Frank Zappa's grandfather had a barbershop—might be a match for her memories.

If the *Tierra Santa* of his imagination was powerful enough to spark new ones in her.

But that was not the kind of walks that Nieves was taking. "Invite your friend for dinner," said Basilio after he'd seen her cross the alley in the middle of night. "Grandpop will love it."

A month of crossing from one narrow yard to another—passion, promises, and threats ("I don't like her, Elisabeth, I never liked the old man, and I don't like his faggot grandson.")—before the map unfolded toward the inevitable.

Take a left at the Spanish café famous for its *txipiroi*, cross the underpass by the old Crown building, and keep walking until you see two-legged trash with "WHITE POWER!" inked across the pale fat of their backs and smell chili.

Duck into the alley behind G&A Hot Dogs—derelicts, dumpsters, and dope—and cop a couple of vials, unaware that the Greek who owns the diner pays an off-duty detective to drink coffee and take pictures of everything that happens from a second-floor window.

[Just like you, Basilio; just as defensible, just as wrong.]

"That's the guy," said Farantos, taking a peek as he brought the two-years-to-a-pension public servant a plate of dogs with the works. "The piece of shit leaning up against Miss Gertie's fence..."

"Who's the girl?" asked the cop, lusting with chili sauce and mustard on his chin as he clicked away: rats and bust-out drunks and mutants getting the evil eye from Gert as she hung her Kon Tiki drawers on the line.

"Who knows?" shrugged Farantos as the young woman in the alley rolled up a torn, long-sleeved work shirt that an old Spaniard wore at the steel mill in the days when anyone in Baltimore with a strong back and a working alarm clock could earn enough to eat like a King.

The cop with the camera waited until she stuck it in—Nieves Boullosa Vega shooting dope for the first time in Estados Unidos —before calling the wagon.

When it arrived, the veteran street junkies and corner boys left Nieves with three balloons of dope (they looked like gumballs, red and yellow) and Elisabeth's wedding band on the ring finger of her left hand, an item soon to be listed on a police report

along with a description of a young foreign national with puncture scars on her arms.

•

Nieves en route to the austere labyrinth of Central Booking
and Grandpop asleep at the kitchen table, forehead in the crook
of an arm upon newsprint as he dreamt of a Galician childhood in
the reign of Alfonso, back in the West Virginia of Spain where he
once carved a bicycle out of pine.

Elisabeth crying at the sink in dishwater up to the elbows, the
cuckold raging behind her: "What do you mean you don't know
where your wedding rings are?"

An electrical storm in the young mother's brain—"Why didn't
she just ask me for the money?"—as Basilio paced his studio, the
storm crossing the alley and falling through the hole in Grandpop's roof: "Find her..."

He yanked the tarp covering the hole in the ceiling to inspect
his completed work, the room flooding with unforgiving light as
Solstice spun toward the 4th of July, no review as harsh as he ap-
praised hundreds of hours of sweat, feeling helpless and stupid.

[*"Please find her..."*]

Shades of green depicting Grandpop in his garden; a rectangular canvas of a beat-up delivery truck ornamented with Farsi
lettering and primitive drawings of Daffy Duck licking ice cream;
the bottle cap factory in silent conversation with the railroad
tracks that have kept it company for a hundred years.

Sail cloth stretched to the limit for love but not commerce.

"What do you mean she a-didn't come home?" demanded
Grandpop as Basilio tried to ransom a distant cousin he didn't
even know he had thirty-three days earlier. Showing her his work
that first night, he explained in ridiculous Spanish, "The cala-
mares ink bubbles up...*trémulo*, deep green, almost black."

"*Chipirones*," she laughed, reaching toward Pepper Plant
Portrait No. 4, Basilio gently taking her wrist before her fingers

touched the image.

"I cooked them for Grandpop and tried painting with the ink."

"*Repugnante*," said Nieves, her laugh filling the studio at the time and filling it now.

Basilio was in love with her—fucked-up, lick turpentine off the work bench, and listen to the same song forty times in a row LOVE—stung in a way that signaled he was not with Elisabeth. On the wall above the row of pepper portraits he'd daubed a line she'd said the on first day beneath the hole in the ceiling.

"It is Morocco that opens the eyes to color..."

Securing the tarp, he left by the kitchen door with a cup of cold coffee and walked into E's yard for the first time, picking up the shovel as he made for the basement door in case her husband answered.

She sobbed: "If I had any lawyer friends I wouldn't be here."

Basilio dropped the shovel and she quickly tossed him the keys to her car as Mr. Assistant Manager rushed up behind his wife to slam the door in his face.

•

Basilio parked a block away from the old City Jail—a 19th century castle of black stone at the corner of Van Buren and Madison, the old cells turned to offices where mothers and grandmothers and girlfriends and bondsmen and attorneys and lovers and predators and preachers sought the release of those charged with violating the laws of the State of Maryland.

High above the 1859 turrets loomed the bland, beige monolith of modern prisons built around it, a penal colony that had long taken over the near east side of downtown, a cranny here and there for a carry-out or a body shop or the rare old-timer who had owned their home forever and was only leaving feet first.

Don't all the great cities put their penitentiaries downtown?

Just as entrenched: a tent city beneath the Expressway where, as Basilio walked toward Central Booking, he caught snatches of conversation between the homeless and the hopeless in the Catholic Worker soup line.

They were all yakking about the same thing: How a couple of hand-cuffed prisoners being unloaded had gotten away when a "Mighty Good" bread truck lost control near the loading dock and rammed the jail wagon, two dead on the scene, two mangled like rag dolls, and two running for their lives.

"Whole gang of 'em runnin' like cockroaches in the kitchen when you turn on the light."

"Naw, man, wasn't but two or three."

"That white girl walkin' slow, just mindin' her bidness while they chased everybody else."

"Where she got the dog to cover up them cuffs—fuckin' brilliant!"

"I seen 'er—mmm, mmmmm, mmmmmmmm!"

The choppers were overhead now, circling, circling, circling as Basilio yelled over the din: "What white girl?"

The men glanced over and turned back to their conversation. Basilio took out $10 from the roll he'd managed to put together and asked again, "What white girl?"

"Don't go inside to ask," counseled a female bus driver waiting to visit her nephew. "If she got away they'll keep you for collateral."

The homeless man closest to Basilio reached for the ten-spot and Basilio pulled it away. "What did she look like?"

"You know," said another guy, stalling. "Young girl..."

Basilio put the money back in his pocket and headed back to Elisabeth's car where he was stopped by a middle-aged woman leaving the soup kitchen.

[He could always tell, somehow, which ones had once been in the convent. This Samaritan wore her gray hair cropped short with a white Fordham t-shirt and a simple wooden cross. Had the icon been a whistle, she'd have looked for all the world like a gym teacher.]

Pointing west toward the Washington Monument, she said,

"Dark hair past her shoulders, large brown eyes, torn jeans, old work shirt."

"And a dog?" asked Basilio.

"A small dog," said the woman.

"Thank you."

"Good luck."

Driving in circles—dipping in and out of the housing projects that ringed downtown—Basilio saw a future that would not blossom until the last years of his life. With both eyes peeled for Nieves, a third began cataloguing the bare walls of abandoned buildings as he moved deeper into the 'hood, blank canvases of red brick waiting for the wrecking ball between seek and ye shall find.

More than forty-seven-thousand boarded up and crumbling buildings—former homes, corner pharmacies, shirt factories, and churches—to choose from. Upon the right one (not today and probably not tomorrow and maybe never if he didn't stop re-arranging the furniture in other people's lives), Basilio would paint his masterpiece.

Deep in the west side now, well beyond anything he recognized, Basilio feared that Nieves might have been safer en route to deportation; prayed that she'd already found her way back home with Elisabeth there to welcome her with bolt cutters and a kiss.

Passing the ruins of Schmidt's Bakery on Laurens Street, Basilio stared up at the shattered and rusting skylights to conjure the mural that would cap an improbable career.

A mystic in a torn blue work shirt with black hair past her shoulders?

Not her.

His own reflection in the dark circles beneath the diary of a young girl.

Basilio's dreams were ludicrous.

If a good word is worth one golden coin bearing the profile of a princess, then silence equals two.

You think you know, but you don't know...

•

The day after Nieves escaped and Basilio drove in larger circles around the city smoking a joint and drinking beer, Elisabeth's husband swung open the wire gate to Grandpop's yard so
hard that it fell from its rusted hinges.

A born-again nut-bag in righteous anger, he strode into
Grandpop's yard like Saint Jerome the Thunderer in heat for a
reckoning. The cuckold kicked over a trash can that woke the old
man from a string of catnaps—had a doll from Iberia really been
living with him or was it just a dream?—but before he reached the
kitchen door Grandpop had taken his piece-of-junk .22 from the
china cabinet where he kept pictures of actresses cut from the TV
pages.

The old man fired before the tough guy reached for the door-
knob, just another ignored gunshot in Baltimore that missed
its mark. Running back across the alley and into the basement
through the door Nieves had passed a hundred times in half as
many days, he shouted up the stairs to the kitchen for Elisabeth
to start packing because they were moving "far, far away."

When Basilio returned, he parked E's car in front of her house
with the key in the ignition, walked down the alley without looking left or right, and, reaching Grandpop's back door, saw the
shattered transom, glad that he had painted a picture of it above
his grandfather's sleeping head before it was destroyed.

[Basilio had loved that transom since childhood, old safety
glass made of hexagonal chicken wire; the number "627" across
it from a hand-made stencil. He saved the frame with the hope of
using it for an as-yet unmade portrait of Nieves.]

The next morning, Basilio took the pistol from the cabinet
(it had haunted him upon first moving in with Grandpop, spoke
to him each night as he tried to fall asleep) and on another fu-
tile search for his cousin dropped it into twenty feet of water at

the end of Clinton Street before walking the three miles home through the alley that ran behind the hot dog joint.

After the first drug dealer called the house, Basilio turned the ringer off on the side of Grandpop's black rotary phone beneath the blue deco clock on the wall. The 1950s Chesapeake & Potomac technology was a real hunk of hardware—you could bludgeon someone to death with the receiver—and the house fell silent, the old Spaniard assuming that people simply stopped calling.

•

No one wanted the paintings that Nieves had inspired during her brief stay on Macon Street and he quickly and cheaply sold every canvas anyone had ever expressed interest in during his failed attempts to find her. Which left him with paintings no one wanted.

In the months that followed, Basilio began a new series based on the stories Nieves had told him, tales that stung him the way a 14-year-old girl sticks pins in her thighs just to know she's alive.

Basilio hung them on old nails so they could be read left to right on the Miro wall below the hole in the ceiling, a small arc that stretched a bit closer to justice each day.

Hicimos el amor.

Every time.

Nosotros lloramos.

When it was time to go.

Ella orino en mi mano.

Once ...

NINE INNINGS IN BALTIMORE

Agitated, so frustrated and angry his skin itched, Basilio left the house on foot and an empty stomach a little after 6:00 p.m. He was looking for reefer. If not that, booze and someone new. Trouble enough to last through to morning.

Something/Anything.

"I might not be much," he heard himself say, walking along the railroad tracks that ran from the bottle cap factory down to the coal yards of the industrial harbor. "But I'm all I think about."

How sick Basilio had become of Basilio. He watched a coal car on the tracks tip its load onto the wharf and wished he could do the same with himself: dump the shit and roll away clean and empty.

It was August 27, 1990, a night he'd remember to his distant grave.

Uptown, the Orioles were getting ready to play the Yankees at Memorial Stadium. There, twenty years earlier, he'd seen Dave McNally hit the only grand slam by a pitcher in World Series history. Basilio had cared at the time (deliriously so, as only a 12-year-old can) and it was a memory he'd committed to canvas more than once. But he didn't think much about it anymore.

He was a broke-ass artist who painted signs and houses and cartoons of monkeys eating banana splits on the side of ice-cream trucks to stay just one step behind instead of two. And hadn't given a shit about baseball—or much of anything, even his palette and the hole he'd cut in the roof of his studio—for a long time.

Not since Trudy left, Grandpop died, and Nieves disappeared.

A crusty, almost-empty bottle of Fundador (Spanish turpentine, a holdover from the days when Grandpop still had friends who vis-ited) was in the basement back home, gathering dust behind a flour sifter. Basilio wished he'd brought it along. Finish it off and smash the bottle against the rails.

He and Nieves had walked these tracks together in the first days after she'd arrived on short notice from Spain, making the last few months of Grandpop's life a miracle with food and stories from a village the old man had left some seventy years before.

Basilio—for whom she'd made life a nightmare—would al-ways be grateful for that.

And then he and Nieves and Elisabeth walked down the Ches-sie line—Elisabeth skipping across the ties, Nieves balancing on the rails—as he led them to a handful of waterfront dives that hadn't been torn down yet, places he could trade some lettering —OPEN DAILY—for a cold beer and a ham sandwich.

And then Nieves and Elisabeth started walking by themselves and Basilio stayed home.

"Grandpop... tell me about playing soccer in the land of base-ball."

"*Donde esta Nieves?*" he answered. "Turn off the light and lock the door when you go out."

There was a time, when he still drew with No. 2 pencils and crayons, that Basilio could have told you about every Oriole from the owner who ran a local brewery to the groundskeeper who raised tomatoes beyond the foul poles.

One evening after his parents had gone to bed, he grabbed the phone book instead of his homework and—with a patience that now failed him—looked up the name of every player and coach on the team.

Eventually, he reached Mrs. George Bamberger, wife of the longtime pitching coach, and blurted: "I think George should tell Earl to use Moe more." Mrs. Bamberger said she would pass the tip along. After their third conversation in a week, she politely told Basilio not to call anymore.

A few years after that (goodbye crayons, hello blonde hash), he was outside of the stadium with a bunch of friends from Trans-figuration High, all of them stoned before an afternoon game. He saw a kid about his age wearing a No. 7 jersey with the name "BE-LANGER" across the shoulders headed toward the good seats.

Basilio had always been quick, could remember things and spit them back with a little mustard. For the longest time (before he got to the part in life where the answers were more than mere fact) this passed for being smart.

"Belanger means warrior in medieval French," he told the kid.

"No," said the boy. "It's from the French *boulangerie*—it means bakery."

"Are you sure?"

"Positive. He's my father."

[Mark Belanger, a chain-smoking shortstop who won eight consecutive gold gloves across Basilio's childhood—a thin and flawless fielder known as "The Blade"—died of lung cancer at age 54.]

Tonight, Basilio had banged the heavy receiver of Grandpop's rotary phone—black steel and Bakelite, Eastern 7-5254—against the kitchen wall, chipping the plaster, rolling the dice for nearly an hour without getting anyone. None of his guy friends had pot or Valium or a little bit of this or some of that.

[It was Nieves who was the addict because Nieves used nee-dles.]

And none of the women who'd been orbiting Macon Street since Basilio had moved in with Grandpop were home or inter-ested or able to lather up enough hogwash to get away. Up until tonight (Monday, a tough day for shenanigans), there'd always been another song on the broken record.

If a man answers, hang up...

Basilio veered off the tracks, passed the ruins of the Standard Oil refinery (back in the 1940s, his mother's grandfather had lost a foot there), and scuffled through the side streets and alleys to-ward Miss Bonnie's bar on the edge of the gentrified harbor.

It was hot and window air conditioners dripped condensation

onto small squares of backyard concrete. A woman with a rag around her head used a hose and a broom to sweep trash down the alley where it would fall into the sewer grate and make its way down the Patapsco to the Chesapeake Bay.

Several miles to the north, up on 33rd Street, "play ball" was about to ring out behind a great coliseum of brick and limestone, a memorial to the dead from America's World Wars upon which hung three-hundred-and-seventeen handmade stainless steel letters.

"Time will not dim the glory of their deeds..."

Trudy was going to the game with her father and India, the daughter born to her and Basilio when the wheels were coming off. Approaching the stadium, his granddaughter's hand in his, Trudy's father pointed to the wall of words and said, "Pop made those letters."

"All by yourself?"

"Almost," said Pop, who liked Basilio but was not upset that Trudy was no longer married to him. It bothered him more that his daughter and granddaughter were living in the city by themselves.

Sometime tonight, between the first pitch and the last out, Basilio would become a father again and India would have a half-brother she wouldn't meet until she had children of her own.

By then, Memorial Stadium would be long demolished, newer wars—some of them permanent—were remembered in silence before ballgames and lost to the wind were most of the letters Pop had made with twenty other men.

Big Ben McDonald was on the mound for the Birds tonight against New York. By the time he threw the first pitch, Basilio was well into his second beer at Miss Bonnie's. And you didn't have to read the sports page to know that the Yankees were cocksuckers and always would be.

•

After being fired from every job he'd ever had [from sweeping floors to the docks where even the longshoremen's union couldn't save him], Ted the Clown's vocation had boiled down to two suspect skills: bumming drinks at Miss Bonnie's Elvis Bar and putting curses on people (usually Bonnie's customers, although neighbors and relatives were also fair game) who had told him to go fuck himself.

"That clown is bad for business," said Bonnie. But she never barred him and her new clientele, young people from outside of the neighborhood coming into the city to drink and carry-on, expected to see Ted on a corner stool, white face and grease paint and a shot of cheap brandy between soiled thumb and forefinger of a white-gloved hand.

["Clowns always wear gloves," said Ted. "Even Mickey Mouse."]

Though Bonnie didn't believe in Ted's horseshit, dust and feathers, she was pleasantly surprised not long ago—"Damn near stupefied," she said—when the evil eye the imp put on Old Lady Kasha led to the bitter invalid's death.

Kasha's tiny rowhouse was next door to Bonnie's and Ted stood outside of it on the sidewalk, fixing his rheumy eyes on the sack of spoiled potatoes in the hospital bed on the other side of a storm window and chanting: "Trizzle, trazzle, drozzle, drome, time for this one to go home!"

Poof!

So long, Kasha.

Good riddance to a dry and vengeful stick of Krakow wood who had outlived all of her relatives and few friends; no one happier than Bonnie Sobotka, who lived atop the tavern that was her livelihood.

"I'll be goddamned if she didn't just shrivel up and die," said the barmaid. "Like Ted dropped a house on her."

The trick ("it's all in the timing," said Ted) was followed a week later by a miracle with which the clown had nothing to do: An unexpected gift to an unlikely recipient, Basilio Boullosa struck sober while sipping an eight-ounce draught of Old German in the shadow of the King.

"Look at that," said Basilio.

"Look at what?" said Bonnie.

In a far corner, a man was listening to the ballgame on a 9-volt transistor, the radio next to his beer and New York ahead of Baltimore 1-to-nothing.

"Yeah," said Bonnie. "Don Joe, in here every night, same spot, five beers and he goes home when the game's over."

"Above his head," said Basilio.

Above Don Joe's head: An oil painting of a ballplayer in a flea-market frame, one of the few images in the bar not of Elvis; a pitcher with a handlebar moustache and baggy gray knickers throwing a ball skewered with forks toward home plate.

A forkball!

Ha-ha-ha!

The work of a longtime regular named Ronnie Rupert, a housepainter who'd lived across the street from the saloon all of his sixty-two years. Rupert liked Basilio and when he wasn't holding forth on baseball, they talked about art.

Basilio was transfixed by Rupert's work, wondered why others could drink and get high successfully—wasn't the proof in the paint?—and he could not.

"Look Bon," he said, directing her to pay attention to an image she never gave much mind. "See how it looks like the forks are spinning with the ball. I'd give anything to be able to do that?"

"Anything?"

Basilio shook his head, sipped his beer. In the backyard kiddie pool that is Crabtown, everyone has peed in the water.

"You're better than him," said Bonnie.

"Maybe when I was a boy," he said, no longer able to ignore a certainty closing in since he moved in with Grandpop.

Living with Trudy wasn't the problem nor was the obligations of fatherhood or the fact that there are only twenty-four hours in a day.

"I smell a rat," said Grandpop at breakfast one morning. "And

I think I'm looking at him."

Bonnie leaned across the bar. "What's eatin' you, hon. You ain't been right all summer. Where's all your little girlfriends?"

"I don't know Miss Bon. Everything is gray."

"If you don't, I do," said Bonnie.

Basilio pushed his glass toward Bonnie for a refill but she didn't move until he looked up and held her gaze. Taking his glass off the bar, she told him something she'd never told anyone in fifty years of serving booze. Opinions were not good for business but Bonnie had never loved anyone—not her kids nor any of her five husbands—as much as she loved the mixed-up, thirty-something man with paint on his pants.

"You're an alcoholic."

•

Basilio sits in an empty ball field a block from Bonnie's front door, a new creature unrecognizable to himself. Boullosa without booze, artist sans sativa. Less than half-an-hour into a sober ride that would last (one step forward, two steps back) the rest of his life.

Above him, bright stars. Clarity and wonder and the hint of a breeze off the harbor. Across the Avenue, a shape came into focus, a white pancake face shining beneath a streetlight.

"What's the score, Ted?" asked Basilio as the clown came closer.

"Here's the score," said Ted, fishing around in the folds of his dirty pajamas for one of Bonnie's pink bar napkins. "Call came in not two minutes after you left."

Bonnie's scrawl on the napkin: "She says it's important," followed by an out-of-state number.

A gnarled gonif in a goof-suit, Ted wasn't much taller than a cross-legged Basilio on the ground and, as the clown offered him a belt from his half-pint, Basilio saw himself floating above it all.

"No thanks."

"No?"

"Leave me alone, Ted."

•

Walking along Eastern Avenue toward downtown, Basilio shoved the napkin into the pocket of his white jeans [the ones with the 1970 World Series patch on them] and discovered a forgotten roach. He never forgot where a last stem or seed might be hiding yet somehow tonight, hurting, he'd had. He flicked it toward the curb and kept walking.

Some lucky bum might find it in the morning lit or it would be squirted down the gutter and into the sewer by an old woman with purple ankles, a broom, and a hose. Or lie there until the next thunderstorm.

If Trudy wasn't the problem and lack of talent wasn't the problem and Grandpop (who'd worked as a machinist at the shipyard for forty years without such worries) wasn't the problem then maybe, just maybe, Basilio was keeping company with the problem as he walked down the Avenue.

Wondering what he was going to do with himself, he hummed an old tune—"*I hope you never had 'em and I hope you never do...*"—when a dented gray Chevy compact pulled to the curb.

"Yo, Ringo, you a street walker now?"

"Officer Friendly," said Basilio. "Where you going?"

"Got a fresh one in Waverly."

"Near the Stadium?"

"Close enough to hear the roar of the crowd."

"Hop a ride?"

"Get in," said the detective, pushing open the dented passenger door. Basilio did and the cop pulled away as he struggled to yank the door closed.

Born the same year as Basilio, Zero Baubopolis was a star of stage and street. A police department phenom, he'd made detective in less than three years on the beat in East Baltimore, the same neighborhoods where he'd grown up.

Zero belonged to Baltimore's first family of clowns, both priests and fools, subtle and disciplined practitioners of the ancient art with roots in Greece. "The art was old when Egypt was young," the Baubopolis patriarch liked to say. "And we were there to perfect it."

Zero, his twin brother Xenos, and their siblings owned a storefront theater called the Clown Gymnasium in a block of restaurants two blocks from where Basilio lived alone, Grandpop now dead about five months and Nieves gone.

Zero lived above the theater where he worked out with weights, practiced yoga and Pilates, and gave private lessons to women of a certain age (some very young, others long broken) drawn to the muscular Greek with the purest of intentions: They wanted to make people happy.

The young meant it, other older ones had failed at making themselves happy so were trying something new.

Raised in the claustrophobic community of Greektown, the cop spoke with a faint accent, even though English was his first language. He showed his students how genuine whimsy could lower their blood pressure and improve their immune system.

"Working on anything good?" asked Zero, turning north on Patterson Park Avenue.

"I could use some work," said Basilio, who in the past had painted the inside of the Baubopolis storefront black for special performances and then white again once the show was over.

"Nothing better to do on a Monday night than come see a dead body?"

"Nope," said Basilio. "Thought I'd take in the game."

"The game? Half over, isn't it?"

As Zero searched for the play-by-play on the radio he stopped on news that Stevie Ray Vaughn had been killed that night in a Wisconsin helicopter crash, dead man's blues playing softly behind the correspondent's report.

"Damn," said Zero. "I heard he just got clean too."

"I prefer Johnny," said Basilio, staring out the window into Patterson Park where a dozen years earlier he and Zero had cut grass, Baubopolis eyeing up the bad guys he'd go on to arrest and Basilio learning the blues from a black supervisor who never traveled with less than one hundred cassette tapes and a straw hat.

"What?" asked Baubopolis.

"No disrespect," said Basilio quietly, "but I prefer Johnny Winter."

"Hard-headed Ringo," laughed the cop, turning for the stadium lights. "Always going his own way."

Zero pulled into the players' lot and badged his way right up to the turnstiles to let Basilio off.

"Aren't you going to be late?" asked the artist, thanking Zero as he got out of the car.

Baubopolis laughed, "They'll still be dead when I get there, ranchero."

•

The game's announced attendance was 24,589 with no one manning the gate when Basilio arrived with the Yankees batting in the top of the eighth. He walked in uncounted and climbed a concrete ramp to the cheap seats as centerfielder Roberto Kelly hit a home run to make it 3-to-0 New York.

His found his daughter with Trudy and Trudy's father in Section 34 of the upper deck. India sat with cotton candy, seeing Basilio first as Trudy and her father—a Sparrows Point steelworker with enough seniority to avoid lay-offs—spoke quietly at the end of the row.

"DADDY!" cried India "You made it!"

Trudy and her father looked toward Basilio as Wild Bill Hagy led the thinning crowd in a tepid O-R-I-O-L-E-S chant, the beer-bellied cabdriver contorting his body into the alphabet as the home team came to bat in the bottom of the eighth.

Basilio and Trudy had been separated for almost two years,

divorce just a signature away and a brief court appearance at which Basilio's presence was not necessary.

India scooted down the aisle to hug her father and he took the empty seat alongside of Trudy with his daughter on his lap. He said hello to his father-in-law and asked Trudy to go with him for a hot dog.

"Can I go?" asked India.

Trudy stood up with India ready to follow. Trudy's father gently reached out and held his granddaughter back.

"I'll bring you some cotton candy," said Basilio.

"No," said Trudy. "She's had enough."

In the tunnel leading to the concessions, a young vendor with Robert Plant hair gave Basilio a nod, raising an eyebrow in a way that said he was open for business. The guy sold hash in the bleachers and Basilio walked right past him. Turning to Trudy, he said, "I've changed."

"You showed up in the eighth inning."

"I'm different Trude," he said as they got in line. "Something happened."

"Well I hope it's for the better. She's going to need you."

"When hasn't she had me?"

And just like that, the old curtain came down. Trudy stepped to the counter, about to order when Basilio interrupted.

"Two hot dogs, two beers, and a cotton candy," said Basilio, handing the cashier money that would have been long gone at Bonnie's. He turned to Trudy with the tray of food and asked one last time.

"Please, I'm begging you, don't sign the papers."

Someone barked for them to keep the line moving and they stepped aside.

"I'm sorry," said Trudy. "Just watch the rest of the game with us."

Basilio handed the food and beers to the girl he'd known since they'd played Beatles records on his grandmother's front steps and disappeared into the concrete cavern that led to the street, the first strides in his five-mile walk back to those same steps accompanied by the applause greeting a worthless Mickey Tettleton double.

The night was hot as he walked east on 33rd Street. Passing the eighteen-foot tall statue of Martin Luther overlooking Lake Montebello, Basilio realized he wasn't angry like all the times before. Neither happy, nor unhappy or angry. Veering from the lake toward Clifton Park, a municipal golf course where duffers were sometimes robbed at gunpoint, he was aware of knowing things he did not upon leaving the house six hours earlier.

Things he wouldn't be able to explain to himself much less Trudy for years to come but one day would have the presence and clarity to share with their daughter. He was no longer what he once was yet aware of what he'd always been.

Tomorrow he would make two calls: One to India to see if she wanted to go to that night's game, just him and her rooting against the pinstriped devils. And one to the number on the napkin the clown had given him between first and second base on the Patterson Park infield.

AUNT LOLA

The gate to Aunt Lola's yard hung limp on broken hinges, closed with a piece of rope. Basilio let himself in from the alley and walked over cracked concrete to her back door. It was nearly dawn on Christmas Eve, stars fading into a gray, cloudy sky, a sea bag of gifts on his shoulder.

He paused before knocking, staring in as Lola moved around the kitchen in her housecoat, sipping coffee. She didn't hear him when he rapped lightly, so he watched a moment more.

Post-war metal cabinets thick with brown paint and wrinkled decals of horses; an old Oriole stove—a tank without a thermostat—next to a top-of-the-line Kenmore fridge, a mourning gift from Lola's kids when their father passed away the year before.

On the wall, next to a one-week-left-in-the-year calendar from Our Lady of Pompei, a studio portrait of the original Bombacci sisters—Mary, Stella, Anna, Francesca, and Amelia—unsmiling in old country sepia before dispersal to orphanages, servants' quarters, and, inevitably, America.

During the Great Depression—when being poor meant nothing more than not having money—the sisters had populated the alley with children, a score or more of first cousins that included Basilio's father, son of Francesca, and Lola, daughter of Anna.

Now, Basilio and Lola, whom he called aunt out of respect, were the only ones left in the 600 block of South Macon Street.

The rest were dead or scattered in a grass-is-greener hopscotch that began in an alley once known for homemade wine and rosebushes before skipping to Dundalk and then Rosedale and White Marsh and now out to the God-forsaken, subdivided pastures of Harford County.

Lola's children had tried for a year to get her out of the house and Basilio, who made ends meet painting seafood on the sides of refrigerated trucks and didn't own a car, sure wasn't hiking out to Fallston to celebrate Christmas Eve.

Lola came to the door and pulled the curtain, her face creased with lines he'd drawn a thousand times over, wisps of Francesca, gentle to the point of naiveté, alive on the other side of the glass. She squinted, recognized him, and unlocked the door as he plucked something from his bag, the satchel immediately lighter by half.

"Hey, hon," said Lola. "Whatchu doin' up so early?"

"Giving out presents," he said, stepping into the warmth of fresh coffee, dishwater, and oil heat. He held a heavy, long-handled cookie iron in front of her. "This one had your name on it."

In the long moment that Lola puzzled over the well-worn contraption, Basilio realized he hadn't been a boy for a very long time. And no one put out shallow, dime store dishes of celery dribbled with olive oil and black pepper before holiday meals anymore.

"What is it?"

"What is it?"

Lola felt around on top of the washing machine that stood between the door and the sink and found her eyeglasses.

"Good God," she said. "I ain't seen one of them in many a year."

As she poured coffee for him, Basilio opened the flat jaws of the pizzelle iron to show what was engraved there: The Miraculous Medal of Our Blessed Mother on one side and a busy weave of diamonds on the other.

Miraculous: A floral "M" in a constellation of petitions, the initial interwoven with a cross surrounded by twelve stars.

Twelve stars: a dozen men on the road sowing truth no one wants to hear.

Truth: spare parts and broken hearts in an East Baltimore kitchen nearly a hundred years after their ancestors had found warm beds, full plates, and simple work in the shadow of a great bottle cap factory.

"Where'd you get it, kid?"

"Where do you get anything in the Third World nation of Baltimore?" laughed Basilio. "From some dummy who didn't know what the hell it was."

He set the iron across a newspaper on the table, yesterday's headlines confirming his cynicism, and looked around the spotless rowhouse, Catholicism a lesser devotion than prayers said on your knees with a bucket and a scrub brush.

Aunt Lola didn't have a tree, but carols were playing on a plastic AM radio and she'd taped Christmas cards to the spokes of the banister in the middle room.

"What the hell am I gonna do with a pizzelle iron? Hang it on the wall."

And, just before Basilio could say that it wasn't a bad idea—hang it on the wall, put up a small shelf and light candles—something better occurred to him.

"Make pizzelles."

"I don't know, hon."

"How hard can it be, Aunt Lol?"

"I turned many a pizzelle iron, but one of the cousins picked up on the recipe, not me."

"No one wrote it down?"

"Didn't have to," she said. "So nobody did."

"We can do it," he said, drumming his fingers across the plastic tablecloth. "I watched 'em do it, you did it every year. Eggs, sugar, flour and butter, like everything else."

"Got plenty sugar," she said. "But baking powder, baking soda—I don't keep that stuff around no more."

"The store does," said Basilio, getting up to peek in the fridge, empty except for a small carton of milk, a big jug of water, and two meatballs in a dish of tomato sauce. An expensive night light.

"There's some vegetable oil in the cabinet," she said. "But the main thing..."

"...is the anise," said Basilio.

Lola moved to a roll top hutch, Pennsylvania Dutch stenciling on the lacquered wood, and found a crusty brown medicine bottle, bone dry.

"Don't let 'em give you extract, it's too weak," she said, handing him the bottle. "Oil of anise. Same as what you're holding."

Lola went for her change purse but Basilio was already at the door, a good year of selling tacky paintings to tourists behind him: Mr. Boh throwing a baseball, Mr. Boh scrubbing marble steps, Mr. Boh eating a pile of steamed crabs.

"Be right back," he said, picking up his sea bag on the way out the front door, counting the houses as he passed them, remembering who used to live in them.

Mr. Kugler, "the German" who made beer in his basement, put on lederhosen to hike in Patterson Park and was head chef at the bottle cap factory down by the railroad tracks when it employed a thousand people.

Miss Helen, a tough Polish lady who shucked oysters in cold packing houses on Boston Street, worked as hard as any man and would tell you without being asked, "We didn't have no women's lib in them days, we just worked..."

His grandparents' house was in the middle of the block and he remembered the Christmas Eve forty years earlier when he'd lost a flying Beatle doll—John—above these tarred roofs; a toy enjoyed for a moment before it disappeared into the cold night sky.

How he'd cried!

Never imagining that a couple of miles down the salty river would find him living on Macon Street the way his widowed grandfather had before him: alone.

Two blocks up, he hit Eastern Avenue and turned left toward the old Chessie underpass, built in 1930 when the factory was supplying millions upon millions of crimped, cork lined "crowns" to bottlers around the world. A train rolled by as he walked beneath the trestle and he stopped to absorb the feel of it, remembering stories of Depression era kids being sent to pick up loose coal to throw in pot-bellied stoves: cheap coal that burned dirty and every now and then blew up a house.

The train passed and he moved into the Highlandtown shopping district, reaching into his bag to give away a baseball cap—the mighty cartoon bird orange, freshly laundered and smiling—to a boy young enough to be happy about it; a repaired rosary to a Salvadoran woman pushing a stroller with two kids in it—he laid a little holiday Feliciano on her and she smiled—unloading everything he had in a short walk to DiPasquale's near the corner of Gough and Conkling.

Sometimes during this annual ritual, passing out unwrapped oddities that people would have stepped over if they hadn't been presented as gifts, he'd see the very thing he'd given away—a plastic action figure or a ball with a few bounces left in it, a redistribution of something more impossible than wealth—lying in the gutter alongside the spot where he'd offered it.

At DiPasquale, around the corner from the Zannino funeral home where his grandfather had lain, Basilio ordered a double espresso from the girl behind the deli counter and drank it down, his duffel no longer a St. Nick sack but a grocery bag as he grabbed what he needed and resisted the urge to linger.

At the register, he took out the anise bottle and asked if they could re-fill it for him, the way Lola said they did back when you got anise at the pharmacy. Studying the bottle like an Indian arrowhead, the cashier chuckled and handed it back to him with a clear, plastic bottle of anise, just as small and $5.95.

In Basilio's wake, someone was buying ricotta and someone was getting hauled out to a hearse. On an opposite corner, Mr. Stan was selling last minute inventory at his custom foam shop: pierced hearts and holly for the cemetery and twinkling lights for fake trees. One goes and the whole string goes out.

"Got it," said Basilio, walking back in the house without knocking.

The kitchen table was covered with wax paper and an empty

aluminum spaghetti pot sat on the counter. Aunt Lola was leaning up against the washing machine, counting on her fingers.

"I think I got it, too," she said. "It'll all come back when I start
working the dough."

She cracked a half-dozen eggs into the pot and tossed everything else in after them, pouring out a couple tablespoons of the
anise oil, Basilio holding the pot steady as she leaned over it with
an electric mixer, the beaters nicking the edges.

And then, she took a dab of the dough and fashioned a small
cross from it, sticking the icon to the back of the stove where
they'd see it as they worked.

"My mother always did that," she said. "For luck I guess."

Basilio turned a knob on the stove and put a match to the
front burner, the oven as old as the railroad underpass, bought at
Bolewicki's and already in the house for years when Lola moved
in on her wedding day.

The iron lay over the open flame—"good and hot," said Lola,
"it's gotta be good and hot"—and soon she was dropping small
balls of dough between the scored jaws. The first few were pale
prototypes; trial and error and an almost good one for every three
that weren't right at all.

"Let me try," said Lola, taking the iron and dipping under the
weight of it. "My God it's heavy."

Basilio held her wrists in his hands, they were soft and pudgy,
like the dough, and helped her turn the iron. They made a keeper
and flipped it onto the wax paper, the cookie flat and crisp and
light brown around the edges, the "M" raised in perfect legibility.

The day (she'd been up since three o'clock and couldn't get
back to sleep) had worn Lola out and she sat down, pooped.

"I'm gonna rest my eyes a little bit," she said, moving to the
couch in the front room, a crocheted pillow under her head. "Just
a couple minutes."

That minute was all it took for Basilio to get the ambidex-
trous hang of making the cookies by himself, as though the iron
and the dough were brushes in his hand: open, plop, squeeze

long enough to say a "Hail Mary," turn the iron, sing a verse of "God Only Knows," open, pluck, repeat, repeat, repeat as Aunt Lola breathed in the warm aroma, the licorice scent of the anise perfuming her dreams.

Awake, we recognize and remember the mystery of more than ten thousand smells through a thousand genes and a thousand receptors. They come together the way letters make words and words make sentences. Asleep, the gift multiplies and the receptors that told Lola pizzelles were piling up in the kitchen had bonded in the shape of a teardrop.

Science promises that in the future, smell may be restored to those who've lost it; a day when appetite, fear, and longing will be given back to people unable to follow their nose.

Until that day...two dozen pizzelles on the table, three dozen, four.

As pictures moved in Lola's gray head—glimpses of a trucking company at Foster and Oldham when it was a pasture, the day when her mother unwittingly burned up the rent money by hiding it from her husband in the oven—Basilio turned the iron and stared into the alley.

Out there in the weeds and litter, he saw moments when he'd been taken into small, dark bedrooms crowded with heavy furniture and crucifixes large enough to plant on Calvary, vanity tables turned to altars for sick old ladies as the Bombacci sisters fell away, one by one.

He never remembered their names, could never tell the difference between Aunt This One and Aunt That One, the rooms smelling of death and Noxzema as the aged brushed their hair below 3-D collages of the Sacred Heart, frames of bleeding butterfly wings that scared and transfixed a boy no taller than the post at the end of the bed.

"Come here, kid," they'd say in broken English. "Let me look at you."

For taking five small steps from the foot of the bed to the head with a little nudge from behind, for letting his cheek be touched,

Basilio would get a quarter. Remembering what a long, hard road those steps had been, he decided that when Lola woke up, they'd retrace them together.

A couple of hours later, Lola found the table crowded with cookies; the aluminum pot, rimmed with crusts of dried dough, soaking in the sink.

"Good Lord, how long was I sleeping?" she said, nibbling the edges of a pizzelle. "What are we gonna do with all these cookies?"

"Give 'em away," said Basilio.

"Sounds good to me," she said. "I slept good."

They packaged the cookies in deco tins Lola found in the basement, dusty things once packed with Goetze's caramel creams, Esskay sausage, and Utz potato chips, old drums she rinsed out and layered with the last of the wax paper.

As Basilio passed her stacks of cookies for the tins, Lola counted them: four dozen, five dozen, six dozen, "seven dozen, just like I thought we'd get from what we whipped up," she said, eating another cookie as Basilio picked up the phone and asked for a cab.

"Where we going?

"Fallston."

"Fallston!" laughed Lola, happy to take a ride. "Wait'll they get a load of us! Should we call and let 'em know we're coming?

"Nah."

The cab honked outside and they walked out the door, Lola in front with one tin, Basilio behind her with two more, his sea bag empty on the kitchen floor; the cold sharp and the late afternoon sky heavy with the possibility of snow.

"I dreamt the bottle cap factory was on fire again," she said as they got in the cab. "That cork burned for a week when we was kids. Didn't think they'd ever put it out."

"It's gonna be new again," said Basilio, telling the cabbie to ride by the factory on the way out. "Just like the old American Can building over in Canton."

"Canton, sure, over in Canton. But not here."

"I'm just saying, hold onto your house Aunt Lol. It's going to be worth a lot of money."

"Where the hell am I gonna go?" she said, a month away from her seventy-fifth birthday. "I'm going straight from here to Zannino's."

The cab turned for the Interstate, over the river and through the woods with pizzelles warming Lola's lap through the bottom of the tin.

THE ROAD TO HIBBING

*"So, you get the third concept—
these two things don't belong together
but somebody put them there
...you get the extra message..."*
—Frank Zappa

Some are dusted lightly, the glint compounded for years in a pestle of Fortuna and hard work to achieve modest success and the occasional, longed-for turn among the stars.

This is Basilio.

Others—like the sculptor Hettleman with whom Basilio haunted the ruined streets of Baltimore—are born with the gift in full; the charge stronger than the filament into which it descends. They seldom live beyond 30 without languishing on locked wards and cell blocks, using toothpicks to make tapestries of Calvary from unraveled socks.

And then there is India, who received the spark in spades and does the work; kin to once-in-a-lifetime prodigies forced to tell the world to back off, that the gift was given to them. From birth, she has had the poles of Basilio and Hettleman before her.

Struggle and surrender; failure as prologue and failure as fate.

"You're taking her where?" asked Hettleman the night before Basilio shoved off from Crabtown.

"Clear Lake," said Basilio.

"She likes to fish?"

"A cornfield—Iowa."

"Where every kid wants to go," said Hettleman, handing

Basilio his old Boy Scout sleeping bag that the young musician would use every night for the next thirteen weeks.

We find father and daughter about to depart the Great Magnolia State a month before India's twelfth birthday, touring the lower forty-eight in a Chevrolet station wagon during the Great Rock & Roll Road Trip.

The adventure took them from Baltimore to the Badlands and back—Memorial Day to Labor Day—up, down, and across the Continent as Basilio painted the history of American music at the longitudes and latitudes where it had descended into upright pianos and busted guitars in the wake of the Korean War.

In the evenings, after long afternoons at public swimming pools where he sketched in a composition book and snoozed beneath an orange floppy hat while India swam, Basilio set up his easel at campgrounds.

The night before in Tupelo, he set aside a stretched and gessoed canvas intended for a still life of a voluptuous fig tree (from a Hettleman photograph: "*I'm swinging over like a heavy loaded fruit tree...*") at 2019 Whittier Avenue in West Baltimore; postponed it to paint the face of the King on the reverse of a wheat penny with a brush made from a single strand of horsehair.

Render unto...

Named for the sub-continent of color—as tanned and smooth as a hazelnut in a pink Elvis t-shirt from the gift shop—India practiced the violin at the other end of the picnic table, the scents of grandiflora and turpentine mixing in the afternoon light over Tombigbee State Park.

A thousand miles away, the girl's mother wondered what the god-forsaken cotton fields of Mississippi had to do with an adolescent girl's summer vacation.

Standard exercises, a few songs of her own choosing for fun—arrangements harder than she could handle; a sip of grape juice with each turned page.

"How much more, Dad?"

The answer was always the same: "Twenty minutes."

"Give it another twenty," he said, working the penny with a magnifying glass, "and I'll make us some sandwiches."

She always complied (for her, not for him, something Basilio wouldn't realize for years), sawing through Shostakovich as Basilio chopped pickles from the ice chest for tuna salad mixed with gas station packets of mayo. They drank cold water from the melted ice and shared a Hershey's with almonds for dessert before twilight games of chess and reading by flashlight in the tent.

"Goodnight, say your prayers, we'll call Mom from the road in the morning."

Living together for the first time since the divorce, they learned to get along as only a couple of a couple of hard-heads trapped for thousands of miles in a moving vehicle are able.

Contentiously inane debates about the difference between reading a map and reading music.

Agreement that better music is often found in Nowhereseville, USA, on the AM instead of the FM.

And, if you sleep in a beat-up station wagon with out-of-state plates and provocative bumper stickers—EAT BERTHA'S MUSSELS—behind a Protestant church deep in the Heart of Dixie, you will encounter the drawn gun and hard questions of a skeptical sheriff before the cock crows.

Is this child your daughter?

[Yes.]

Is this man your father?

[Yes sir.]

Why did you choose to park here?

[It seemed safe.]

May I search your vehicle?

[Yes.]

What are all these paintbrushes?

[I'm a painter.]

Can you prove this child is your daughter?

[Fold and spindle: a copy of India's birth certificate from a yellowed envelope that Trudy insisted he bring along.]

Boss Man left with the finest of the wheat pennies—Louisiana Hayride Elvis, touched up that morning—and a parting word.

"Churches get broken into all the time, even in Mayberry. If you need to sleep in the car, pull into a nice hotel somewhere and park between the other vehicles. No one will bother you and you can go in and use the bathrooms in the morning. Grab a free coffee and some corn flakes for the kids."

Basilio hit the highway immediately, west along the top of Mississippi as India slept; dawn breaking over the Father of All Waters as they crossed the Memphis/Arkansas Bridge on Highway 61 of lament and lore: Polly Jean by way of Bob as bequeathed by an earlier, nimbler Robert of darker hubris.

The rising sun on India's side of the car struck the curve of her forehead in a way that reminded Basilio of his father and, moved by this, he touched her hair. Half asleep, she stirred and asked what would have happened.

"What do you mean?"

"If he didn't believe I was your daughter?"

They were in West Memphis now—Arkansas—headed for St. Louis where Basilio knew an Italian guy from his grandparents' neighborhood who would make them lunch. He pulled into a gas station for coffee and on the way back leaned in the passenger window to give India a bottle of orange juice.

Flipping down the visor in front of her, he angled the cracked mirror so it filled with her dark eyes, brown hair, round cheeks.

"Look."

"Yes?"

"No one will ever believe that you are not my daughter."

•

Fourteen hours, two fill-ups, a bag of cheeseburgers, half a milkshake each, a dozen homemade Italian cookies from Genovese, and 820 miles later, Basilio slipped the wagon between other vehicles-on-vacation at a Best Western in the Land of 10,000

Lakes, dazed from the road and one tank of gas away from broke.

He could call his father (he could always call his father, any-time from anywhere), but it didn't feel like an emergency. He could call Trudy—a thousand miles from home with nothing in his pockets but Elvis Presley pennies—but that would make it an emergency.

And all Hettleman had to spare was the sleeping bag.

"Sit tight," he said to India as she shimmied into the bag in the back of the wagon with the last of the St. Louis cookies and her mother's college copy of Karamazov which, like the Shosta-kovich, was far enough beyond the child's understanding to hold her interest.

From a payphone at a gas station next to the motel, he called Miss Bonnie, a barmaid he trusted like a grandmother who func-tioned as his agent. It was just past 11:00 p.m. in Crabtown and the bar sounded dead on the other end of the line.

At Bonnie's, he'd left a pair of quick-sale paintings—*Baltimore Coal Pier, 1957* and *Sunrise Over the Bottle Cap Factory*—a steal at $200 each.

"Sorry darling, things are slow. Only the rum-pots been com-ing around. You okay?"

"Yep. Just checking."

"How's my girl?"

"Having the time of her life."

"Some folks been asking about the Grandpop pictures. Ain't from around here. Wanna see if I can sell one of those?"

"No, no, take those down" said Basilio quickly. "I'll call you later."

"Suit yourself."

•

Pumping gas the next morning—topping the tank with seven bucks and some change left over; not a grain of oatmeal to mix with warm water from the wash room spigot—Basilio watched his daughter brush her teeth in the passenger seat.

She swished water around in her mouth, opened the door to spit on the ground, and spied her father at the rear of the car.

"Morning, Dad."

"Morning, hon."

Through the wagon's long windows, he watched her dig out an almost-empty jar of peanut butter and pop open a can of garbanzo beans. She jiggled a dozen or so chick peas into the peanut butter and, with a Popsicle stick from the day before, mixed them in the jar.

Les haricots avec sauce aux cacahuètes.

Basilio returned the nozzle to the pump and moved forward half-a-foot for a better view. Diligent and contented—riding some brio far beyond the dirty hood of a station wagon in Minneapolis—India balanced a single glazed bean on the end of the stick and brought it to her mouth.

Cranium shaped garbanzos (Basilio knew folks back home with heads shaped like chick peas, several ran their mouths over 75-cent drafts at Bonnie's) slathered with peanut butter and eaten from the end of a stick; a balancing act, a game.

Basilio knew (just as India knew they were down to beans and nickels, thrilled with an errant quarter buried beneath cassette tapes) that if she hadn't found the ice cream stick she would have used a twig or a pencil—whatever worked.

And in that moment, wiping his hands on a paper towel as he came to the driver's side, he sensed something in the girl that his prejudice kept him from seeing in her mother. It was a part of himself—his most valued trait, a near-reckless surety that came with the sparkle—that Trudy (and those before her, those during her, those after her) found attractive until it wasn't.

Knowing it was hard-wired into his daughter, as it had in Basilio's grandfather for whom he'd been named, gave him an idea on how to invest this last tank of gas.

["YOU PIMPED OUR DAUGTHER ON THE STREET?"

"I was teaching her to work."

"SHE'S 12 YEARS OLD."

"It beats taking out the trash and doing the dishes for allowance."]

He turned the ignition and pulled away from the station, India not paying attention until Polly Jean came out of the dash and Bobby Z went in: "...*where the winds hit heavy...*"

With the skyline of Coon Rapids before them, he let the song play through once and hit rewind.

Anoka and Sandstone, red iron pits running empty.

"Can you learn this by tomorrow morning?"

India's finger on the rewind: Cloquet en-route to 2410 Seventh Avenue East.

Once more with feeling, empty can of beans at her feet as she chewed the flat wooden stick.

"I know it now."

HOWIE WYETH

[1944 to 1996]

"Holy ancient American piano..."

A little more than five years into the new life inexplicably granted him, Basilio sat in a booth at the Sip & Bite reading the obits over a plate of chopped steak and onions with mashed potatoes and gravy, midnight comfort after another failed attempt to shepherd Petey the Polack toward recovery.

HOWARD PYLE WYETH, 51, DRUMMER

The musician's famous uncle—Helga and secrets, a woman in tall grass yearning for a farm house on a far hill—would outlive Howie by a dozen years and be remembered forever.

[Beaded with his own rosary of Helgas, Basilio Boullosa had been taking aim at Andrew since he'd been struck sober at Miss Bonnie's Bar on August 27, 1990.]

"The difference between me and a lot of painters," the great painter once said, "is that I have personal contact with my models...I have to become enamored."

Howie enamored of a drum a kit made of pots and pans and garbage can lids; his ride cymbal where most drummers put their high-hat, the bass like someone stomping the mud out of a cardboard box, snare sans snap, much less crackle and pop...

Howie bleeding to death in his sleep while some quack tried to wean him off of dope...

A left-handed Quaker who disliked travel, foul language, and wastes of time—a grandson of N.C. Wyeth charting his own archipelago of treasured islands—Howie was an exceptional talent who made every band he was in better.

A man who'd only be remembered in the liner notes of other people's albums, for as long as those who loved him were alive and, for the rest of her long and fruitful life, by Basilio's daughter each time she took her violin from its case.

"This is a triad," Howie told India, moving to a piano between sets of a show in Manhattan toward the end of the ten-thousand mile, once-in-a-lifetime road trip Basilio and the girl had taken in 1992. "Simple three-note chords a fiddler can use when backing up a singer. Mix them up and see what you get."

The next day, Wyeth agreed to sit for his portrait, posing by a window with a cat in a Village apartment that reeked so powerfully of feline piss and shit that Basilio sent India to a movie on the corner, regrettably fibbing to Howie an hour-and-a-half later that the piece was finished.

Saying goodbye to his guests at the curb, Howie reminded India: "Those triads come in handy when you're taking a solo. Just don't overdo it."

Good advice not taken; not for years by Basilio ("I'm okay, Pop") nor Petey (stumbling down his front steps, "I've got it this time, Chief"); and, certainly, not by Howie.

When Basilio first floated the idea of a father/daughter road trip by India's mother he'd only just begun to be okay.

He'd long stopped running cheap reefer through his grandmother's flour sifter in the basement with Petey; no longer kept a $5.99-a-case beer in the fridge at all times; had ended the insanity of asking the girl on Quail Street (one of India's old babysitters) to bring over her father's Valium when she came to sit on the couch and listen to records.

["*Take all the tea in China...put it in a big brown bag for me...*"]

No, not quite okay as the Summer of 1992 approached but a good two years into a sobriety authentic enough for his ex-wife to give her blessing to a month-long vacation during which India practiced her fiddle at campsites from coast to coast and Basilio painted portraits of Elvis on pennies; a crucified Johnny Winter on the side of a Leland liquor store; and Howie Wyeth on canvas.

Howie's portrait was on loan to the Cat's Eye Pub across from the tugboats on Thames Street, where Wyeth once backed-up a local band. It hung near Charlie Newton's mural of the history of Ireland, a narrative that meant nothing to Basilio, who only cared about the joint because his father and his waterfront pals had passed countless hours at the Eye.

Though Basilio often found it harder to make ends meet than the years when he was getting high every day, the Wyeth portrait had not been for sale before and it certainly would not be now. He'd been doing a lot of sign painting lately to pay the bills, getting leads from his good friend Petey, a house painter.

"I got it this time, Chief," Petey had said to him earlier in the evening, his pants torn, knees bleeding. "I'm gonna get a grip."

In Basilio's family, particularly among the Lithuanians on his mother's side, there was never any over-doing it.

Just on-and-off.

Advice hopefully heeded by the genetically pre-disposed India—15 now, a freshman at the Baltimore School for the Arts, in a chamber group with classmates and a hillbilly band with older friends about whom Basilio was suspect.

The wire-service obit said Howie's memorial was held at the Quaker Meeting House in Stuyvesant Square and quoted Robert Ross, the guitarist who'd introduced Basilio to Wyeth.

"People were testifying," said Ross, a bluesman who guessed he'd played a thousand gigs with Howie. "Some didn't know he played drums, they only knew him as an amazing piano player. Others didn't know he played piano, only as an amazing drummer."

Most of the mourners, Ross said later, "spoke of Howie's kindness...reserved, often depressed but always willing to help another musician looking for work. He had a little black book with the names and numbers of a million cats."

Ross knew most of them, had played with everyone from

Victoria Spivey to J.B. Hutto, and never encountered anyone as exceptional as Howie Wyeth.

"He can play anything—AN-EE-THING!" Ross had told him before the New York City gig. "Ragtime to rock to folk to fusion to blues to bluegrass. Just call the tune."

It was a loud obituary—Dylan's Rolling Thunder, Link Wray and Robert Gordon, even a mention of a session with Leslie West —for a quiet man; five paragraphs made noisier by all the stuff it left out.

How—no matter how ill or tired or miserable he felt—Howie never allowed his ailments to affect his playing.

[Hear that, Keith Moon?]

That he knew what someone was going to play before they knew it themselves.

"And if you weren't at your best he'd bury you," said Ross, noting that the only other drummer who came close was S.P. Leary.

And how he once indulged an obscure artist from Baltimore and spoke seriously about music with an 11-year-old girl, one musician to another.

Basilio stared out the diner's plate glass window—red neon SIP, blue neon BITE, the Greek forgot the ampersand—to a mailbox that had stood at the corner of Boston and Van Lill since the area was nothing but canneries and lumberyards.

He'd launched missives to many a Helga from the rusted blue box across the street and took another, just about finished, from his jacket.

The new girl was a student at the Institute, in her third year of pursuing the kind of art that needed more explanation than appreciation. They'd met at the Greek Folk Festival in Basilio's neighborhood a few weeks earlier and talked in a pew at the back of St. Nicholas Orthodox Church.

Pointing to an icon of the Blessed Mother, she told him with the assurance of a novice: "What you do is picture making."

The letter was his first communication since the festival. He took it from the envelope, the message interrupted a few hours earlier by Petey's latest calamity.

Basilio used a ballpoint to sign his name and with a pair of green pencils—one forest and one the color of the Chesapeake —sketched her likeness from memory across the bottom of the page.

LULU: Green Gown.

He put a first-class, 32-cent Georgia O'Keefe stamp to the envelope and set it aside his coffee cup.

From the same deep pocket that had held the pencils and Lulu's letter, Basilio pulled a postcard of Holy Rosary Church around the corner, the place where his dear and disturbed friend Francis Peter Pietrowski had gone to grade school with his hair combed nice, attending daily Mass in Polish and missing the Good News while off in a corner, counting his sins.

"Dear Petey," he wrote, "If I could drink like a normal man I would do it all day every day..."

[Pietrowski would not be as fortunate as Howie; suffering longer and by degrees indecipherable to all but the scared little Catholic kid deep inside a saint they called Petey.]

On this note Basilio put a generic postcard stamp—Old Glory—and, as the waitress cleared the table and refilled his coffee, got up and walked to the box.

He took Lulu's letter, kissed it, and dropped it in.

He took Petey's postcard, held it against the dark clouds above the black harbor, kissed it, and dropped it in.

A BANQUET OF ONIONS

"It's hard to imagine civilization without onions..."
—Julia Child

It was a negotiation worthy of a stevedore's strike: protracted, rough, hammered out in the back of a waterfront saloon, and, at the eleventh hour, resolved.

"Deal?" asked Sister Dolores, extending a dark, heavily veined hand.

"Deal," said Basilio, taking it.

The aging Franciscan's grip—firm, bony, and without compromise—pinched like a message, one that Basilio missed in the relief of knowing that India was in school.

This is how a 12-year-old named India Jean Boullosa—a prodigy of promise and pluck, a kid bouncing between parents wrestling with problems they didn't know they had—joined the last graduating class of St. Stanislaus Kostka in Baltimore.

"One more thing," said Dolores, draining her glass of beer.

Anxious to tell India's mother that he'd taken care of everything, Basilio stood up.

"No," he said. "We shook on it."

"You're right," said the nun. "We did."

Down the road, Basilio would forget the singe of her eyes but not the voice and never her fingers (too long, as though they carried an extra knuckle) or the tops of her hands—a blackish purple, paper-thin and bruised from brushing against a font or statue or the edge of the Formica table in the convent where she took her meals alone.

A stone, a leaf.

An unfound door carved with the faces of the faithful.

Basilio would paint those hands over and over in the years to come—floating above the tarred rooftops of Baltimore, at the end of the wrists of other artists—and he'd flinch at his impatience, how he'd stupidly talked beyond the sale.

O Lost!

And by the wind grieved.

Trudy, come back …

•

Labor Day weekend, 1993.

Two days earlier, Basilio Boullosa had been stared down by another woman.

"Get her in a good school," said Trudy, threat unspoken. "I'm out of ideas."

She hit Basilio the moment he walked through the front door of her house (briefly theirs) after a summer long road trip he'd taken with India.

A summer without having to care for her daughter had left Trudy exhausted, defeated by a crippled city's crippled schools —"…broken words never meant to be spoken, everything is broken…"—and sickened by the suspicion that all of the men she'd trusted since leaving Basilio were just like him, only worse.

Trudy had changed in the months that Basilio and India were away, two clicks to the left of the Yaquis and still turning: burning sage at dawn, solitary dinners of cucumber and yogurt (pretzels for protection, nutmeg for power) as father and daughter traveled ten thousand miles in a station wagon someone had given Basilio in exchange for an oil painting of Moe Drabowsky.

Whatever she was surrendering to, it did not include her soon-to-be ex-husband.

"Jesus Trudy," said Basilio. "School starts Monday."

India had nearly forgotten these conversations over the

months away. Breaking free of her mother's embrace, she took her backpack and violin, went upstairs to her room, and closed the door. Trudy took the plate of grapes she'd been eating, passed Basilio on her way to the stairs without looking at him, and left him alone at the bottom of the steps.

"Get her in a decent school," she said from the landing. "Or I'll take her someplace where good schools are free."

"THAT WOULD BE KANSAS!"

She disappeared at the top of the steps and he shouted louder—"TRUDY!"—detonating months of manicured hope that she would miss him enough (the three of them together) to keep trying. "WHAT THE FUCK DO YOU EXPECT ME TO DO OVER A HOLIDAY WEEKEND?"

Trudy opened her bedroom door and said, without emotion, "You're Mister Baltimore. You know people."

•

"How do you know Tony Abato?"

"He cut my mother's hair when I was a kid."

A far corner of Zeppie's in the last true neighborhood gin mill on a waterfront where—back when St. Stan's still had its own priest, in the days before containerization—the pastor would bless crates of Krakow ham poached by the stevedores before the booty was divvied up.

A couple of hams for the poor (as long as they were Polish) and the rest sold from behind the bar or traded for one of the thousand favors that blew through the cobbled streets where the tugboats tied up, all of them named by Limeys more than two centuries ago: Lancaster, Durham, Aliceanna, and Shakespeare.

"Mine too," said Dolores, remembering when Tony cut hair at the convent; two dozen nuns living together in the 1950s, before the first Roman Catholic president of the United States was here today and gone tomorrow.

Before hippie shit and personal fulfillment and the trouble-making

Berrigans began calling the sisters not to the world but into the world, where, of course, they lost their way.

Tony Abato had a Franciscan aunt—half-Polish, half-Italian, all Baltimore. Two, maybe three times a year, after weeks-long binges of booze and dope, guilt and remorse, he'd show up at the convent with combs and scissors and his trumpet.

Free haircuts and Glenn Miller numbers after supper, the sisters dancing together and laughing; Tony redeemed, if just for an evening. Dolores was younger than the rest, and Abato played "A White Sport Coat and a Pink Carnation," especially for her. Now she was the last, alone in a small castle of granite where she'd lived since taking vows as a teenager.

"It was cloistered when I was little and it was an honor to help the sisters clean," said Dolores, wiry at 80, a tough old hammer running what was left of the show. "When Mother Superior wasn't around, we'd sneak and peep and see what we could see."

"What did you see?"

"Floors you could eat off of."

Dolores lived alone a few doors up from the tavern in the three-story convent—twenty-three cells, large parlor and a dining hall, a chapel identified with the word *kaplica*, and life-sized plaster statues of saints and martyrs succumbing to all manner of atrocious death and rapture.

Principal, janitor, math teacher, boiler tender, and charwoman—laundering cafeteria dish towels along with the altar linens—Dolores did everything at St. Stan's except say Mass and hear Confession. The other day, someone saw her balanced on a bosun's chair a hundred feet above the ground and thought she was trying to hang herself or jump when she was simply washing the convent windows.

Still, there were enough old-timers left in the gentrifying neighborhood to stop Dolores at the market, her canvas shopping bag with just enough in it for that night's dinner, and dump their troubles.

"Goddamn Greeks threw me out of the diner, Dee. Put me on

the shit list," said Miss Josie the other day. "Banned me."

"How come?"

"'cused me of stealin', made me empty my pockets."

Dolores feigned sympathy, shook her head—*tsk, tsk.*

"Stealing what, Josie?"

"Sugar packets, right there for anybody to use. That ain't stealin', Sister."

"What is it, Joze?"

"That's just taking."

Dolores took Josie's hand, her small gold cross lost in the burrs of an old blue sweater, and offered succor if not absolution.

"Forget about it."

Basilio had not come to Zeppie's to confess, certainly not the dead-to-rights trespasses that led Trudy to walk away. All those hours on the road with India as she slept or read or stared out the window led him to conclude that Trudy would have left one day no matter what, that his shenanigans simply made it easier for her to go.

"Tony and I belong to the same club," he said.

"The crybaby club?" laughed Dolores. "The ones who sit down our basement on Thursday night drinking coffee and boo-hoo-hooing? Throwing their cigarette butts in the gutter?"

"Woe is me," smiled Basilio.

"Good for you, I'm having a beer," she said, raising a finger in the air to get the bartender's attention. "Thank God for that basket they pass around. It's a big help."

Zeppie came out from behind the counter, something he did for no one else, with a tall draught for Dolores and a bottled soda for Basilio.

"There was a heavy faith around here back when drunks knew what an act of contrition was," she said, licking the froth from the lip of the glass. "You could almost touch it."

"I came up with Vatican Two."

Dolores sniffed: "God is love."

"Right," said Basilio. "God is love."

And tuition at St. Stanislaus was $2,300, about $2,220 more than Basilio could get his hands on at any one time.

"Has she been baptized?"

"Yes."

"Communion?"

Basilio shook his head.

"We dropped the ball."

"What does she believe?"

"You know," he said. "Don't cheat, don't lie, don't steal."

"Do unto others," said Dolores and Basilio brightened. But the nun did not, holding Basilio's gaze just long enough to make him feel like he'd stepped in dog shit.

"Her God is music," he said; the truth abrasive enough for Basilio to hope the old woman would get up and leave.

"Where did she go last year?"

"Public school."

"Why not keep her there?"

"Not safe."

"Grades?"

Basilio shrugged, so-so.

"Why aren't you with her mother?"

"It's not safe."

Silence.

"That was a joke, Sister."

"Funny," said Dolores and she asked the question again.

"I was not a good husband," said Basilio. "She threw me out."

"But you're a good father and I like you," said Dolores. "I'm gonna help you out."

Voila!

"We need more people at Mass. I want her to play at the Sunday folk Mass."

"No."

"No?"

"Come on, sister. A Catholic folk group? She's too good to pick up bad habits."

"Both of you have to be invested."

"She can teach," said Basilio, unsure of where the idea came from.

"Teach what to whom?"

"Music to the little kids. The ones who want it."

"Want what?"

"Something they can be good at."

"Has she ever taught before?"

"I learn something from her every day."

Dolores's mind scanned decades of obituaries in which violins and clarinets survived the forgotten polka stars of yesterday, wondering how many kids would be content with an accordion; remembering the weddings and church hall dances that rocked St. Stan's every Saturday night and Sunday afternoon of the year.

"I like it," she said.

"She's in?"

"You're in."

•

India taught (usually music but sometimes math) and—along with an African-American kid who went to a Baptist church near Johns Hopkins Hospital—joined the other kids preparing for Confirmation. She was not required to attend religion class (though often she did) and used the free time to worship her God in one of the many empty classrooms.

Some of the kids—goodie-goodies and bad-asses alike, one boy who was already shaving and would do something very stupid to get India's attention before the year was out—spied on her when her violin echoed in the halls.

Until Dolores marched down the hall and broke it up: "This isn't a concert, children, move it along..."

She put Basilio in touch with a businessman who supplied the paint. He brought his own brushes and found scaffolding in the basement.

"No blas-feemin' once you're up there making it pretty," she said.

"What are you talking about?"

"I know you artist types," said Dolores. "Don't get any big ideas."

And this is how Basilio Boullosa—a sign painter with ambition so big it embarrassed him, a fine artist who put the face of Elvis Presley on a hundred and one wheat pennies over the summer, trading them for gas and food when the adventure was close to collapse—exchanged weeks of back pain and neck cramps below the ceiling of a century-old Polish sanctuary in a city holding on by the skin of the few teeth it had left.

One Sistine Chapel on the Patapsco for a year of Catholic education.

He'd done what Trudy had demanded and still managed to upset her.

Baptized in infancy (as was Basilio) and long dutiful (as Basilio was not), Trudy had come to despise Catholicism and the scold of its patriarchy; once nailing a crucifix above the front door to haunt her husband's comings and goings (replaced by a watercolor of a toad, the cross of rosewood now in a forgotten drawer) and, finally sick of pulling the sled by herself, had no interest in a trip to the rectory for a load of sacrificial blah-blah-blah from a man in a dress.

Basilio got up to leave and Dolores stopped him.

"How'd she get that name?"

"What?"

"India," said Dolores. "What kind of name is that?"

"Colors," said Basilio. "Because of the colors."

•

India in the backyard, reading under the Fleckenstein tree when Basilio came home with dinner and sheet music for gypsy folk songs she'd been asking for. India closed her book, a door stopper she'd picked up at a junk store on the road, and looked up to see her father smiling.

"You're in," he said holding up a large, brown bag streaked with grease. "Crab cakes from the Sip and Bite! French fries and gravy!"

India almost smiled. She knew kids who went to the Catholic school near her mother's house—an oasis in the city with big ballfields and a huge kitchen for spaghetti dinners—but not one squeezed between bars and tugboats and places where, if you knew what day to show up, you could still get a freshly butchered duck.

Basilio gave her the sheet music—"Keep it away from the food"—and asked her to bring out glasses of water. As she did, he stared up at the Fleckenstein tree and considered all that had happened in the past thirty-six hours.

It was to the maple's majesty ("that tree's too big for the yard," his father had said more than once, the roots eating into the terra-cotta sewage pipes, back-ups in the basement and complaints from the neighbors) that Basilio had prayed since getting sober.

A stone rolled.

Leaves falling across a door open just wide enough for unexpected grace to greet an unlikely candidate.

["I like you kid. I'm gonna help you out..."]

Less than a month after Bessie Fleckenstein became a widow her son moved her into his house somewhere out beyond the Beltway. About to hang her last line of wash on Macon Street after a lifetime there, the kindly German Catholic leaned over the wire fence separating her yard from the Boullosa's—the last neighbor who had known Basilio's grandparents—and said, "Hon, do you want my house?"

She just about gave it away for nothing (just about nothing was all Basilio had), saying with the serenity of someone who's life has been well-lived. "I know you'll take care of it."

The unerring punctuality of chance.

To Miss Bessie, who shed a tear: "Thank you."

To the tree, rustling its response: "Thank you."

India returned with the water and Basilio set a crab cake in front of her, lump back fin, as big as a softball.

"Not only are you in," he said, "but you're in the eighth grade."

Another hiccup in a long weekend of surprises. India nodded. She would have been happy to quit school and travel the world as a minstrel, acquiring songs the way other girls collected false friends. Or go the other way and earn a Ph.D.

It was all the same to her, for the first gift she'd received from the God of the Fleckenstein tree was her talent (no other musicians on either side of the family) and the second was knowing that the black case lined with velvet held everything she needed to survive in this world.

"Come on, kid," said Basilio. "Let's eat."

He set out a Greek salad to go with the crab and fries. Rice pudding sprinkled with cinnamon for dessert along with a couple of kebabs for India's first-day-of-school lunch the next day.

Skewers of lamb and vegetables on which the old man, still working the grill at 80, always put an extra hunk of onion in memory of his family's misfortune—*megalos limos*—before making it in America.

Whenever Basilio came to the diner—sometimes to eat, sometimes to sketch faces that didn't exist anywhere else but Baltimore—the Greek would tell war stories as he flipped eggs.

"For months, dinner was just an onion, maybe roasted, not even oil," he said, his back to Basilio as though he were regaling the bacon and eggs. "If you had two onions you were better off than other families. Three and you were rich."

And now they used a thousand pounds a week and the grill was never cold.

In dreams, the appearance of an onion—red, white, or purple; sweet or tart—symbolized strength to overcome grief.

And green! Wisps of translucence, a thin leafy stalk in your hand like a brush dipped in crimson. If you are eating one in a dream it is promised that better days are coming.

Who but the very few have experienced smell in a dream, waking up to wipe the sting from their eyes?

A breeze blew the napkins away. Basilio got up to chase them and used India's book for a paperweight, the red and black cover showing a shifty rake and his three sons.

"Your Mom was reading this when she was pregnant with you."

India put a forkful of crab on a saltine—a golden rarity anywhere outside of the Chesapeake watershed, a lesson she learned the hard way on the road trip.

"I know," she said, taking a bite.

"What's it about?"

"Well," she said, sipping water. "The part I just finished was about a mean old woman, a witch."

Basilio nibbled feta.

"Did she fly on a broom?"

"She was selfish."

"How selfish?"

"Super-duper selfish."

Licking her fingers and wiping them on her shorts, India opened the book, a bit of olive oil on her pinky staining the page.

"...there was an old woman who died and found herself in hell. She complained to Satan that her damnation had been a mistake."

"What'd old Scratch say to that?" asked Basilio.

India spoke in a devil voice: "You've been a greedy, selfish woman all your life. Surely, this is where you belong."

Now the desperate shrew, she picked a crescent of onion from the salad and held it in the air.

"I DID A GOOD DEED ONCE!"

India threw the onion over her shoulder.

"I GAVE AN ONION TO A BEGGAR!"

Devil voice: "Oh, yes, I recall. You pulled a puny onion from your garden and handed it to a supplicant at the fence."

India jumped onto the bench of the picnic table and raised

her right hand in the air like a magician.

"POOF!"

Dropping the book, the napkins blew away again as she spread her arms wide to recite the tale by heart.

"An angel went down into hell holding a stalk of an onion for the woman to grasp. She grabbed it with both hands and was miraculously pulled up and out of hell."

"A way up," said Basilio, taking a long drink of water, "and a way out."

India plopped back down: "Everybody in hell wanted to leave."

Basilio laughed: "It was hell!"

India brushed some dirt off the book and continued.

"Legions of the damned grabbed the old woman's legs and feet and ankles and were pulled up along with her until it seemed that the very bowels of hell clung from a single onion. Though the weight was immense, the onion held and the angel continued to lift everyone up and out of Gehenna."

"Exodus," said Basilio.

"Miraculously, the doomed—millions of abject sinners—found themselves raised from agony by the grip of a selfish wench upon a single onion."

"Set me free," sang Basilio, "why don't you babe?"

"And still the onion held, halfway to heaven and a long way from hell. The selfish woman looked down to see the endless chain that had hitched a ride with her, resentful that others could be redeemed simply by clinging to her withered and spindly legs.

"She shouted: 'If all of you grab on to me like this, the onion will break'...the woman began to kick and smash the people hanging from her and one by one they fell, each causing tens of thousands of others to plunge back into hell."

Basilio began gathering the trash from their meal and India brought the story home.

"With each kick the load became lighter yet only now did the onion begin to fray. Believing the weight of the others tore the onion, the woman kicked more ferociously."

"Finally, only one person was left, an especially wretched soul pinching the woman's big toe. She kicked and kicked, screaming, 'THIS IS MY ONION!'

"As the man lost his grip, the last thread of the onion tore. Near enough to the gates to catch a glimpse of paradise, the woman fell back into the lake of Hell.

"The angel wept and went away. To this day, the woman burns in hell...her only memory the caress of the onion between her singed fingers..."

•

The Fleckenstein tree began to shake, rhythmically and then violently as storm clouds rolled in from the harbor. India grabbed everything she could and ran into the house as Basilio tossed the trash in a can by the gate and followed her, ducking inside as the first drops fell.

A late summer, hit-and-run thunderstorm, the kind that scrubs the air.

Basilio put the left-overs in the 1948 Westinghouse refrigerator that had replaced his grandparents' ice-box. India took one of the rice puddings and plopped down on the red leather couch in the middle room, sinking a plastic spoon into the confection as her father shut the kitchen window, gusts of suddenly cool air blowing old newspapers and the new sheet music to the floor.

"Am I living here now?"

"For now," said Basilio.

"How long?"

"Until we get the schedules straightened out."

Suddenly tired, India knew it was more complicated than that. Speaking with her eyes closed, she ran the cinnamon on the curve of the spoon across her lips and asked: "How come Mom couldn't do it?"

"Do what?"

"Get me in a new school."

Basilio grabbed the other pudding and sat down next to her on the couch, licking the bottom of the lid just as his India had done, as he had done as a child.

"It took some finagling."

"What's that mean?"

"It's an engineering term," said Basilio. "Like juggling lobsters while you're roller skating."

India laughed, a grain of rice on her lips, "Mom can't finagle."

"Nope," said Basilio.

"We finagle."

"You'll probably be spending most of your time here."

India scraped the last of the pudding from the corners of the plastic cup.

"What's wrong with Mom?"

Staring into his own pudding—storm raging, the sky dark enough for the street lights to come on—Basilio decided to tell his daughter the most accurate version of the truth available at the moment.

"When I was really little, I mean like three years old, I found my mother crying in her bedroom, face down in a pillow, sobbing."

India had seen her own mother do the same.

"She died when you were my age," she said.

"Just about," said Basilio. "But that doesn't have anything to do with it. Nobody else was home, just me and her and I stood in the doorway, not much taller than the hinge. And I asked the same thing you just asked me: 'Mommy, what's wrong?'"

India set the empty pudding cup on the floor just before a crack of thunder, a fractured bolt of lightning turning the backyard brilliant, illuminating the inside of the house for half-a-moment.

"What did she say?"

"She told me to shut the door and go play. Never even took her face out of the pillow. I went away thinking that whatever was wrong was my fault and I had to fix it."

India did not seem moved.

"What's wrong with Mom?"

"I really don't know," he said as trashcans blew down the alley. "Whatever it is, it doesn't have anything to do with you."

•

By early October, the month of the Holy Rosary and John Lennon's birthday, Basilio was making good progress on the ceiling and trusting that his daughter, who kept busy and seemed happy, was doing so as well.

One Friday afternoon, during a lesson with a third-grader who cried that she hated the violin and wanted to be an Olympic volleyball player, India left the music room and slipped into line for Confession.

"When you're finished, it's like you're brand new," a classmate had told her. Dolores saw her and went about her business. Kids whispered and Basilio never knew.

When it was her turn (the kid leaving the box looked at her and smirked), India went in and sat in the darkness until the priest slid the screen on the other side and she saw his face in shadows.

What does a 12-year-old confess who has never done it before?

That her father gave her his bedroom but she wished he'd kept it instead of sleeping half-naked on the couch in the middle of the day? That she hated the smell of turpentine and blamed her mother for everything?

Perhaps she was most upset that the God she'd created from music was no longer keeping time.

From the other side of the screen: "You may begin."

Silence.

Before the priest could speak again, she blurted: "I miss my mother."

"That's a virtue," he said. "Is your mother still with us?"

"I'm not with her."

"Where is she?"

"On the other side of town."

A modern-day circuit rider, the young priest was responsible for Mass and Confession at eight parishes in six neighborhoods from the waterfront out to the county line. Not long out of seminary, he was good at the job—he truly loved people, gave away more than he kept—and would leave the priesthood long before India accepted that her parents were just people, extraordinary, perhaps, in their idiosyncrasies, but pretty much like everybody else.

"Do you see her?"

Through tears: "Not enough."

"You're the violinist?"

"Yes."

"You're good."

Sobs and "Thank you."

"And you haven't made your First Communion?"

"No."

"Do you want to?"

"My mother wouldn't like it. She wouldn't like what I'm doing now."

"Maybe she would. Who knows? When will you see her again?"

"I have to wait until she calls."

"Call her," said the priest. "You have no sins to forgive."

•

Here she comes again.

With her Pepto-Bismol, warm glass of milk, and a dusty blackboard of complaints written in the strictest Palmer Method, Sister Dolores Hyacinth Karcz shuffled into the sanctuary in torn canvas shoes and a ragged red sweatshirt bearing the image of a white, crowned eagle and the words: POLISH NATIONAL ALLLIANCE.

The usual agitations of old age typically kept her up—leg

tremors, toe cramps, an itch just beyond her reach, and a weak bladder. Sometimes she just lay there saying the Rosary the way other people count sheep. But tonight was different; tonight Dolores was spooked.

Click!

Basilio's painting music—old soul from a 9-volt transistor on the altar, the protestant petitions of the Reverend Al Green floating up to the ceiling—went silent.

Under his breath, high above the pews: "Shit."

In the daytime, Dolores's thick Baltimore accent (vaguely Cockney, profoundly ridiculous) had a harsh bark to it. It softened in the evening and, late at night, faltered toward a mumble. Still, it carried easily to the ceiling where Basilio lay on his back, biting his tongue.

"I told you not to blas-feem."

Dolores was directly beneath him, the pew scarred and black with a century of sweat, hairspray, and the grease from the necks and arms of the faithful long departed.

"Didn't I tell you?"

Yanked out of his contemplation, Basilio wondered how canonical law might judge the accidental nudging of an open can of oil-based robin's egg blue.

KA-POWIE!

Right in the kisser!

The God of Mercy would most certainly forgive him.

The spot Basilio was working on called for complete restoration of a portrait of Blessed Stanisław Papczyński (defender of those "wronged by society") and a touch-up of the Five Holy Martyrs of Miedzyrzecze, monks killed in their hermitage and set ablaze by robbers. Tradition holds that their bodies did not burn.

Instead, with the tip of a horsehair brush, he'd manipulated the original figures into a long line of sinners attached to the rotting feet of a shrew, the bitter hag fast to an onion extended by a cherub that looked a lot like India Jean Boullosa.

Cracks in the stained glass near his head brought the cursing and false laughter of rumpots stumbling home from last call at Zeppie's to wives who'd locked them out of the house. Before the road trip with India, Basilio often joked that he and Trudy had split the family home 50/50.

"She got the inside," he'd say, back when the beer was going down easy. "And I got the outside."

Dolores craned her neck for a better look and said, "You know Michelangelo didn't do it that way. That's just the movies."

"Is that right?"

[He didn't know.]

"The Pope had some kind of contraption built that let him stand up. Not everything's the agony and ecstasy."

Sometimes he could paint while Dolores talked, depending on how worked up she was. Tonight, she'd been woken by a nightmare so vivid it was like watching the news on TV.

"Huh," he said, trying to stay inside of his story, leaving a small area near the cherub to portray himself as a servant, a nod to his sapling recovery.

A servant!

Good God of Grandiosity, how much ego does it take to be Gandhi or Dorothy Day or Jimmy Carter?

What had he ever given away?

"Gristle," he decided, putting the lids back on the paint. "Not even an onion."

"Well?" demanded Dolores.

Basilio hit a switch on an extension cord and a small, powerful light illuminating the just-about-finished section—fingertips scraped raw, ankles twisted in desperation—went dark. The only remaining light came from pinholes of street light boring through the stained glass as he climbed down.

"What's wrong, Sister?" he said, wiping his hands on a rag and trying a light "Haven't you ever seen pictures of Hell before?"

In the dream, Dolores wandered the St. Stan's playground in the long black habit she'd worn until the late 1960s and moved toward a pile of trash near the street, the Niemann organ.

Reduced to kindling and scrap metal, stepped on by laborers and sifted through by junkies and junk men, the grand instrument a nuisance to developers turning St. Stanislaus Kostka into condominiums.

Then she was a kid again, Dee-Dee in untied saddle shoes running up to a man with a crowbar in his hands, screaming: "STOP! STOP IT!"

The wooden pipes of the organ splintered, the ones made of tin were crushed; Mexicans (they were all Mexicans even if they weren't, just like once upon a time everyone on South Ann Street was a dumb Polack) hauling the trash to the curb.

"*ZATRZYMAC!*"

No one answered, as though they were deaf or she was mute or both.

The dream rattled in her mind—"Don't you foreigners understand ENGLISH?"—the cornerstone a weight upon her chest: 1889.

Rage from the nightmare spilled into the now as she pointed to the ceiling with a crooked finger: "You got somebody up there wearing flip flops."

"You know I don't, Sister," said Basilio, sitting down next to her. "It's a Bible story like all the others."

"Not in any Bible I ever seen."

"What is it, Dolores," asked Basilio gently. "What's wrong tonight?"

"Can't sleep."

"Did you try..."

"I tried it all. When you can't sleep, you can't sleep."

"I've got a lot to do here, Sister."

"Remember when you first came to me—all worked up, half out of your mind?"

"Yes."

"I was trying to tell you something but you wouldn't listen."

"I was desperate."

"Well I'm desperate now."

"Are you sick?"

Dolores shrugged; she felt sick.

"You didn't have to paint this ceiling. I could've let your daughter go to school for nothing."

Now she had his attention.

"What do you mean?"

"It's all over," she said. "*Gotowe—kaputski.*"

Basilio thought of all portraits of Baltimoreans—a parade of people, Doloreses of all ages, who made the city what it was—all the canvases he might have completed in the months spent on his back; all the sleep lost as he burned the paintbrush at both ends.

He stood up to keep from pushing her—"What?"

"Sit down," she said, leaning her head back to stare at the good work Basilio had done; not what she would have chosen but clean and bright, the colors almost floating down from the ceiling.

"I used to sit here as a little girl, just looking up at the ceiling making up stories to go with the pictures," she said. "The Mass was in Polish anyway. I knew a few words."

She laughed.

"All the bad ones."

Oh brother, thought Basilio, still pacing, his own dark road stretching out before him while Dolores took another turn down memory dead-end lane.

"I could have been married," she said. "You don't think I coulda been married?"

All those neighborhood boys who'd asked her to dance on the roof of the Recreation Pier, boys who became stevedores with good union paychecks (the ones who didn't drink or eat themselves to death); seated with their families at Mass, smiling politely as she brought the bread and wine to the altar.

Could have traded one habit for another back when all the folk singer nuns were running off with peace nuts from the seminary.

"What was I gonna do? Teach? I was already teaching. Get a

job? I had a job. I had a calling."

"Don't I know it," said Basilio, taking the pew in front of Dolores.

Unsolicited and inescapable callings; such a dreadful thing to fall into the hands of the Living God.

Dolores pointed to the cherub Basilio had just finished and he was sure the hammer was coming down again.

"She's a good kid," she said.

"Thank you, Sister."

"You know it hasn't rained since you started? More than a month now. Not much to speak of anyway."

Basilio wondered if rain was some sort of Salem litmus used to prove blasphemy.

Dolores pointed to a far corner of the ceiling, a spot Basilio hadn't noticed, where the plaster had buckled.

"The roof leaks," she said.

Basilio was floored.

"The roof leaks?"

"Something terrible."

"The day we first met it rained like hell," said Basilio. "I was here the next morning and nothing leaked."

"Yeah," said Dolores with weary non-chalance. "Hell doesn't always get in."

Basilio jumped up, flushed with an anger he only thought Trudy could cause.

"WHAT AM I DOING PAINTING THE CEILING IF THE ROOF LEAKS?"

Dolores waited for the echo to die.

"I was going to tell you at the bar—one more thing, remember? But you were peeing your pants to tell Missy Fru-Fru that you'd saved the day. We shook on it and you ran off."

Basilio remembered, sat down again.

"Why didn't you take somebody else's tuition to fix the roof?"

"Wake up," said Dolores. "You ain't paying attention to what goes on around here."

A police helicopter hovered overhead and it seemed to Basilio that he could see its looking-for-bad-guys spotlight through a thousand holes in the roof. A siren wailed down Eastern Avenue and faded.

"Not my problem no more. It's been sold."

"What's been sold?"

"The ceiling you're painting and the pew I'm sitting in. Archdiocese signed the papers last week. Church, school, convent. Everything. They'll probably rip the goddamn poor boxes off the wall and shake the nickels out of 'em."

"How long was it for sale?"

"Since before you came begging."

"I didn't beg," said Basilio, shamed by the lie.

The calendar was pushing toward All Souls' Day, which Dolores liked better than All Saints' because it meant everyone got in (or out) for free. Just about time to start the furnace—the pride of 1934, patched up for free when the congregation was made up of working families, steelworkers bringing whatever was needed home from the mill to keep their kids warm as they learned the catechism.

Dolores wasn't raising Lazarus anymore.

Sins of omission, sins of commission.

The trespass of delusion.

"So what am I doing?" asked Basilio.

"Taking care of your family," said Dolores. "You were smart to give up drinking."

"It was mostly marijuana."

"Booze, dope, women, whatever," shrugged Dolores. "Ruined my family and I wanted out. My brother lied about his age and got into the Navy. My mother had a fit when I told her I wanted to go into the convent. I was a baby, but *mamusia* had herself a good cry, gave her blessing, and watched me go. It was only a block away anyways."

[Blessings are not what came with heavy rains just before Thanksgiving when the waterfront flooded from Caroline Street all the way down to the mailbox in front of Zeppie's, the regulars drinking up as cars floated by; a long week of storms when the ceiling panel with the shrew tethered to an angel by the tuft of an onion fell onto a bank of 50-cent votive candles.]

"I just wanted to see it beautiful one more time before I died."

O Lost!

"Where did everybody go?" said Dolores, assuring Basilio that India would finish out the year before kicking the kneeler out of the way, needing to get up in a few hours for Josie's funeral Mass.

And by the wind grieved.

"All those Catholics..."

Ghosts, come back.

Dolores stood up and turned to go.

"Where the hell did all them Polacks go?"

THE GANGES OF BALTIMORE

"You always love the city you die in..."
—Tom Nugent, Trouble Maker

<u>Side One</u>

This is a five-sided box of clear glass made of broken transoms and shattered diner china salvaged in alleys from the slums of West Baltimore to the rubble in the east.

It hangs on spider silk, a half-bubble off plumb, deep in the bleeding heart of the Holy Land.

In 1995, from Thanksgiving weekend through the last day of the year, Basilio Boullosa received a series of letters from one of his few peers, an artist who'd abandoned Baltimore to live alone in the woods.

X-rays written on scraps of paper stained with paint, dirt, and glue, rings from coffee cups and marijuana ash.

Sent to 21224: "Dear Ringo..."

Posted from 21520: "Hettleman."

Bragging letters, pissed-off letters, and crying letters; a self-absorbed dirge for things Hettleman professed to care nothing for.

"Don't miss it at all..."

If not his mind, then surely Hettleman's talent—substantial, acknowledged for a moment and then forgotten—was failing him.

Hettleman made his splash assembling reliquaries: shrines to Irish railroad workers near Fourteen Holy Martyrs, black oyster shuckers along the harbor rim, household saints and scraps—

half-a-handkerchief, a missing house in the middle of Smallwood Street—from his own family.

Basilio lived in a reliquary inherited upon his grandfather's death.

He slept in the bed where his father was presumably conceived and shaved before a wooden medicine cabinet whose mirrored door bore a log his grandfather had kept with a carpenter's pencil, tracking the life of each razor blade—when purchased, how many shaves he'd gotten out of it, when it was time to buy a new one. The last date was from the summer of 1989.

Basilio boiled eggs in a sauce pan his grandmother bought on Eastern Avenue a few days before her wedding. He stretched canvas and built frames on his grandfather's work bench, worried over the rosebushes in the backyard, and weaved all of it into portraits of women who'd come to visit over the years before going on their way.

"Dear Ringo," wrote Hettleman. "Do you remember how we met?"

Long time ago, whispered Basilio.

"... it was your first one-man show. First time I'd ever been to Miss Bonnie's. She sure must have liked you to take down all that Elvis for your work. That rich broad bought the painting of your grandparents in bed when they were young."

Grandmom and Grandpop, thought Basilio, closing his eyes to see them as they were in the painting, half his age and entwined in the bed he slept in every night.

"Deep blues and dark greens," wrote Hettleman. "The money goes in a day—we spent some of it on hash that night. Blonde like the attorney who bought the painting. We both could have nailed her that night. When you sober up the money is gone you wish you had the canvas back.

"Still sleeping in that bed?"

I am.

Basilio hadn't seen Hettleman in years and rarely thought of him before the missives began landing from the other side of the state.

"Out here, man, the air is pure out here and the soil is rich... I'm breathing like I haven't breathed since I was a kid."

Basilio—lost in sauce-stained cook books his lover brought over when she could get away—never wrote back.

<u>Side Two</u>

If a great man were to paint a landscape of the two hundred miles between the City of Baltimore and the far reaches of Western Maryland, where might the line fall between braggadocio and despair?

"Instead of watering down the gesso," wrote Hettleman, "I rub it into planks of wood and work on top of the swirls."

New work by Basilio—a dirty wineglass on a zinc counter—leaned against the wall near the door. He would sell it cheap for quick Christmas money and turn 40 by spring. The longest relationship he'd had beyond an extended adolescence with his daughter's mother did not last five months.

The vestibule door was made from a dozen panes of pink milk glass, each framed with wood painted to look like wood: undulating striations of brown and gold made with a craftsman's comb, one of ten thousand inherited relics.

The door the same, save for a new generation of nicks and chips—one long scratch from an especially large painting carted to market the day before—as it was when Basilio the boy waited for guests to arrive on Christmas Eve. The holiday had not been celebrated on Macon Street for more than twenty years.

Outside, the aluminum storm door with the letter B encircled in the center creaked. Basilio had begun waiting for the sound that announced the day's mail since the arrival of Hettleman's first, unexpected letter.

Bills, junk, and a supermarket circular dropped against octagonal tiles, the shadow of the mailman passing the curtains as the storm door banged closed.

Basilio stepped gingerly across tangled strings of lights and scattered ornaments to get the mail. He sifted it on the couch (nothing marked *correo aereo*, there never was) and stopped when he saw Hettleman's hand across a smudged envelope that had been used before.

He'd spent the morning mopping the floor, pushing all of the ornaments that hadn't been broken to the side. Now he lay stretched out on a couch where, a few hours ago, Aubergine had moaned with one leg in her jeans and one leg out. She'd lost half-a-cup of blood; he a third.

"Dear Ringo—"

"This county issues the fewest number of building permits in Maryland. No dope, no murders, no beggars, no bullshit."

It was the day after Thanksgiving and Basilio—pained and exhausted in the front room, staring at the vestibule over the top of the letter—wondered if he should get up and make another turkey sandwich from the carcass Aubergine brought for soup.

"I should have done this a long time ago," wrote Hettleman. "Don't miss that shit hole at all."

Basilio was preparing for a one-man show at Bonnie's Bar —big pieces, frames made of scavenged wood, scratches on the door from hauling them out to the car.

[He might sell a painting. Maybe two. And if the mood struck him—if she was pretty, if she was sad, if she was old and remembered when Baltimore was Baltimore—he might give one away.]

Basilio made more money painting provincial Christmas scenes on decorative pillows—Baltimore the most provincial of cities: big-hearted, duckling ugly—than he did telling the story of Life on Earth as it is Idiosyncratically Lived along the Crumbling Holy Lands on the Patapsco.

"My studio is a stand of ancient hemlocks, sky high," wrote Hettleman. "They filter the light before it reaches the old barn planks I'm using. Natural sunlight, Rings. Won't paint by anything else."

Basilio wondered if Hettleman was painting at all.

"You know what's really weird? Everybody out here is white. I mean everybody. The town sits under a big hill they call Negro Mountain but there aren't any black people. You think you know what it means. But you don't. You don't know until you move to a place like this. You can forget that you grew up in a black city..."

Piss and bravado in Western Maryland.

And blood on the tracks in the 600 block of South Macon Street.

•

Since they'd met under the whirligig at the Visionary last summer—Aubergine chaperoning her daughter's field trip, Basilio looking for colors—his lover had brought the best version of herself to his door, one in opposition to a day-to-day life she no longer recognized.

This morning, as always, they were on each other before she had time to take her coat off.

Aubergine dropped a bag holding potato and parsley salad, mumbling "Walter Hasslinger's recipe," as Basilio smothered her words with his mouth. Any trace of the Baltimore that was gone pleased him. Anything they could share together pleased her in turn.

Basilio waltzed her across the maze of decorations on the floor as buttons and zippers broke loose, tossing her gray beret across the room just before they fell onto the couch.

It was great, it always was, great until they rolled from the couch to the floor and Aubergine screamed like a teenager in childbirth; stabbed in the soft, dimpled flesh of her rear-end with the ice pick point of a steamed crab shell, a holiday ornament painted by a hand far less patient than the one decorating pillows.

The ornament was precious to Basilio, a bauble from a moment bigger than all that had occurred on Macon Street, more than the story told in the brushstrokes of the green and blue painting that Hettleman liked so much.

[Every Christmas since Grandpop died, Basilio promised to put the shell in a safe place—better to protect it in a china closet than hang it on the tree—and every year he let it sit out until December rolled around and hung it on the tree.]

The wound ran deep and Aubergine refused to go to the hospital.

Since the whirligig had spun: buckets of spousal salve lathering friction burns across her shoulders, bruises on her thighs, books laying around the living room by authors no one had ever heard of and a receipt for $28.95 worth of rotisserie chicken (all of Aubergine's appetites were blue-ribbon) in a part of town her husband only knew from crime reports.

But stitches in your ass from a puncture wound delivered by a Christmas crustacean?

"Jesus," said Basilio, running for a towel, stepping on the same shell in his bare feet—"FUCK!"—his blood pooling with Aubergine's on the floor.

Blood on the rug, on strings of blinking lights that Basilio had plugged in before she arrived, in the grooves of the hardwood floor.

Blood running down Aubergine's leg as she ran up to the bathroom where after sex they rested in a clawfoot tub below a skylight; where during the Depression newlyweds had washed their dinner dishes when Grandpop rented out the second floor.

Dime-sized drops of blood that Basilio wouldn't notice for years and then, on his hands and knees when he couldn't get the colors to mix the way he wanted, when Aubergine's successors walked out, he'd assume it was dirt or chocolate.

Aubergine left Macon Street limping, her backside dyed with the last drops from a twenty-year-old bottle of mercurochrome that Grandpop had used on shaving cuts and a thick wad of paper towels affixed with masking tape.

Basilio lay on the couch with half a crab shell upon his belly, the bloody rug in the backyard where it would be rained on, crapped on by birds, baked in the sun, and one day thrown away.

"I'm in heaven, Rings... "

Basilio pinched the bridge of his nose with the envelope, tears smearing Hettleman's penmanship.

"Come see me when you're tired of getting shit on in the Third World."

Side Three

The second week of December, into a house whose every baseboard supported painted canvas—histories within histories, the covers of Long Playing record albums, endive trampled among a thousand odors—came a package.

"Dear Ringo... I made you something..."

Wrapped in newsprint on a bed of straw, lay a mask—unyielding and crude.

Painted to resemble flesh that looked like wood, it had eyeholes, an opening for the mouth, and twine attached behind the ears.

"Made it out of some cereal boxes that blew out of the trash and got rained on in the field," wrote Hettleman. "I set them next to the wood stove in the kitchen and when they dried out, I saw your face."

"Whose face?" demanded Basilio, walking the mask to the basement where a pot of cabbage had simmered since morning.

Basilio stirred the pot and contemplated Hettleman, a man with his troubles behind him making a witch doctor mask out of soggy cardboard in the wilds of western Maryland. And remembered the day he watched as a crab shell was transformed from garbage to gem.

Remembered is not quite the right word, since he thought about her—and all she'd done with him, to him, at him, and for him in fourteen weeks on Macon Street—all the time. No matter who was in his bed or sitting for their portrait, he thought of her.

Nieves Boullosa Vega of Galicia, named for snow in a land of hot springs, a distant cousin close enough to touch, on Macon

Street just long enough to reverse the tides.

She fished a crab shell from the trash in the backyard, squirted it off with a hose, and across its back painted a winter scene of a stone *horreo*, snow dusting the cross at its peak. Nieves worked with a focus Basilio had rarely seen, patiently drilling the point of a safety pin through the carapace to make a hole for twine.

A summer of extreme memories more than seven years past yet not much evidence of it: a hurricane that roared down the alley in the last months of his grandfather's life. A few notes left on the kitchen table saying she had gone out, a glass earring he attached to a broken rosary, and a pair of bright yellow shorts on the line she had every intention of retrieving.

Basilio had offered her everything: a backyard just wide enough for two trash cans and his grandmother's rosebush—arms spread wide: all this can be yours—and in return was told that Grandpop was still alive and what right did he have to make such a proposal?

My heart?

Take my right eye.

Basilio stirred the pot—his mother's recipe, there'd be plenty of time for Spanish meals between now and the *caldo gallego* on New Year's Day—and sat down in a basement perfumed with the scent of cabbage and peppercorns.

Kapusta.

Hettleman had stopped working with canvas because he didn't like the "give" of it, said he was using old boards and cabinet doors, things that "held their own."

"Yeah, Rings…this one is you!"

Having Lithuanian mothers—one on either side of the Messiah—had connected Basilio and Hettleman early on. They'd supported each other's work, followed Nugent like field mice, and stayed up past dawn smoking pot and drinking beer in the alley behind Miss Bonnie's bar.

Hettleman's mother grew up near Druid Hill Park. Basilio's came of age around the Hollins Street Market, dead since Basilio was 13, run over on a supermarket parking lot with an arm full of groceries.

He was ashamed to admit—which he hadn't, not to Aubergine or any of her predecessors—that he missed Nieves more.

He'd never made a picture of his mother but he had a few photographs of her, kept one in a drugstore frame next to the stove. It showed her as a kid during the Depression, posing in a kiddie wagon and holding the reins of a goat in front of the Hollins Street Market. It was the source of a great family story.

She'd seen one of her girlfriends posing on the goat and cried until her mother fished out enough quarters, dimes and nickels to buy a pork chop dinner so that the crybaby (known in the family as "Squeaky Oil Can") could have what she wanted. Not so much to have what she wanted. Mostly so she would shut the hell up.

And the crab ornament crumbling to dust in an old Noxzema jar in his grandparents' bedroom, the only proof that Nieves had ever been on Macon Street at all.

On the sink, the mocking mask: What are you looking at?

Not long after Nieves disappeared for good (early on, he jerked between wondering if she was really gone or just lost), Basilio overheard a man talking about his daughter at a bus stop.

"I'd kick her ass," he said. "But it would be like kicking myself..."

How much of Hettleman's anger had leeched into the mask?

Rain on cardboard, heat on rain, paint on heat, Hettleman on paint, resentments chewing on Hettleman.

"You live in your grandparents' house...my Bubbie's place on North Smallwood Street? Jesus Christ, Rings. She used to chase the little *schvatzas* with her broom like a crazy woman. They thought it was a game and laughed so hard no one bothered her. Last twenty years of her life she was the only white person for a dozen blocks in every direction.

"All those years I could have been lighting candles and eating good. Instead I was just fucking around. Some half-ass artist. Fuck that. I'm not fucking around anymore."

Basilio set out a bowl (Limoges, rosettes with gold leaf, 1950) and spoon (stainless) while scanning Hettleman's grievances.

The night cramps in his legs, how Bubby Klein was knocked down and robbed after she got too old for the chase; how High-landtown might have taken a beating for fifteen minutes but Res-ervoir Hill had been in the toilet for more than forty years by the time Hettleman came to his senses.

Envy, anger, and a hollow vengeance worthy of Bobby Fischer.

"I hate that I didn't move in and take care of her like you did with your grandfather...I fucking hate myself..."

Hettleman knew well the one painting Basilio was known for—"her hair was black, as black as an olive"—and he was at Miss Bonnie's the night the rich lady bought it. But did he know that it is easier to admire the picture than to be in it?

Basilio left the letter on the table and walked on a still-tender foot to the mask. It lay on a drying board between the sink and stove.

The cabbage bubbled slow and thick, the color of the corri-dor where Basilio was told his mother's injuries were fatal. The stew smelled like the mess Nieves left in Grandpop's old bedroom when she disappeared.

Basilio picked up the mask with his left hand and stirred with his right, permanent indentations on the tip of his index finger and the inside of the middle one from years of gripping pencils and brushes.

Basilio brought the mask to his face and stared into the holes. Not through but into...deep into Grandpop's funeral some half-dozen years before. At the wake, Basilio stood next to his father with one eye on the door to see if Nieves would show.

A Spaniard—even one as fucked up as Nieves, a half-click away being one of the all-time greats in a life where any differ-ence is all the difference—is a Spaniard. And in her heart—the foot vein is connected to the ankle vein—she loved Grandpop more than dope.

She walked into the funeral parlor at the corner of Conkling and Gough looking like shit and Basilio left his father's side for the first time in three days. He moved quickly but not quick enough as Nieves knelt at the casket, made the sign of the cross, nodded to Basilio as though to an acquaintance, and fled into a car at the curb.

Basilio saw it all as though they'd buried Grandpop that morning.

As though...

BANG!

The pot of cabbage flew off the stove—Basilio struggling to pry the clammy mask from his face—and struck the photo of his mother riding the goat, cracking the glass. The pot hit the far wall and fell, viscous broth and bits of potato in puddles on the floor.

This very thing—pots sailing off of stoves like cannon balls— supposedly happened now and again; once to the best friend of Basilio's grandmother. He'd heard them talking about it at this table in this basement when he was a kid.

"Frances, I'm telling you, it shot off the stove and gave me a black eye."

But he'd never believed it.

Aubergine in the détente of counseling she neither needed nor wanted.

Nieves in the wind.

The mask fell into the mess on the floor, its edges beginning to fray from the acid in the cabbage.

He picked it up—dripping, stinking—set it on the table and cried: "Come back..."

But one wasn't talking and the other never listened.

Side Four

Christmas Eve in the 600 block of South Macon Street.

The mail came late, the storm door banging as Basilio dressed for dinner, waiting for his daughter.

Then to Cousin Donna's for the meal: empanada the Galician

way; calamari from Ikaros up at Eastern and Ponca; pasta with tuna; smelts, thin lengths of celery in shallow dishes of olive oil and cracked black pepper; crusty bread soaked in wine and sprinkled with sugar.

At the center: salted cod baked in fresh cream and bread crumbs.

Bathed and shaved, Basilio opened Hettleman's letter with one of Grandpop's penknives while walking upstairs to dress. He unfolded it on his grandmother's vanity and read while buttoning his white shirt, his grandfather's cuff links—mother of pearl inlaid with an onyx B—next to the Noxzema jar.

"Dear Ringo,...

"How'd you like the mask?"

[Loved it, thought Basilio. Couldn't get enough.]

"Remember what Nugent used to tell us when he was bombed and shitting his pants at Bonnie's and she'd run us out and tell us not to come back?"

[Maybe you, thought Basilio, but Miss Bonnie never ran me out.]

"He'd preach: 'Everything profound loves a mask...'"

The mask hung in a window upstairs, Hettleman's pigments—something like cochineal mixed with lead white—holding its own against the early winter sun.

"Skin is reflective," wrote Hettleman. "It mirrors everything."

A shimmering 360: Grandpop's cufflinks; the cobalt Noxzema jar; a portrait of the Sacred Heart of Mary made with butterfly wings by a long-dead relative in Argentina; silver vanity mirrors, also like wings, spotted with gray.

On the bed, an unopened gift from Aubergine, forgotten when she'd hurt herself, found when he went looking for the last rolls of his grandmother's wrapping paper. Basilio made a triangle knot in one of Grandpop's old ties, a short one from the '30s, ox-blood with cream swirls, and moved toward the bed, Nieves's bed when she lived here but never Basilio and Nieves's bed.

"I hope the mask didn't piss you off," wrote Hettleman. "If it did, don't toss it. One day it will hang at the Visionary..."

And Basilio laughed—his laugh—as high as a pigeon.

The Visionary!

He ran a comb through his thinning hair and paused to open the gift from Aubergine. She had found a can opener, the same vintage as Grandpop's tie, the kind that worked on elbow grease. It had a smooth wooden handle, painted red down to a rounded white tip. If she had left it in the basement during one of their dinners, Basilio would have assumed it had been there for sixty-years.

He laid it next to the comb on the dresser, shoved Hettleman's letter in his pocket and went downstairs.

On the couch—floor gleaming, tree twinkling, door open to the vestibule—Basilio sat with Hettleman's letter and waited like he used to on Christmas Eve when the dinner was held here, two dozen people in a narrow basement kitchen where Basilio now ate most of his meals alone.

The basement where his grandmother's lady friend, Miss Leini, sipped coffee from a bowl, a scar from a deep cut across her brow, and told his grandmother—almost blind, naïve in her blindness—how a stewpot flew off the stove and knocked her to the ground.

The letter was one more in a recent flurry from Hettleman and Basilio had filed them chronologically in a wire napkin hold-er. Each letter, even the amusing ones, revealed a Hettleman a little shakier than the last.

"Did I ever tell you about the Christmas ball factory? I bet some of your relatives worked there ... it was up by the bus yard on Ponca Street."

[Basilio didn't know and it nettled him. He remembered walking his grandmother up to Ponca Street to visit Miss Leini. But a Christmas ball factory? Three blocks from his house? It pissed him off to learn it from Hettleman.]

"It was my great-grandfather's business, Bubby Klein's father. The goyim called him 'the Old Jew.' I think some of my relatives even called him that when they didn't think there were any kids around."

Basilio had once done a series of paintings based on things he'd heard when the grown-ups didn't think children were afoot.

That's how he'd learned that his mother had had a few "high-balls" when the car hit her; that his grandfather had been deported as an illegal during Prohibition; and his grandmother was Miss Leini's only friend because the proper society in a neighborhood of shipyard workers and housewives shunned the orphaned Greek—so good looking it caused pain in others—for living as she pleased.

"They worked the line the way their husbands worked at Bethlehem Steel. Like their men who walked out the gates with enough steel to build a destroyer, these broads robbed us blind. They had to be able to letter and draw," wrote Hettleman, who'd doodled reindeer and elves in the margins. "Trite greetings, glue and sparkle...usually in script but lettering too, simple stuff."

Basilio glanced at the front window, listening for the sound of a car door.

"My father worked in the factory on summers and weekends. All women, Polish and Italian, a couple of Greeks. Some blacks when he couldn't find anybody else, but not for the lettering. All of them could draw, though. More people knew how to draw then."

Basilio considered the ancient balls on the small plastic tree in the front window, the ones he'd found wrapped in newspaper in shoeboxes the first Christmas after Grandpop's death.

Happy Holidays, Merry Christmas, 'tis the Season....

God Bless Us.

Everyone.

"The God-fearing Catholic women of Highlandtown eating meatball sandwiches on the line and robbing us blind one Christmas ball at a time!

"One day, a flat-chested woman (she wasn't Polish or Italian, my old man said the other women called her "American" but she was just a hillbilly), one day, Rings—no-tits Fannie had a rack! My father gives it squeeze and—crack!—two of the biggest balls they made, one green and one red, broke like stale crackers. Christmas falsies!

"My Dad was just a kid, helping out over the holidays, Rings. He had no interest in the Hebrew Piano, he wanted to be like us. Or maybe he wanted to be like you. I have some of the stuff he did before he knocked up my Mom and had to get married.

"He was a natural born cockhound, Rings. The shit you can't teach. I bet he got as much pussy as Sinatra. Of course, it was Baltimore pussy, but hell, the worst I ever had was great."

Nice talk, chuckled Basilio, nice talk on Christmas.

"But Fannie could draw...she could *draw*, Rings—you know what I mean—so the broken bulbs came out of her bra and out of her pay and she got to keep her job."

The car Basilio was waiting for—he knew the sound of his daughter's mother's exhaust—stopped outside and he waited for the vestibule knob to turn.

Now it was Christmas.

On the way outside—trying to do nine things at once, his arms full of presents, car keys in his mouth, receipt for the paid-in-advance calamari between his fingers—Basilio thought he'd shoved Hettleman's letter in his pocket.

But the wind caught the pages, sending the missive sailing across Macon Street toward the railroad tracks where the bottle cap factory used to be.

Side Five

New Year's Eve, 1995.

Up from a very late nap, Basilio walked up two flights of stairs to his studio on the third floor, a new letter from Hettleman in one hand—the last he would receive—a cup of black coffee in the other.

"I'm so fucking broke, Rings, I ain't got change for a grasshopper and that's a pizzy ant and two crickets..."

Basilio laughed, settling in for a night at home on the last night of the year. Not because he was broke (he was, having sold just enough paintings and some sign work to get through Christmas) but just because.

"In the middle of nowhere, dead ass, bent-dick broke," wrote Hettleman. "Who you gonna sell a painting of Memorial Stadium on the back of a hubcap to out here? No one. Fucking nobody."

Basilio entered a long, open room; paint spattered across bare floorboards, a hole in the ceiling. He hugged a wall in the darkness to the middle of the room, a deckhand on a rowhouse schooner; a length of heaving line holding a tarp across the opening in the roof.

As he loosened the line from a cleat on the wall, the tarp dropped to the floor.

Swoosh!

Above his still-groggy head—waking up on the far side of 10:00 p.m.—a large, squared hole opened onto a sharp, crisp night, clouds sailing like nocturnal zeppelins through chilly moonlight.

Wind knocked over an unfinished portrait of Aubergine, her blood in the brown of the birthmark on her shoulder. As it fell, it knocked over an incomplete portrait of her predecessor.

[He'd opened the roof once for Nieves, not knowing that she had come up on her own all the time while he was out of the house, expertly dropping and replacing the canvas tarp, stealing a peek at the view before she began stealing from Grandpop.

The one and only time they'd been intimate (that's how Basilio preferred to think of it) had occurred here, under a gaping hole on the anniversary of the Day the Beatles Met Elvis; Grandpop out for a late summer walk with the young mother across the alley who ran interference the way Basilio's grandmother once did for Miss Leini.]

He stood directly beneath the hole and looked up.

New Year's Eve had become a night to mull the accomplishments of the past year, pushing work by degrees from the studio to the vestibule and out the door, never finishing all he'd attempted; a night to sketch a plan for the year ahead.

An annual date with solitude for when you were as chronically mixed up in other people's domestic strife as Basilio had been since he was a teenager, New Year's Eve was a difficult night to be out in the world.

Pathetic?

What are *you* doing New Year's Eve?

Basilio sat on a threadbare Persian carpet and looked up at Nieves spread across the ceiling like a crow, the ones that dive-bombed *la tornaratas* back in Galicia, her pale, thin face spreading out in vapors of red and gold from the edges of the hole.

He'd made the mural in the wake of her brief and turbulent time on Macon Street; Elisabeth's husband—only half the pussy that Aubergine's husband was—banging on the kitchen door with his fist.

"Do you know where they are?"

Basilio invited him in for a drink.

"I wish I did."

"I bet you do, asshole," said the cuckold, slamming the gate on Grandpop's fence so hard it fell from its rusted hinges.

•

Basilio put a pillow under his head and stretched out. With a sip of coffee, he took the letter from his pocket as the studio —one large room, from the street out front to the alley behind him—absorbed the cold from open sky.

Hettleman: "It's full-on winter now and I'm late working the berries. Possum haw, good for the bluebirds.

"Those beat-up little seagulls still pecking away at frozen French fries on Pratt Street?"

[Basilio thought of the one he'd seen that morning—filthy gull struggling under the weight of a chicken wing—when he'd walked to get a paper to see what he'd be missing tonight.]

"Wanna know the truth, Rings? My ass is dragging. You play make-believe with the ponytail of the month beneath those cathedral skylights and all I've got is a shard. A dented oyster bucket missing a handle.

"I didn't leave Baltimore because of Smallwood Street or the fuck ugly hotel they put up that blocks the Bromo Seltzer tower. Let Nugent write those stories. What did he used to tell us when we were getting high in the alley behind Bonnie's?

"You always love the city you die in. I never knew what he meant until now."

Basilio had known since August 27, 1990.

"I left when my dog died," said Hettleman. "Crying on the steps, 101 degrees at 10:00 a.m. and one more mutant—why this guy, why that moment, I don't know cuz I seen it a million times. One more retard eating shit out of a box and dropping the trash on the sidewalk as casually as wiping his ass. I snapped, Rings. It was leave Baltimore or kill somebody."

Basilio knew the feeling, doubted there was anyone in the city that didn't. The week Grandpop died—week fifteen of Nieves in the wind—he planted two pink dogwood trees in front of the house and had Petrucci the bricklayer build planters around them at the curb.

And then stood sentry over the saplings, watching from the front window with all the vigilance he'd once used to stare across the alley at Elisabeth's house; watching to make sure no one fucked with them.

Once he caught the local urchins—kids whose mothers shepherded them with admonitions like "eat your grilled cheese motherfucker"—jumping on the thin branches and hanging like monkeys, limbs snapping like chopsticks.

Basilio had fantasized about shooting them from the branches and rehearsed his testimony.

What does Baltimore City need more, your honor?

Strong, beautiful trees—shade and color and a filter for the air; birth and re-birth for spring beats death—or another mouth to feed in juvenile prison?

Both the trees and the kids survived and Basilio never told anyone of this most shameful of all lusts, hovering just below his desire for Nieves.

"I began packing the truck on the spot," wrote Hettleman. "Moe still warm, in the back of my truck in a broken dresser drawer. And then I lit out for the territories, one last drive by the missing tooth that was my Bubbie's house."

Basilio stroked the carpet beneath him as Hettleman described the Baltimore heat—Calcutta, the Serengeti, New Orleans on Labor Day—weather as different from the one pouring through the hole in the ceiling as kale is from corn flakes.

"I jumped on the expressway at North Avenue and ran to the headwaters of the Falls. Ten miles north of chicken bones getting washed into the storm drains and dumping into the harbor where Maggio used to catch rubber balls with a crabbing net.

"Parked the truck and carried Moe to the riverbank. Water was a little cleaner up there. Set the drawer down and took off my clothes. I waded in and poured the Falls over my head with a sauce pan just to say I'd done it.

"Didn't do any of the authentic stuff. Just waded in, held my nose and went under."

And people think I'm nuts, thought Basilio. Sections of the Jones Falls were easily as filthy as the Ganges. He held Hettleman's letter to the sky, the words translucent.

"Moe as dead as Smallwood Street and the dresser drawer—the cabinet gone to splinters...I was going to save it Rings, was going to glue it, clamp it, strip it, and stain it, was gonna, was gonna, was gonna...

"The dog in the dresser, easel rags tucked around him on all sides. Took him to the water's edge, doused it with turpentine and dropped a match...nudged Moe out into the current and he burned beautiful, absolutely beautiful headed down to the harbor...just like a proper Hindu...wouldn't George—what is life anyway, Rings, what the fuck *is* life—wouldn't George have loved it?"

Basilio took a sip of coffee, now cold. "Viking, you idiot...not Hindu."

"So, Moe sails toward Pratt Street and I fill an old oyster jar with river water, put the jug on the passenger seat and roll away..."

Basilio rubbed his eyes. There was stirring on the street and a premature string of firecrackers popping in anticipation.

In the summer—many humid summers down the road from the summer—a ballgame on the radio would help Basilio measure how long he'd labored over the precise constellation of freckles across Nieves' nose.

Keep going to the fifth inning, the black and orange of perennial doormats bleeding into portraits of women, Grandpop and abandoned buildings. Two more outs 'til the seventh-inning stretch. Extra innings and he could get the down along the curve of her ears and the little chunk of flesh missing from a knife-game back in Vigo.

Across the ceiling, he painted Nieves spreading like vapor from each right angle of the hole, the rippling mercury of Luna making her teeth shimmer against splintered wood.

Black eyes—"I got a crow on a wire," wrote Nugent in his Library of America edition, "...ever look into a crow's eye? Think about a hunk of black ice..."—and wings of orange.

This bird has flown.

"Nothing out here," wrote Hettleman. "Nothing I want to paint..."

The story of the cremated mutt impressed Basilio in a way Hettleman's art never did. Someone shot a gun in the alley, premature but not by much. A gust swept through the hole and rattled the mask where Basilio had arranged it to stare at the house where Elisabeth used to live, his grandmother's Fatima rosary weighing it down from the same nail in the wall.

He held it in front of his face and looked himself dead in the eye, holding his own gaze for a long moment, as if trying to decide whether or not to take a hit of acid.

[Once you get on that bus—cabbage stew all over the floor,

the stink of it in the cuffs of your pants—you don't get off until it runs out of gas.]

Basilio brought the mask to his face and counted the moments left in the year as Nieves shook herself loose from the beams and sat cross-legged at his feet.

"Nice mask..."

Basilio struggled to sit up, caught a splinter in his palm.

"Hettleman made it."

"Never heard of him."

"Where'd you go?"

"*O Camiño de Santiago.*"

"What?"

The edge of the mask cut into his jaw as he tried to freeze her face in front of him.

"I didn't go anywhere."

Basilio had neither seen nor heard from Nieves in more than six years, not since Grandpop's funeral when she showed up dressed in black—frayed cuffs of a men's dress shirt buttoned at the wrists—and looking like shit.

Now, the harder he tried to see her, really see her, the more the roads she had traveled in the last six years rolled out before him.

Living it up in New York, a belle of hipster Brooklyn.

In the back of a white Chevy Impala squealing through the streets of Mexico City.

Kicking up grain after grain of desert.

And right here, as Basilio confessed to a ghost that she is the love of his life, right here in the Holy Land with seconds to go.

A bang of pots and pans on the street, the rat-a-tat-pop of firecrackers as Nieves took Hettleman's letter from Basilio and read it aloud.

"I love Baltimore," she said, sailing away through the hole in the ceiling, the letter falling back upon Basilio's chest with the first flakes of a light snow as the New Year erupted. "No one can say I don't."

ADULTEROUS JERUSALEM

I.

"I have been searching for time past all my life..."
—Jeanloup Sieff

Cookie sure could splash the purple around.

Like bruises on Grandpop's thin skin or the swelling of an old woman's ankles. The tint of a grape snowball on the tip of Basilio's tongue.

In a reporter's notebook, she described her connection to Basilio as "a violent crush," one that lasted just about as long as it took to demolish Memorial Stadium. Around quotes about what the ballpark meant to the locals, she reflected upon what might have been: "I would have run away with the veil on my head."

Past-tense promises in a generic notebook not generic enough to escape perusal. Across their summer—ten thousand smacks of the wrecking ball on 33rd Street, grown men sobbing outside a chain-link fence—Basilio was lost in the sugar wafer motherhood that was Cookie in despair.

"I can't grasp my life anymore," she said over a plate of French Fries and gravy, waiting for cheesesteak subs at a carry-out on the eastern edge of the Holy Land. "Every night I'm tortured about what to cook for dinner."

The Greek who called himself Heracles (the distinction lost on locals who called the proud man's diner Hercules) did business near what remained of Sparrows Point in the dying days of steelmaking in Baltimore. Not counting buttered toast and coffee

on the way to the airport the next morning, it was Heracles who
served Basilio and Cookie their last meal together.

Of that hour, no one knows and, believing the end of their
delight was a long way off, they indulged moments of post-indus-
trial transcendence Cookie believed possible only with Basilio.

"They used to run Esskay pigs in a tunnel under this street,"
he said, "and over there was a German butcher shop where the
junkman bought trotters for stew..."

Cascades of tingles and tides of thrills: boom-boom upon her
arrival, the next morning, just because and a dance party for two
in their underwear—"*Sha-la-la-la-la-la-la...hey!*"—belly-buttons
quivering thimbles of sweat.

Basilio made Cookie's portrait in front of the limestone face
of the crumbling stadium upon which hubris was bolted in stainless steel: TIME WILL NOT DIM THE GLORY OF THEIR DEEDS.

He used a pebble to scratch the words across the orange and
yellow horizon of the canvas, Cookie staring straight ahead in a
one-piece bathing suit and unbuttoned blouse, torn canvas gym
shoes, and the slightest of smiles: "Stadium Study No. 4."

The painting lay against a wall in Basilio's studio, oxidizing
as he sipped root beer, a golden fry at his lover's lips, salt on her
tongue.

A portrait in bee's wax and ivory...

Basilio was about to describe the simple dinners he used to
make for his daughter when in whirled the guy voted by his high
school classmates as the person most likely to become a roadie
for Foghat.

Timothy Tukulski, with whom Basilio had gotten stoned
nearly every day when Gerald Ford was president, "Tasmanian
Tookie" skidding to a spastic stop at their table.

"RINGO!" he cried. "One time for Tookie!"

Basilio was astonished, wondering how—how the fuck— could
the specter of his once charismatic and now dissipated friend
hover before him if Tookie's long-ago compatriot in cannabis no
longer existed?

As Tookie babbled—"How you been man...you never call...
Naw, who told you I was dead?"—Cookie covered her mouth to
keep from laughing.

Basilio was amazed: "Timmy Tukulski..."

They'd fancied themselves the greatest rock-and-roll pot
heads of the bicentennial, driving to get their Transfiguration
High School diplomas in Basilio's mustard yellow Pacer, passing
a sticky bowl of Thai stick and hash—"the heavy-heavy"—while
singing along to "Jelly Roll Gumdrop" on the 8-track, the morning sun dancing through a gaseous asphalt haze.

For years, Tookie relived the moment in a stream of un-re-
turned messages on Basilio's answering machine.

"Remember man, remember? We were running late—always
late—and I jumped out of the shower and got dressed in the car?
Stuck my head out the window to dry my hair and you passed
over that fat Fidel-burger. Shit, Rings, sailing up Charles Street
like a hood ornament on a Mercury."

Remember, man?

That night, Basilio's Italian grandmother (on whose sheets
Cookie slept, sipping coffee from Francesca's wedding china,
bare-chested and cross-legged in Nonna's bed) took her last
breaths at Johns Hopkins as Basilio and Tookie did bong hits with
people they didn't know.

Remember?

Who could forget?

The next day, Basilio signed on to an ore ship out of the long-
gone SIU hall at Baltimore and Central and sailed for Peru at
dawn, his father's tugboat pulling alongside to whistle goodbye
as the freighter left the pier.

By the time the ship passed Annapolis, a hung-over Tookie
was late for work at his parents' pet supply store, launching a
career of lugging fifty-pound bags of dog food from trucks to the
shelves and shelves to cars for customers who dropped coins in
his hand like he was a little kid.

A hundred-and-one idiotic jobs later—light bulb salesman,

grub worm eradicator, button hole grinder—Tookie floated on an air-mattress in his dead parents' above-ground pool, a beer in one hand and a joint in the other as he embellished the graduation story for a wayfarer he'd found walking alongside a highway near the airport.

Basilio was his hero and he loved telling Ringo and Tookie stories to anyone who still gave him the time of day, strangers mostly.

"Once he paid me to make an inventory of everything in this house."

"*Todos?*" asked Nieves.

"Every toothpick," said Tookie, paddling the joint over to her.

"Kill it," he said, having cashed his last unemployment check just before picking her up. "We got plenty."

La vagabundo savored the reefer on a chaise lounge, sipping iced coffee and scribbling in the margins of a book as Tookie drifted from one end of the pool to the other.

"Driving up Charles Street with my head out the window... last I ever saw that crazy motherfucker."

II

"I could no longer trust what I was seeing..."
Charles Harbutt

Basilio sketched Cookie as she did a small load of clothes at the coin-op next to the diner, a Pulitzer nominee drumming her fingers against the top of a "Super Spin" in a canyon of stainless steel, her belief in Arm & Hammer stronger than her regard for a husband who had not read a book in five years.

He tinted the image with watercolors from his Schmincke pan —gray, pearl, and white foreshadowing his Kitchen Period—before closing up his paints and setting the image aside to dry.

He kissed the back of her head at the folding table; separates and lingerie tossed into a backpack as night fell on adulterous

Jerusalem, an umbrous moon above the aging steelworks, once the largest in the world.

Basilio turned Cookie's chin toward the soon-to-be ruins along the Patapsco and said, "Look close and you can see it vibrating."

"Don't see it."

He told her about the green flash he'd seen on that long-ago ore ship, a phenomenon that must be glimpsed at the exact moment the sun falls below the horizon.

"You make a pin-hole with your thumb and forefinger," he said. "And you have to be lucky."

Cookie saw neither and they went next door to eat, trading dates on the calendar like bubblegum cards.

•

Cold fries and a third of Cookie's sandwich were left on the tray as Basilio dug in his pocket for the tip. They were headed for snowballs when a racket of clanging pots and loud voices came from the kitchen.

Entrance music for a freak, an autodidact who long ago had frayed the wire between Mensa and mental; Tookie Tukulski dragging the cleats of ragged cowboy boots across blue and white tiles.

"RINGO!" bellowed Tukulski. "One time for Tookie!"

Basilio astonished, Cookie laughing out loud.

Tukulski made a bee-line for the booth, his crazy eyes all over Cookie—no bra, small breasts, thin cotton tank-top—Detroit Symphony Orchestra, Est. 1887—until she flushed crimson, wiped her mouth with a napkin, and grabbed a sweater from her bag.

"Tookie," marveled Basilio. "Tookie Fucking Tukulski."

His long-lost friend was humping crabs for an ex-heavyweight boxer and strip-club bouncer named Stitchell, two bushels of females hauled into the walk-in cooler for crab cakes and soup.

Cookie excused herself to make a phone call as Tukulski pulled a $5.99 disposable camera from his pocket and hit the button.

"Gotcha," he said.

Cookie and Basilio caught by the click and frozen in the flash; one chilled with premonition, the other flabbergasted that the most reckless person he'd ever know was alive.

Basilio caressed her hip as she edged by, Tookie plopping down the moment she was gone, scarred fingers smelling of crab guts and grime as he finished the last fry.

"She's pretty," said Tookie. "You guys going steady?"

"Yes," said Basilio as Tookie chewed with his mouth open. "Jesus Christ, Took. You look terrible."

Tookie nudged his friend's shoulder, the smell of cold brown gravy mixing with the dirt under his fingernails.

"You're funny, Rings."

Tukulski's face was heavier, his nose fleshier, lined with veins and bent to one side. His small brown eyes still carried traces of uncommon intelligence (drunk, he used to win bets by naming all of the presidents in reverse order) but without the sparkle.

Shouting came from the kitchen in the foreign languages of Greek and East Baltimore as Heracles and Stitchell fought over the bill, the size of the crabs, and how many dead ones lay on the bottom.

"Same thing every time with these Greeks," said Tookie. "Wanna catch a quick one while they fight it out?"

"Don't get high anymore, Took."

"Once in a while won't hurt you."

"Never been able to do anything once in a while," said Basilio as Cookie returned from the pay phone.

"We should go," she said.

"Want me to take one of you guys before you split?" said Tookie as Basilio stood up. "What's your address, Rings? I'll stick it in the mail."

Cookie snatched the camera from Tookie and ordered the

boys across the room—"Over there..."—pointing toward an RC COLA menu on the wall, inch-high black letters and numbers pushed into the slots of a plastic board yellowed with grease.

Basilio and Tookie sneered like bad-asses on the cover of *Highway to Hell*. Cookie snapped and tossed the camera back to Tookie—"Rock on..."—who fumbled the catch.

Tookie used the last exposure as the couple turned for the door—Cookie's head on Basilio's shoulder, exhausted as they moved toward a sun that wasn't green as it set behind a steel mill that wasn't vibrating.

"Told you he was an asshole," whispered Basilio, reaching for the door as the crab mean screamed "TUKULSKI!" and Tookie scrammed into the back.

Old Lady Heracles called to Basilio from her stool behind the register, pointing to the camera Tookie had left behind in his haste.

Basilio handed the camera to Cookie on the parking lot, chuckling as the crab truck roared off, Tookie getting yelled at like a school boy. Cookie dropped the camera in her backpack and off they went.

III

"A photograph is a secret about a secret..."
Diane Arbus

Back in Detroit ...

At the age of eight, Cookie decided to become a reporter between bites of meatloaf as her father told the family how he'd pulled over Denny McLain for driving drunk after the Tigers won the 1968 World Series.

Still in uniform, he sipped Stroh's from the can and nudged Cookie's mother as if she were his partner in a squad car.

"Thanked him for a great year and let him go."

Cookie pushed peas around her plate, her mind an engine of

language and worry, her sister the pretty one. She read the *Free Press* every day, front to back on the floor beneath the dining room table, searching for her father's name in the crime blotter and looking up all the words she didn't know, discerning, somehow, that people acted differently when reporters were around.

Same city, more than thirty years later...

Cookie threw her bags in a corner, ordered pizza for the kids (they were leaving for swim camp in the morning, her husband was out getting last minute stuff they needed) and went to bed early. Her story was due tomorrow.

She fell hard asleep, mumbling something about how great it was to be a reporter.

That's what she'd told Basilio a year before when they'd met in the Motor City at an exhibit of paintings; kitchen appliances named for women—Judith the Cheese Grater, Helen the Egg Beater—and tools with masculine names—Gene the wrench and a push mower called Herb.

The paintings were hung with clothespins on fishing wire strung across the rafters of an abandoned storefront, the whimsy of an old Baltimore friend of Basilio's named Billy Ray Gombus who'd moved to Detroit to buy a house for a dollar and make pictures on butcher's paper with house paint.

Cookie was there to grab eight paragraphs for the back of the Saturday paper. Three quotes, atmosphere, no photos, and a bit of PR cribbing. It should have taken less than half-an-hour.

"To be honest," she said as they stood near Betty the Vacuum, running her left hand through light brown hair, blushing as though confessing a crime. "I'm married."

A month later, in bed with Basilio in Baltimore, she told him that the beauty of being a reporter was that you could be anywhere at any time under any circumstances and call it work.

She'd once wanted to capture in a book what Basilio attempted with line and color, wanted it very badly.

"Newspapers can do the same thing," said Basilio as they sat on his couch listening to records. He didn't believe it and she knew that he didn't.

The hogwash behind this adventure was the death of old ball-parks. The razing of Memorial Stadium provided context to the looming destruction of the tin-roofed cathedral at Michigan and Trumbull in Corktown, the neighborhood where her father and his father had grown up sneaking into ballgames.

Cookie worked on the story for a month, a good and sad read built upon three economic realities.

The impact a major-league ball park has on its neighborhood when games are still played there.

"Hey Ringo, let's go to the game. Nickel beer night!"

The extant liabilities when a ballpark stands vacant for years.

"Rings, gimme a call man. We're gonna break in and steal some seats before it's all gone."

And what transpires after the wrecking ball swings.

"Hey sweetheart," said Cookie, staring over a parking lot that was once the Cass Theater. "It's me."

"Need it now," called the weekend editor.

"Call you back," she said, hanging up to read the story one last time.

"More than three hundred people are murdered in Baltimore every year and all the natives seem to care about is that their be-loved Memorial Stadium is being torn down."

She filed, called home to say she was on the way, and gathered up her stuff.

"Nice work, Cook," said the editor as she left the newsroom, not telling her he'd toned down some of the more extravagant passages. "A-1 Sunday."

Above the fold, thought Cookie as she left the newsroom, though she thought wrong.

On the way home, she went out of her way to visit an 89-year-old abandoned house called Tiger Stadium as it moldered in the summer heat.

KEEP OUT!

Cookie thought about the spectacle that was 31-and-6

Denny—"No one is above the law," her father had told her, "but I let him go"—and meeting the players when Dad had ballgame duty, sitting behind the home dugout, Sergeant Cook on the field between innings, protecting a diamond now overgrown with Devil's Grip.

Pulling alongside of turnstiles through which millions had passed, she rolled down the window to stare into the dark and fenced-in portals, noticing little things that would have made her story.

But as her Irish grandmother often said, you can't put ten pounds of shit into a five-pound bag.

Wouldn't it be nice if Basilio could make a picture here before it was too late?

She could buy one of his paintings (not a chance of bringing home a blender named Brenda but maybe a sketch of his grand-father's deco alarm clock) and tell Basilio to use the money to fly in for a day.

They could take Billy Ray to dinner in Hamtramck, order the *czarnina* Basilio said he'd always wanted to taste. They could and they did and surely, they would again.

Cookie had achieved a lukewarm détente in her marriage. She knew her place and had no plans to abandon it. Writing in the margins now and again was her way of easing hostilities, hiding out from the other life.

Was not Detroit the Paris of the Midwest?

"Happy once," she thought, parking between the maple trees in front of their house. "Happy enough."

Maybe tonight they would go to the movies.

Cookie grabbed her leather bag from the back of the car, kicked a soccer ball so hard it nearly cleared the gabled roof, and walked in the front door with the greeting she loved best: "Going A-1, honey!"

Setting her bag between the door and the sofa, she turned the corner for the kitchen and found her husband at the table with a dozen snapshots arranged like solitaire, the latest work from the goof most likely to become a roadie for Foghat.

"Big story," he said, looking up. "Above the fold."

Cookie did not immediately recognize the photos (her husband was a coupon clipper, the table always cluttered), but as she moved to give him a kiss they came into focus.

Tookie holding a crab with his bare hand, thumb and finger pinching the spot where the back fin flipped; five pictures of a dirt-brown mutt staring directly into the camera; Stitchell scrubbing the crab truck, a pissed-off look on his face; somebody's bare, white ass; and Tookie on a crabbing dock, giving the world the finger.

Cookie's husband picked up a picture of Tookie and circled his face with a black marker.

"At least tell me it's not this guy."

Cookie sat down across from him, trembling slightly and hoping it wasn't obvious, palms sweating as her husband looked at her as though trying to put a name to a face.

Like her father, Cookie's husband was a cop though he hadn't been on the street since the kids were little. The department had paid his way through Wayne State and more than once he'd given his wife information that had furthered her career.

Cookie scanned the table for the rest of the photos. Maybe they hadn't turned out. If so, she might ride out a lie.

No, that's not me.

This is me.

"What are you looking for?" he asked.

"I don't know," she said quietly. "Nothing."

He gathered up the photos, tossed them toward her and said, "Maybe you're losing your mind."

•

Unto the moment of their very different deaths, Basilio and Tookie held fast to the fiction that the last time they saw one another was graduation day, 1976.

About a year after running into Basilio at the Heracles, Tookie persuaded Stitchell that he was trustworthy and the crab man had him drive down to Tilghman Island for a half-dozen bushels of number one Jimmies.

On the way back to Baltimore, Tookie rewarded himself with half-a-joint and a can of Wiedemann's, "Fool for the City" on the oldie's station...

"I'm like a fish out of water, just a man in a hole..."

...and plunged off the side of the Knapps Narrows drawbridge, Stitchell's bounty swimming free, Tookie trapped.

By then, Basilio's portraits of women—whether ankle deep in urban relics or leaning against a desert trailer full of *mementos mori*—were giving way to paintings of sinks and stoves.

Decades later, during his own exit—*Ciao, tierra Santa!*—Basilio did not think of his daughter for whom he'd sautéed soft shelled crabs after school or his long-dead parents, conjured neither Grandpop, himself, nor the long parade of beauty for which he'd beaten the drum.

Falling from scaffolding on bad ankles—glare upon glaucoma, that last step is a doozy—he saw Tookie Tukulski's face in the wind as they raced to graduation at the Basilica of the Assumption of the Blessed Virgin Mary some seventy years earlier.

A hologram of the wildest wild man he'd ever known vibrating above the filthy sidewalk that rushed to meet his face, a plunging pint of Hellenic blue about to mix with the thin blood of an 86-year-old artist who'd never received his due.

•

Cookie buckled and took a job on the copy desk, a grind of grammar and the certainty of regular hours; never again to chase a story beyond her own backyard. By the time she and her husband had forged a new covenant, the land on which Memorial Stadium was built had been developed into senior housing.

Tiger Stadium stood vacant for another ten years after the

Summer of Cheesesteaks and Snowballs. The final game had been played there on September 27, 1999, an 8–2 Tiger victory over Kansas City, the home team coasting on a grand slam by a journeyman named Robert Fick.

Fick's blast—the final hit, home run, and RBI in Tiger Stadium history—left the park in the eighth inning, banging off the right field roof before falling back onto the field. The whereabouts of the ball remain unknown.

ABOUT THE AUTHOR

A lifelong Baltimorean, Rafael Alvarez began publishing poetry during the Ford Administration by rewriting the lyrics to Robin Trower songs. His early pieces appeared in the *News-American*—a defunct afternoon paper for the city's working class—and *Chicory*, a literary magazine published in Baltimore from 1966-to-1983.

The son of a tugboat engineer and a dedicated homemaker, Alvarez was educated in local Catholic schools, graduating in 1981 with a degree in English literature from Loyola University of Maryland.

For twenty years, he worked as a City Desk reporter for the *Baltimore Sun*, specializing in the folklore of city neighborhoods. He quit the paper in 2001 to work as a laborer on cable ships and soon after began writing for HBO's police drama, *The Wire*.

Since 2009, Alvarez has concentrated on writing books and screenplays for independent films.

Basilio Boullosa Stars in the Fountain of Highlandtown is his fourth collection of fiction.

Alvarez is currently at work on a novella titled, "Orlo the Chicken Necker."

ACKNOWLEDGMENTS

I would like to thank all of the editors who helped me along the way, particularly the unsung heroes who—for nothing but the love of the game—publish unsung literary journals around the globe.

Gratitude and a cheesesteak sub goes to Eric Mithen—with whom I put out an annual chapbook of stories and photos—and a hot cup of tea to Jay Reda, proofreader extraordinaire.

Special thanks to my publisher, editor, fellow Baltimorean, and friend, Gregg Wilhelm, who first introduced my fiction to the world.

ADDITIONAL PHOTO CREDITS

"I Know Why I Was Born"
Credit: Jennifer Bishop

"Conkling Street Christmas"
Credit: Jennifer Bishop

"Too Rolling Tookie"
Credit: Jennifer Bishop

"Wedding Day"
Credit: Art Lien

"The Fountain of Highlandtown"
Credit: Jennifer Bishop

"Basilio & Grandpop & Nieves"
Credit: Aiko Alvarez-Gibson

"Nine Innings in Baltimore"
Credit: Jim Burger

"Aunt Lola"
Credit: DeCarlo Family Archives

"The Road to Hibbing"
Credit: Richard "Guantes" Snyder

"Howie Wyeth"
Credit: Philip Edward Laubner

A READER COMMENTS

The fictional world of Rafael Alvarez is familiar but exotic, encompassing fragile beauty and matter-of-fact brutishness; a mythopoetic place populated by immigrants and sons of immigrants: sailors, musicians, junk collectors, and other demi-heroes. Broken men who have eaten all their seedcorn and now subsist on a woman's forbearance. Families cashing in their remaining luck on the indifference of a slipshod god. Meals prepared for a lover, dressed with oil and affection. A blood roux. An immaculate conception.

Frank and lyrical, Alvarez tells just enough for the reader to fill in the blanks. Each sentence is alluring. There are the ones that eagerly glide you along, the ones that induce a reverie, and the ones you call back for another read to encounter the moment of second understanding. A phrase about a girl "shipped to America like fresh linen tied with string" will cut your heart.

There's a calming rhythm to the narrative. The characters speak their lines and then some unseen but palpable presence —a *spiritus sanctus*—envelopes the scene and reveals more—the hopes and regrets and glimpses of the past and future.

Sidewalk, rowhouse, backyard, fence, alley.

The secrets of the sally port, stars through a skylight, Baltimore in high summer.

Our town.

Linda Lee Singh
Valentine's Day, 2017

ABOUT CITYLIT PRESS

CityLit Press's mission is to provide a venue for writers who might otherwise be overlooked by larger publishers due to the literary nature or regional focus of their projects. It is the imprint of nonprofit CityLit Project, Baltimore's literary arts center, founded in 2004.

Baltimore magazine named the press's first book a "Best of Baltimore" and commented: "CityLit Project has blossomed into a local treasure on a variety of fronts—especially its public programming and workshops—and it recently added a publishing imprint to its list of minor miracles."

Thank you to our major supporters: the National Endowment for the Arts, the Maryland State Arts Council, the Baltimore Office of Promotion and The Arts, Maryland Humanities, and various foundations. Information and documentation about the organization is made public at www.guidestar.org. Additional support is provided by individual contributors. Financial support is vital for sustaining the on-going work of the organization. Secure, online donations can by made at our web site, and simply click on "Donate." (Thank you!)

CityLit Project is a member of the Greater Baltimore Cultural Alliance (GBCA), the Maryland Association of Nonprofit Organizations (MANO), Maryland Citizens for the Arts (MCA), and the Writers' Conferences and Centers division of the Association of Writers and Writing Programs (AWP).

Please visit us at www.citylitproject.org.

ALSO BY THE AUTHOR

Fiction
> *The Fountain of Highlandtown*
> *Orlo and Leini*
> *Tales from the Holy Land*

Non-Fiction
> *Hometown Boy*
> *Storyteller*
> *A People's History of the Archdiocese of Baltimore*
> *The Wire: Truth Be Told*
> *The Tuerk House*
> *The Baltimore Love Project*
> *Crabtown, USA*

1997

2017

CPSIA information can be obtained
at www.ICGtesting.com
Printed in the USA
BVOW09*2316300717
490280BV00001B/1/P